3

5/4.

THE UNITED NATIONS
AND THE POPULATION QUESTION
1945–1970

THE UNITED NATIONS AND THE POPULATION QUESTION 1945–1970

RICHARD SYMONDS
AND
MICHAEL CARDER

Published by
CHATTO & WINDUS
for
SUSSEX UNIVERSITY PRESS
1973

Published by
Sussex University Press
*
Distributed by
Chatto & Windus Ltd
40 William IV Street
London WC2N 4DF

ISBN 0 85621 006 4

Printed in Great Britain by
Butler & Tanner Ltd, Frome and London

CONTENTS

CONTENTS

PART SIX

The Development of an Action Programme
(1967–1970)

Preface

THIS book was written whilst the authors were at the Institute of Development Studies at the University of Sussex and was originally intended as part of a wider study. It had been our intention on the one hand to study some of the major economic and social questions with which the United Nations and Specialized Agencies had been concerned over the past twenty-five years, and on the other to obtain a picture of how future prospects appeared in those fields from the point of view of the international agencies.

The most useful way in which to consider the future seemed to be in the form of essays contributed by several officials of the UN and Specialized Agencies in their personal capacities: these have been published as 'International Targets for Development.'[1] The past could hardly be treated in the same way, since international officials could not be expected to write critically on the role of the agencies which they served. Moreover, when we came to consider major and interlocking issues, such as the involvement of the UN agencies since 1945 in malaria eradication, food, population, education and employment, it became evident that the complexities were such that each of these questions could in itself be the subject of a book.

That we started with population was to some extent accidental. The Institute of Development Studies held two seminars for officials of overseas governments dealing with population problems. To our surprise we found that no comprehensive account existed of the role of the UN agencies in this field. A lecture turned into a lengthy article; but at the point when this might have been published, one of us was appointed temporarily as a consultant by the Secretary-General of the United Nations to advise on the use of the new United Nations Trust Fund for Population Activities. The experience suggested that our academic approach had neglected a number of important factors and drove us back to further research, mainly on documents of the UN Agencies, which resulted in this book.

As the book goes to press both of us are in the service of international agencies, one as European Representative of the United Nations Institute for Training and Research (UNITAR)

[1] Richard Symonds, editor: *International Targets for Development*, Faber, London, and Harper and Row, New York, 1970. The essay in it of H. Gille on 'Population' is an essential complement to this book.

vii

and the other with the International Labour Office. It is there-fore necessary to state that neither the United Nations, UNITAR, nor ILO have any responsibility for the views expressed, and that no materials have been used in it which were not or could not have been available to us in our previous academic capacity. It had been our intention to end the book in 1969. Develop-ments in 1970 were, however, so important that we have revised it to take these into account, although our new occupations have prevented us from covering these in as much detail as earlier periods.

Many international officials and others have generously given us their time, advice and criticism. We wish to express particular appreciation of the kindness of Dr Milos Macura, Director of the UN Population Division; of Mr Halvor Gille of the UN Fund for Population Activities; of Mr K. C. Abercrombie of the Food and Agriculture Organization (particularly for use of an un-published lecture); of Mr Paul Lamartine Yates, formerly of FAO; of Dr V. Zammit-Tabona of WHO; of Dr Karl Evang, Director-General of Medical Services of Norway, and Miss Julia Henderson and Mrs Frances Dennis of the International Planned Parenthood Federation. None of them can be associated with our analysis and conclusions, but the book would have been considerably less well informed without their help.

We wish to express our gratitude to the Carnegie Endowment for International Peace and to the Population Council of New York for travel grants which enabled this book to be completed. Finally we wish to thank Mrs Shirley Gurgo for the cheerfulness, patience and skill which she has shown in typing the book through its various stages.

RICHARD SYMONDS
MICHAEL CARDER

Institute of Development Studies
and
Institute of Study for International Organization
University of Sussex

List of Abbreviations

ACAST	Advisory Committee on the Application of Science and Technology to Development
ACC	Administrative Committee on Coordination
ECA	Economic Commission for Africa
ECAFE	Economic Commission for Asia
ECLA	Economic Commission for Latin America
ECOSOC	Economic and Social Council
DTRC	Demographic Training and Research Centre
FAO	Food and Agriculture Organization of the United Nations
FPA	Family Planning Association
GA	General Assembly
IBRD	International Bank for Reconstruction and Development
ILO	International Labour Organization
IPPF	International Planned Parenthood Federation
IUSSP	International Union for the Scientific Study of Population
NGO	Non-Governmental Organization
TAA	Technical Assistance Administration
TAB	Technical Assistance Board
UN	United Nations
UNCTAD	United Nations Conference on Trade and Development
UNDP	United Nations Development Programme
UNESCO	United Nations Educational, Scientific and Cultural Organization
UNFPA	United Nations Fund for Population Activities
UNICEF	United Nations Childrens' Fund
UNIDO	United Nations Industrial Development Organization
WHO	World Health Organization

Introduction

THE subject of this book is the discussion of and action upon the population question which took place within the agencies of the United Nations system and in the League of Nations system which preceded it. In addition to the United Nations itself, several of the Specialized Agencies have been deeply involved, notably the World Health Organization and to an important extent the International Labour Organization, UNESCO and the Food and Agriculture Organization. The Director-General of each of these agencies is responsible to a separate legislative body, has his own budget, and recruits his own staff. The headquarters of the organizations are dispersed throughout North America and Europe. Each agency is thus independent, though with a responsibility to present reports for information to the Economic and Social Council of the United Nations. The Executive Heads also meet together regularly as the Administrative Committee on Coordination.

The looseness of the United Nations system is not accidental. In the system which preceded it between 1919 and 1939 the League of Nations was responsible for a number of functions, including those carried out by its Health Organization and by the International Institute for Intellectual Co-operation, which are now entrusted to Specialized Agencies. Whereas the growing political tensions made the League powerless to maintain international peace and security, its economic and technical activities had grown in volume and importance. Moreover, when the League disintegrated in the Second World War, the International Labour Organization survived. From this experience the Americans, who took the initiative in the establishment of the United Nations system, drew a functionalist lesson. 'The ILO should stay in Geneva', suggested President F. D. Roosevelt in 1942, 'the international agricultural function in the United States; education in China; religion at the Taj Mahal and health at the north of Panama City; economics and finance in Russia and art in Paris'.[1]

In fact, in the post-war system, the United Nations was established in New York and the World Bank in Washington. The major Specialized Agencies were located in Europe: ILO and WHO in Geneva, FAO in Rome and UNESCO in Paris.

On the role of the United Nations itself in the economic and

[1] *The Roosevelt Letters*, vol. 3, London 1952, p. 445.

social fields there could be two views. One was that it was essentially to deal with whatever business was not the responsibility of a Specialized Agency unless or until this became important enough for a new agency to be created to take it over, as happened when the International Atomic Energy Agency, the UN Committee on Trade and Development and the UN Industrial Development Organization were created. An alternative approach was to see the United Nations as not only having a specific mandate to take care of what was left over, but also as having a general position of leadership in the economic and social field.

When the new system of Specialized Agencies of the UN was set up at the end of the Second World War it was not envisaged that the provision of technical assistance would become their major function. The creation of the Expanded Programme of Technical Assistance in 1950, of the UN Special Fund in 1958 and of UNDP in 1962, led to a situation in which most of the Agencies received more money from these sources than from their own regular budgets. Whilst there was a growing body of opinion, culminating in the Capacity Study of 1969,[1] in favour of more centralization, the period was characterized by competition between the agencies to establish their competence or authority in fields which were of interest to several of them. Population, because of its controversial nature, was an exception. Here, on the contrary, there was a tendency for each agency to hope that another would take the lead and the political responsibility for doing so. It is noteworthy, however, that none of what seems likely to be regarded as the three great issues of the seventies—population, the destruction of the environment, and unemployment—was given special attention in the UN postwar system, though Julian Huxley, the first Director-General of UNESCO, was 20 years ahead of his time in emphasizing the importance and inter-relationship of the first two of these.

Relatively little research has been done into how decisions of international agencies are made in economic and social fields. Sometimes they are the result of determined individual action. Well-known examples are Henri Dunant's campaign to obtain protection for the wounded through the Geneva Red Cross Convention, and David Lubin's success in the establishment of the International Institute of Agriculture. A less familiar one is the achievement of a junior UN official in promoting the General Assembly Resolution which called for a UN Development Decade.

Often it is the Executive Head of a Specialized Agency who is

[1] 'A Study of the Capacity of the UN Development System' (Jackson Report), UN Document DP/5, 1969.

responsible for an initiative, as in B. R. Sen's World Food Campaign in FAO, David Morse's World Employment Programme in ILO, or WHO's Malaria Eradication Programme. Sometimes an Executive Head fails in an initiative because he cannot carry with him the members of his governing body or legislature, as Huxley did in putting forward a general philosophy for UNESCO in 1948. The US Government, because it is the major financial contributor to the UN agencies, has not infrequently been responsible for successful initiatives. When an initiative comes from governments, however, power can be divorced from responsibility. An example was the creation of the UN Capital Development Fund, voted into existence by a majority of the poor countries in opposition to the rich countries, who refused to contribute to it.

This book is an attempt to trace, in relation to one particular question, population, the way in which the policies of the agencies of the UN system have evolved, in response to what forces; and in turn what influence the decisions of United Nations agencies have had on developments at the national level. It could not have been written without considerable use of the summary records of the UN agencies. Since these are now in many cases being drastically curtailed in the interests of economy, the book may be the last, as well as perhaps the first, of its kind.

The subject is of considerable interest, for there are few on which such fierce passions have been aroused, and few too on which national as well as personal attitudes have changed so dramatically over the period. Glancing through the records of debates on the involvement of the UN agencies in population programmes, even within the last ten years, a Latin American representative can be found urging the General Assembly to heed the lesson of the fall of the Roman Empire, which he attributed to birth control; a European representative informed the same session that if birth control were admitted 'it would only be a matter of time before such monstrous practices as abortion, mercy killing and the destruction of the old were accepted'; whilst an African representative at the World Health Assembly opposed the provision of the family planning services on the grounds that it would lead to prostitution.[1] Yet, by 1969, a special UN Fund for Population Activities was in operation whose main emphasis was on population action programmes.

When the UN was set up in 1945 the factors which produced what came to be known as the 'population explosion' were

[1] Official Records of the General Assembly, 17th Session, 1962, Summary Record of the 1197th Plenary Meeting and of the 869th meeting of the Second Committee: Official Records of WHO, no. 152.

already beginning to make an impact. Meagre as they were, the public health measures introduced into dependent territories and tropical countries in the period between the two World Wars upset the balance between high birth rates and high death rates which had kept population growth at a low level. People not only began to live longer: more children survived to the age at which they could marry and have children. It is now estimated that the rate of population growth in the less developed regions increased from around 1 per cent per annum in the period 1940/50 to over 2 per cent per annum in the 1960s.

The implications of this situation were not immediately recognized. On the one hand, with the partial exception of India, little was known of the demographic situation in Asia, Africa and Latin America, while on the other, the countries which played the major role in the establishment of the United Nations were preoccupied with falling birth rates and fears of population decline. During the 1950s there was a slow awakening to the fact that world population was growing at an unprecedented rate, but discussion of what should be done was hampered by the prejudices and passions which the question aroused. The results of the population censuses carried out in and around 1960 marked a turning point, for they showed that population was increasing even faster than the highest projections had suggested. During the 1960s a growing number of the less developed countries came to the conclusion that rapid population growth constituted a serious obstacle to hopes for substantial improvements in living standards, and embarked upon programmes designed to reduce fertility. Not unnaturally they looked to the United Nations and the Specialized Agencies for advice and assistance in carrying out these programmes. The provision of technical assistance for family planning thus became a key issue in the deliberations of the UN agencies on the population question.

There are, of course, many reasons why couples should want to plan the size of their families and why governments may be willing to provide the necessary advice and services. In the debates in the UN agencies, involvement in population programmes has been urged, and opposed, for a variety of reasons: Because rapid population growth could adversely affect economic development; because population pressure was a source of international tension; because an over-growing population placed impossible demands on the finite resources of the planet; because fewer babies meant healthier babies, and because couples had a basic human right to the knowledge and means to enable them to plan the size of their families. Some of those who opposed UN involvement in population programmes did so, not because they denied these relationships, but because they considered that the use of contraceptives was immoral and because they felt that family planning was not a legitimate area for state intervention.

In considering the role of the UN agencies in relation to the population question it is necessary to see who wanted them to do what. The population question has not only aroused stronger emotions than any other activity in the economic and social field; it has also cut right across familiar international divisions, producing strange coalitions, and, at times, more than usually equivocal resolutions.

Economists, national and international officials, as well as some academics and businessmen wanted the United Nations to provide comprehensive up to date statistical information and population projections. Whilst the UN Population Commission may at times have been considered unimaginative and the UN Population Division under-staffed, there was never any opposition to this role, which an international and inter-governmental institution was uniquely fitted to carry out.

The birth control or family planning movement saw the UN stage as one on which authoritative and widely publicised inter-governmental resolutions could be obtained, confirming that access to contraceptive knowledge and means was a basic right for every couple. Such statements by international agencies could be used to put pressure on governments at the national and local level in order to amend legislation or to provide ser-vices. Margaret Sanger's decision to devote her life to the birth control movement was taken as a result of visiting slums in the course of her work as a health visitor, where she found that women frequently died after illegal abortions because the medi-cal profession and public authorities refused to give or allow to be given information on contraceptive methods. The movement was only secondarily interested in the direct involvement of the UN Agencies in action programmes. These, they felt, might often be carried out more cheaply and more rapidly by non-governmental agencies.

The origins of the birth control movement are to be found in the writings of Thomas Malthus. From the 1920s, however, the movement became more concerned with individual welfare than with the problem of over-population. The Malthusian tradition was kept alive by another group, composed mainly of biologists, zoologists and conservationists, with some demographers: they were concerned by the damage caused by population pressure to the environment. Allied to them, particularly in the sixties, were an increasing number of those professionally concerned with the economic and social development of poor countries and with foreign aid who saw population increase as an important factor in the failure to achieve development targets. These groups not only wanted international organizations to put pressure on governments to adopt anti-natalist policies but also wanted the UN agencies to assist governments in carrying out such policies.

The officials of the UN agencies had various objectives. To some, the cohesion of their agencies was the most important consideration. Advance in such a controversial field could only therefore be gradual or might have to be halted if there were serious disagreements between their member states. Others were frustrated at the inability of the UN system to try to deal with what Dr Brook Chisolm of WHO called the 'Problem of Problems'. And then, subconsciously, there was the instinctive interest which international bureaucrats, like national bureaucrats, have in the expansion of the activities of their organizations by embarking upon new programmes.

The influence of Christian religious groups was of great importance. The Roman Catholic Church, as will be seen in the course of the study, put pressure on governments to prevent any resolutions or action by international agencies which might encourage the practice of what were regarded as illicit methods of birth control. In compensation it favoured the promotion by the UN agencies of international migration. The Protestant Churches altered their position from one of opposition to birth control in the League period to that of neutrality in the early United Nations period, and finally to enthusiastic support of the involvement of the UN agencies in family planning and population policies. Most other religions, while generally favouring high fertility, have no strictures against the practice of contraception. At the international level, they exercised little influence on the course of the debate.

The Communist position was somewhat ambivalent. Though the Communist countries found themselves in a strange alliance with the Roman Catholics in opposing UN action programmes, a distinction can be made between the attitudes. The Catholics were in opposition both to UN involvement in population control policies and in the provision of family planning services. The Communists, whilst considering that there would be no need for public authorities to control population growth in a socialist society, had no objection in principle to family planning. They suggested, however, that assistance in population control was being proposed as a cheap and ineffective alternative to economic assistance.

For those unfamiliar with the procedures of the UN agencies a word may be necessary on the setting of the debate. The UN and each of the Specialized Agencies has a General Assembly or Conference of all its member governments which meets annually, or in some cases every two years. In between these sessions a smaller Governing Body or Council, elected by the Conference, meets about twice a year, to deal with business in more detail. In the United Nations itself this function is carried out in the economic and social field by the Economic and Social Council (ECOSOC). Each agency has its own permanent secretariat, headed by a Secretary-General or Director-General, sometimes known as the Executive Head of the agency. It is not without significance for this study that throughout the period the Executive Heads were appointed for a limited period but were eligible for re-election.

Membership of all the UN agencies is composed of governments, with the exception of the ILO, in whose Conference and Governing Body not only governments but employers' and workers' organizations are represented.

Recognized pressure groups are the non-governmental organizations (NGOs). These are usually international federations of national associations: they can acquire formal consultative status which enables them to make statements at sessions of Councils and Governing Bodies and gives them facilities for lobbying. In the population field among the most important have been the International Union for the Scientific Study of Population, a scientific body consisting mainly of individual demographers, and the International Planned Parenthood Federation which co-ordinates the work of national family planning associations. Although it was not until 1964 that the IPPF acquired consultative status with ECOSOC, both in the evolution of attitudes with regard to population and in the development of family planning programmes, the Federation for many years exerted an influence far beyond that suggested by the lack of formal recognition. Various Christian groups also have NGO status. The Roman Catholic Church has the additional advantage that the Holy See, in its temporal capacity, is a member of several of the Specialized Agencies and has observer status in the United Nations itself.

The debate on the role of international organizations in relation to the population question moved to and fro from the legislative and executive bodies of one agency to another. At times the focus was on organs of the United Nations itself; the Population Commission, ECOSOC and the General Assembly. At others it was in WHO or UNICEF. And though their legislatures were less involved, the Executive Heads of UNESCO, of FAO and of the World Bank made important interventions. Rather than treat the history of each agency's involvement separately, we have preferred a broadly chronological approach which comprehends developments in all the agencies. Whilst trends can be broadly identified, these cannot always be limited within precise dates. There is therefore some overlapping between the periods into which the book is divided.

Part I

PRELUDE—THE LEAGUE OF NATIONS PERIOD
(1919–1939)

'A practice abhorrent to a large section of religious belief and contrary to the national laws of certain countries.'

Index to proceedings of League of Nations Assembly, 13th session, 1932, referring to discussion on birth control

Attitudes Towards Population

THE most striking feature of the late nineteenth and early twentieth century, as far as attitudes towards population were concerned, was the eclipse of Malthusian ideas. Not long before Malthus wrote the first edition of his essay in 1798, world population, in particular the population of Europe and areas of European settlement, had begun to grow at an increasingly rapid rate as a result of reduced levels of mortality. Despite the rapid rate of population growth, however, Europe was more prosperous than it had ever been. Agricultural output increased considerably as a result of the extension of the amount of land under cultivation and through the use of more efficient farming techniques. The spread of industry and trade and the opportunities provided by the acquisition of colonial empires made a larger population seem not only possible but also desirable. Where population continued to press on the means of subsistence, migration provided an outlet. Thus, between 1800 and 1930, an estimated 40 million emigrants left Europe, mainly for North America. Although fears of overpopulation were liable to return in times of economic distress, the notion that population would, if unchecked, outstrip the means of subsistence was largely discounted after 1850. The belief in human progress and perfectibility, which Malthus had challenged, seemed to be confirmed by ever-rising prosperity. Indeed, to many the main danger seemed to be not 'overpopulation' but 'depopulation'.

Towards the end of the nineteenth century birth-rates also began to fall. Population continued to grow but the rate of growth decreased, in some cases dramatically. The fall in the birth rate produced remarkably similar reactions wherever it occurred. Demographers warned that if current trends continued population would begin to decline within several decades. Economists and manufacturers stressed the dangers of a shrinking market and of an ageing population. For political and military leaders the situation threatened the very existence of the nation; grim comparisons were made with the Roman empire, whose decline was authoritatively attributed to depopulation. Power and prestige were thought to be dependent on a large and growing population. In colonial powers, statesmen and men of letters stressed the need for adequate numbers of men and women to people the overseas territories and to maintain the Empire.

Fears of population decline began first, and were most keenly felt, in France which had been the earliest country to experience a fall in the birth rate, around 1800; and in which throughout the nineteenth century the rate of population growth was considerably slower than in other European countries. At first the slow rate of growth was considered an advantage, and it was not until the Second Empire that the low level of fertility began to arouse concern. The defeat of France by Prussia in 1870 transformed the situation. Defeat was attributed to the relative decline of France's population in comparison with that of Germany. In the years which followed, pro-natalist agitation stressed the military and political implications of a stationary population. Victory in 1918 afforded no more than a temporary reassurance, and pressure for 'demographic rearmament' recommenced with renewed vigour after Hitler's seizure of power in Germany.[1]

Government attempts to influence demographic trends began effectively in 1919 with the creation of the Conseil Supérieur de la Natalité, attached to the Ministry of Health. However, the commitment of the governments which rapidly succeeded each other in the Third Republic was far from complete, and it was not until 1939 that the basis of a coherent policy was established. In 1920 religious and pro-natalist forces combined to obtain a law which prohibited the dissemination of contraceptive knowledge. This was followed, in 1923, by an amendment aimed at making more effective the law of 1810 which prohibited abortion. Between 1917 and 1939 the government was gradually persuaded to take over and to extend the family allowance schemes which had been introduced by private employers during the first World War. Family allowances had originally been given to assist wage-earners who had large families, and not as a way of stimulating the birth rate. However they came increasingly to be viewed as a key part of pro-natalist policy.[2]

Elsewhere in Western Europe the birth rate began to decrease in the last quarter of the nineteenth century. As in France, this gave rise to fears of population decline and to pro-natalist agitation. In Belgium events followed closely the French pattern.[3] In Italy and Germany pro-natalist measures were introduced by the Fascists when they came to power. In both countries the policies were more thorough than in France and reflected the importance

[1] J. J. Spengler: *France Faces Depopulation*, Duke University Press, 1938, chapter VI. For a highly influential contemporary statement, see P. Leroy-Beaulieu: *La Question de la Population*, Paris, 1913. Similar fears are very evident in the work of the leading French demographer of this period, A. Landry. See, for example, A. Landry: *La Revolution Demographique*, Paris, 1934.

[2] D. V. Glass: *Population Policies and Movements in Europe*, London, 1940, chapters III and IV; and J. J. Spengler, op. cit., chapter X.

[3] D. V. Glass, op. cit., chapters III and IV.

attached by their ideologies to a young and growing population. In Italy, for example, in addition to family allowances and repressive measures against birth control and abortion, strict controls were placed on emigration, and the taxation system was modified so as to favour large families and penalize bachelors.[1] Marriage loans were a novel feature of Nazi population policy, and their apparent success led to their imitation in Italy and in France.

Fears of population decline spread to Scandinavian countries in the mid-1930s. Government reaction was however significantly different from that in other European countries. In Sweden, for example, a Royal Commission set up in 1935 recommended that the role of the state should be to create an environment in which people would be willing to have children. The Commission's report pointed out that family planning, because it would help to ensure that every child was a wanted child, would help improve the quality of the population.[2] Consequently, incentives to child-bearing were not accompanied by repressive measures against birth control or abortion. Indeed, during the same period there was a liberalization in the laws relating to abortion, and the government assumed some responsibility for the provision of contraceptive advice and services. To a greater extent than elsewhere, the measures adopted in the Scandinavian countries formed a conscious and coherent population policy.[3]

Of the major countries of Europe, Britain was the least affected by fears of depopulation. As early as 1895 a demographer, Edwin Cannan, had warned of an imminent population decline[4] and during the early years of the twentieth century there was talk of prohibiting birth control because of the danger to the future of the nation. Malthusian thinking, however, remained dominant. A League of National Life was founded in 1926, but its propaganda, unlike that of pro-natalist bodies on the Continent,

[1] Ibid., chapters V and VI. In his Ascension Day speech in 1927, Mussolini said: 'To count for something in the world, Italy must have a population of at least 60 millions . . . It is a fact that the fate of nations is bound up with their demographic power.' Quoted in D. V. Glass: *The Struggle for Population*, Oxford, 1936, p. 147.

[2] Sweden, Socialdepartmentet, Befolkningskommissionen: *Betankande i Sexualfragen*, Stockholm, 1936. See also Gunnar Myrdal: *Population — A Problem for Democracy*, Harvard University Press, 1940. It was a book by Gunnar and Alva Mydral, *Kris i Befolkningsfragan* (Crisis in the Population Question) published in 1934 which had precipitated public discussion of the subject and fixed the broad lines of the debate.

[3] D. V. Glass, op. cit., chapter VIII.

[4] E. Cannan: 'The possibility of a cessation of the growth of population in England and Wales during the next century', *Economic Journal*, December 1895, pp. 505–15.

made virtually no impact and the League soon went into demise.[1] In 1936 there was a new scare following the publication of projections which showed an eventual decline in the population to 31 million in 1975 and to 4 million in 2035.[2] Parliament debated the danger and suggested the creation of a Royal Commission to investigate the whole problem.[3] Demographic considerations played some part in the decision to introduce measures, such as family allowances, to give economic support to the family at the end of the Second World War. The chief architect of these measures, Lord Beveridge, had been involved in a celebrated controversy with J. M. Keynes over the latter's assertion that Britain was over-populated.[4]

Meanwhile family size continued to decrease while the birth control movement had overcome the remaining obstacles to its freedom of action. It was never really in any danger from the pronatalists, and after 1920 began to win over the medical profession and the Anglican church.[5] The high rate of unemployment seemed to confirm Keynes' contention that the country was over-populated. Moreover, in the late 1930s and early 1940s, when measures to stimulate the birth rate were being discussed, evidence was available that repressive measures against birth control and abortion were ineffective and that governments could not 'buy' babies. The freedom of the individual to have access to the knowledge and means to control reproduction was recognized, though the obligation of the state to provide such knowledge and means was not yet acknowledged.

Concern with falling birth rates also seem to have influenced Soviet attitudes towards population in the 1930s. Despite Marx's criticism of Malthus and marxist opposition to 'neo-Malthusianism' on the grounds that it diverted attention away from the class struggle, the Soviet Union was the first country in the world whose government attempted to make birth control advice and services freely available. In 1920 the new government repealed the Tsarist law forbidding abortion and made provision for induced abortion to be carried out free of charge in public health clinics. At the same time, attempts were made to spread information about contraception.[6] During the 1930s, however,

---

[1] P. Fryer: *The Birth Controllers*, London, 1965, pp. 264–6.

[2] E. Charles: 'The effects of present trends in fertility and mortality', *London and Cambridge Economic Service*, Special Memorandum, no. 40, 1935.

[3] UK Parliamentary Debates, House of Commons, 10 February 1937, vol. 320, cols. 482–537. The House resolved that 'the tendency of population to decline may well be a danger to the maintenance of the British Empire'.

[4] *Economic Journal*, December 1923, pp. 447–75 and 476–86 and *Economics*, February 1920, pp. 1–20.   [5] P. Fryer, op. cit., 160–72.

[6] Frank Lorimer: *The Population of the Soviet Union*, Geneva, League of Nations, 1946, pp. 126–9.

alarm at the high rates of divorce and abortion led to the introduction of measures designed to reinforce the family, including
a regulation restricting induced abortion to cases where pregnancy endangered the health of the mother.[1]

In North America during the nineteenth century high fertility
and the large number of immigrants caused population to grow
more rapidly than in Western Europe. The rapid increase in
population was considered appropriate for a land of opportunity.
When the birth rate did begin to fall this failed to arouse public
concern because of the initially high level of fertility and large-
scale immigration. President Theodore Roosevelt in his message
to Congress in 1906 warned of the dangers of 'wilful sterility . . .
the one sin for which the penalty is national death, race death.'[2]
Fears of 'race suicide' were however short-lived and the noted
demographer who had coined the phrase made famous by
Roosevelt joined the majority of his colleagues in attempting to
counteract the propaganda of the 'population boosters'. At the
same time, however, the higher fertility of immigrants caused
alarm and, from 1924 onwards, the government imposed increasingly stricter controls on immigration.

In the other areas of European settlement the demographic
pattern was similar to that in the United States. A larger population was considered desirable, although no serious attempts
were made to stimulate the birth rate. Whereas in America the
higher fertility of immigrants of certain races had led to
stricter controls on immigration, in the Dominions the policy of
selective immigration obviated the need for such restrictions.

The demographic situation of Asia, Africa and Latin America
was relatively unknown and aroused little interest even among
European demographers except perhaps for the British interest
in India. The data available in the inter-war period was scanty
and frequently contradictory. Records indicate that the decline
in mortality began in Asia in the early 1920s. However it was
not until the 1950s, when death rates began to fall dramatically,
that the implications of this trend began to be widely realized.[3]

The general lack of interest in the population trends of
tropical areas was not shared by the birth-control movement,
nor by indigenous elites. When Margaret Sanger visited Japan
and China in 1922, she found many people, both men and
women, anxious to learn about birth control. The Japanese

[1] Frank Lorimer, op. cit.; see also M. Hindus: 'The family in Russia', in
R. N. Anshen (ed.): The Family, its Function, its Destiny, New York, 1949.
[2] State of the Union Message, January 1906.
[3] Carr-Saunders, for example, thought that in India the growth of population would be 'slow and fluctuating'. A. M. Carr-Saunders: World Population
—Past Growth and Present Trends, London, 1936, p. 275.

government, under the influence of the military leaders, would not allow her to lecture publicly on the subject. Nevertheless, her visit encouraged some of her listeners to mount a campaign for the emancipation of women which included birth control in its programme.[1] In 1935 a clinic was opened in Tokyo, but was forced to close down two years later. In 1941 the military government embarked upon a pro-natalist policy which lasted until defeat in 1945.[2]

In India, there was some reluctance on the part of the intelligentsia to emphasize overpopulation. Some of them feared that the British might use this to resist the expansion of public health programmes or counter the nationalist argument that Indian poverty was caused by imperial exploitation.[3] In the League of Nations, no reference appears to have been made by Indian representatives to India's population problems.

Nevertheless many sections of the Indian educated classes were aware of these problems. Immediately after the First World War, a neo-Malthusian League had been set up in Madras. In 1930 the state of Mysore opened the first government-sponsored birth control clinic in the world.[4] Pandit Nehru, who had been in contact with the Birth Control International Information Centre while in England, was, in contrast to Gandhi, a firm believer in birth control. The Congress National Planning Committee, set up in 1935 to prepare for independence, convened a special subcommittee to investigate family planning and population policy. Its report, which did not appear until after the war, recommended that: 'in the interests of social economy, family happiness and national planning, family planning and the limitation of children are essential, and the state should adopt a policy to encourage these.'[5]

In 1933 the Birth Control International Information Centre organized a conference to discuss the population problems of Japan, China and India and the obstacles to the adoption of birth control in Asian societies.[6] The All India Women's Con-

---

[1] M. Sanger: *An Autobiography*, New York, 1938, pp. 316ff., and Takuma Terao: *Outline of the Birth Control Movement in Japan*, Tokyo, Japanese National Commission for UNESCO, 1959, p. 10.

[2] I. B. Taeuber: *The Population of Japan*, Princeton University Press, 1959, pp. 366–8.

[3] Gunnar Myrdal: *Asian Drama: an inquiry into the poverty of nations*, New York, 1968, pp. 1483–5.

[4] *Family Planning in India*, New Delhi, 1959, pp. 1–2; and B. L. Raina and G. R. Amrithal: *The Family Planning Programme in India—Retrospect and Prospect*, New Delhi, Central Family Planning Institute, no date, pp. 2–3.

[5] Report of the National Planning Committee: Population, Bombay, 1947, p. 145.

[6] *Birth Control in Asia—Report on a Conference held at the London School of*

ference, whose London agent was Lady Rama Rau, invited the Centre to send a representative to India to put the case for birth control. As a result, Edith How-Martyn visited India in 1934, and in 1936 Margaret Sanger spoke during the debate on birth control at the annual meeting of the AIWC. When the work of the Centre was transferred to the newly formed Family Planning Association in 1939, the international subcommittee decided to concentrate on providing support for the expansion of birth control activities in India.[1]

The British colonial administration made no attempt, either in India or elsewhere in the Empire, to encourage birth control. In the case of India the explanation was not ignorance of the demographic situation. Censuses had been held since 1881. As early as 1931 the Indian Census Commissioner, J. H. Hutton, considered that the rate of population increase was from most points of view a cause for alarm rather than for satisfaction; but, he pointed out, 'It appears to be the general opinion of Indian economists who discuss the population problem that the only practical method of limiting the population is by the introduction of artificial methods of birth control, though it is not easy to exaggerate the difficulties . . . A definite movement towards artificial birth control appears to be taking place and is perhaps less hampered by misplaced prudery than in some countries which claim to be more civilized: thus not only is artificial control publicly advocated by a number of medical writers, but Madras can boast a neo-Malthusian League with 2 Maharajahs, 3 High Court Judges and 4 or 5 men very prominent in public life as its sponsors.'[2] A few years later the director of the Indian health service, Sir John Megaw, also drew attention to the problem.

British policy towards the promotion of social change was profoundly influenced by memories of the Indian mutiny of 1857 and it was feared that the promotion of birth control would provoke accusations of genocide. Moreover, the last years of British rule were marked by increasing tension between Hindus, Muslims and Sikhs whose representation as communities in legislatures and government was related to their numbers. In this situation, in which there were allegations that census figures were exaggerated in areas in which there was communal rivalry, the prudence of the imperial power in relation to the population question was perhaps inevitable.

Hygiene and Tropical Medicine, November 1933, edited by M. Fielding, London, Birth Control International Information Centre, 1933.
[1] Vera Houghton: 'The International Planned Parenthood Federation: its history and influence', *Eugenics Review*, October 1961, p. 153.
[2] Report of the 1931 Census of India, Delhi, 1933, vol. I, pp. 29–31.

France and Belgium, on the other hand, showed no reluctance in extending their laws prohibiting contraceptive propaganda and abortion to their colonial territories. In Africa, colonial employers were particularly preoccupied with the shortage of native labour and this determined metropolitan attitudes towards colonial population size. The French, in particular, sought an increase in the population of their overseas territories in order to swell the ranks of the French army and to help offset the low birth rate in France.

2

The League and Population Questions

THE early years of the twentieth century were in many ways the high point of internationalism. Between 1900 and 1914 no less than 304 international unions were formed.[1] The birth-control movements which had been set up in several European countries around the turn of the century were no exception. Advocates of Malthusian ideas from Britain, France, Holland and several other European countries met for the first time in Paris in 1900. They set up an international union known as La Fédération Universelle de la Régénération Humaine. Further international neo-Malthusian conferences were held in Liège (1905), the Hague (1910), Dresden (1911), and London (1922). The sixth conference, organized by Margaret Sanger, was held in New York in 1925.

One of the topics most frequently discussed at the conferences was the relationship between 'overpopulation' and war. For the advocates of birth control, population pressure was a major cause of international tension because it exacerbated economic rivalries between countries and because it led to demands for territorial expansion.

In 1919 the British Malthusian League had adopted a resolution calling on the League of Nations to refuse membership to any country which did not 'pledge itself so to restrict its birth rate that its people shall be able to live in comfort in their own dominions without the need for territorial expansion'.[2] At the sixth International neo-Malthusian and Birth Control Conference in New York in 1925 a similar resolution urged 'the appointment of a commission to study this question of birth control with a view to making recommendations to the constituent nations'.[3]

The appeals of the birth controllers were ignored. Margaret Sanger was nevertheless determined that the question should be discussed at the international level. She believed, as she has explained in her memoirs, that the League of Nations should include birth control in its programme and proclaim that an

---

[1] F. S. L. Lyons: *Internationalism in Europe, 1815–1914*, Leyden, 1963, pp. 11–15.
[2] Report of the 41st Annual General Meeting of the Malthusian League, London, 27 June 1919.
[3] *Proceedings of the sixth International Neo-Malthusian and Birth Control Conference, New York, 1925*. Resolutions.

increase in numbers was not to be regarded as a justifiable reason for national expansion, but that each nation should limit its inhabitants to its resources as a fundamental principle of international peace. She therefore proposed that a world conference on population be held in Geneva. Unlike the New York conference and the earlier neo-Malthusian conferences which had been attended almost exclusively by birth control propagandists, the world conference would bring together experts in economics, sociology, demography and biology to discuss population problems and to recommend solutions.[1] She hoped that the League of Nations would participate.

A. M. Carr-Saunders, the British demographer, was originally invited to be chairman of the conference but was not available. He was replaced by Sir Bernard Mallet, a former Registrar-General of the United Kingdom. Margaret Sanger, in her determination to make the conference respectable, was influenced by the fact that Sir Bernard's wife had been a Lady-in-Waiting to Queen Victoria, and thus might be expected to exercise a useful social influence in League circles.

Margaret Sanger had however underestimated the controversial nature of the subject. Before many of those invited would agree to attend, the organizers had to promise that any mention of birth control or Malthusianism would be forbidden. Accordingly, the prospectus sent to participants stated that 'propaganda of any kind, or for any objective or doctrine whatever will find no place in the conference. Its viewpoint is that of the scientific laboratory or study rather than that of the pulpit or hustings.'[2] Moreover, it was conveyed to Margaret Sanger by Sir Bernard that the Secretary-General of the League of Nations, Sir Eric Drummond, considered that the eminent scientists whom she had taken such pains to gather together would resent the fact that a woman had been responsible for organizing the conference. Reluctantly she agreed to the removal of her name and that of her co-workers from the official programme.[3]

The reaction to the conference within the League Secretariat was mixed. Drummond declined an invitation for the League to be represented on the grounds that the dates were inconvenient, as they immediately preceded sessions of the League Council and Assembly. It was perhaps unfortunate that Dame Rachel Crowdy, Chief of the Social Questions Section, in seeking his permission to attend, told him that this 'was really a conference on birth control'. Although Mallet explained to him that birth control would not be discussed and that he himself would have

[1] M. Sanger: *An Autobiography*, op. cit., pp. 376–8.
[2] *Proceedings of the World Population Conference, Geneva, 1927*: Notice.
[3] M. Sanger, op. cit., pp. 385–6.

had nothing to do with the conference if it were, Drummond insisted that the conference was going to discuss questions 'which arouse the strongest national feelings and which were of a delicate character' and that the League could not therefore be represented. In vain, Mallet made a plea for benevolent neutrality from the League. Drummond replied drily that 'I should prefer neither to show benevolence or malevolence, but to maintain absolute neutrality'. He admitted, however, that he could not prevent members of the Secretariat from attending privately, though he expressed the hope that they would not attend many sessions in view of his official reply to the invitation.

A number of League officials received invitations to attend. Some, like Sir Arthur Salter, the Director of the Economic and Financial Division, as well as several officials of the Health Division, accepted. Others in addition to Dame Rachel asked the Secretary General for advice, including Pierre Comert, Director of Information, who lamented that whilst this was a very delicate subject, which would put League officials in opposition to the Catholic world, he hardly saw how to avoid the invitation.

Eventually, the question of attendance at the Conference was raised at one of the regular meetings of the Secretary-General with his Directors at which Avenol, as Acting Secretary-General, suggested somewhat tentatively and ineffectively that the Secretary-General's office should in principle be consulted about replies to invitations to attend conferences. The suggestion brought a strong reaction from the Health Division, whose Acting Director, in a note to the Acting Secretary-General after this meeting, recorded his view that, 'I consider that several of the problems which this conference is to consider are of very great importance from the point of view of future League activities. I am also convinced that the League will have to take count of several of these problems whether it desires to do so or not ... Should officials of the League ignore completely this conference, which is taking place in Geneva, their abstinence would certainly be taken as indicating the League's lack of interest, and might give rise to adverse criticism among people whose opinion and co-operation are worth possessing.'

Even the Health Division, however, whilst giving considerable encouragement to the organizers, explained to them that, although sooner or later the League must take cognizance of the problems which were to be discussed, when a sufficient number of Member States became convinced of the necessity, meanwhile official representation at the conference was impossible. Dame Rachel advised Mrs Sanger that she would do more harm than good if she tried to get from the League Assembly an expression of opinion on the subject of birth control. Drummond's policy did not prevent the Economic and Finance Division, as well as the Health Division, from nominating representatives at the end of the conference to a private meeting to consider the establishment of a continuing organization to carry on its work.[1]

The response of Albert Thomas, the Director of ILO, was very different from that of Drummond. With Louis Varlez, Chief of the ILO Migration Service, he gave Margaret Sanger constant encouragement and arranged research, interpretation and services for the conference, which he saw as a means of drawing attention to migration problems. He wrote to Mallet to express the hope that the conference would be a great success and would 'be the beginning of an international movement which will contribute much to the solution of world problems which are largely the result of a bad distribution of the population of the globe'.

In a Minute to Varlez he speculated, 'is it possible to imagine a world organization in which an international authority arbitrates on population questions? Lands are under-populated in countries of determined sovereignty. Can one conceive in the name of the general interest that new populations can be admitted on these lands and under what conditions? That is the immense problem with which the world is confronted, but which no-one, I believe, has dared to raise in a positive manner. It will cause a scandal, but it seems to me important for the future of the world that the problem be faced.' Eager as always to obtain publicity and support for the ILO, he added, 'I will not forget the individual immediate profit which we shall get out of the conference for the Office.'

He gladly accepted an invitation to address the conference, though he insisted on doing so as 'a free man and a citizen of the world' rather than as Director of ILO, in which capacity he would have had to consult his Governing Body and would have felt constrained. In his speech he asserted that there was an optimum population for each nation and that migration was the most immediately effective way of bringing it about. If there was no solution to the migration problem, there was likely to be conflict between nations, but international organizations refused to discuss the problem. 'What is the use of having international institutions,' he asked, 'when each time a serious problem comes up the States drop back and refuse to discuss it?'

He threw out the idea that 'a sort of Higher Migration Council be set up with the power of deciding the right of over-populated countries to occupy other territory', but recognized the difficulty of imposing on a people the presence of national minorities. He stated too that countries which were asked to receive migrants

[1] References for pp. 12–14 from League of Nations Archives. General/40/59774, 1927.

should have the right to demand that over-populated countries should first try to solve their population problems internally. No doubt, he concluded, the Higher Migration Council was premature, but the Conference would have done good work if it brought about the establishment of a private institution with the scientific role of carrying out research on population as well as propaganda.

Julian Huxley considered that Albert Thomas' idea of an optimum population inferred that population exporting countries should take steps to lower their birth rates. This was not, however, Thomas' concern. His colleague, Varlez, noted that neo-Malthusian biologists, mostly American, had dominated the Conference and that ILO's ideas on migration had been relegated to the second level. Margaret Sanger also deplored the fact that Thomas' initiative on migration had not carried more weight. 'Unfortunately', she wrote to him, 'the biologist is a laboratory man and does not of his own accord have the wider social viewpoint.'

Thomas attended the meeting at the end of the conference which took the first steps towards the establishment of the IUSSP, but he was disappointed with the result which he found un-imaginative. Poor Varlez, who had handled negotiations, received one of the Director's magisterial rebukes, 'Vous avez été décidément trop discret'.[1]

Margaret Sanger did not take part in the meeting to establish a permanent organization. It was felt that the new organization, which was set up primarily to bring together social scientists concerned with the study of population, would stand a better chance of success if it were not associated with her name.

Even without birth control, or Margaret Sanger, the International Union for the Scientific Investigation of Population Problems which emerged from the 1927 conference found it difficult to avoid being used as a 'pulpit'. Until 1939 the proceedings were marred by Franco–German rivalry and by Nazi attempts to use the conferences to legitimize their anti-semitic policies and demands for 'lebensraum'.[2]

Meanwhile the League had begun to collect and analyse population data. The League's Economic Section published a Statistical Year Book which included information on population size, birth and death rates, age structure, occupation and migratory movements for a number of countries. Shortly before

[1] References for pp. 14–15 from International Labour Organization. Archives.
[2] See for example the Proceedings of the third General Assembly of the IUSSP in Berlin, August–September 1935: H. Harmsen and F. Lohse (eds). *Bevolkerungfragen*, München, 1935.

the World Population Conference an International Economic Conference had met in Geneva under League auspices to discuss ways of removing economic barriers between countries. Although the preparatory committee for the conference had considered it inopportune to include population as a separate item on the agenda, the documentation for the conference included several papers on migration and a short report on the natural movement of populations written by the Health Section.[1]

The Health Section does not appear to have shared the fears of imminent population decline which were prevalent in many European countries. Commenting on the continuing excess of births over deaths, the report observed: 'Leaving aside abnormal war years, it is becoming more and more evident that the natural increase of the population is soon bound to slacken (*although not to cease*[2]) in the most densely populated parts of Europe.' Elsewhere continued improvements in the control of mortality would ensure a continuation of the high rates of natural increase experienced in the first quarter of the twentieth century.[3]

The volume of international migration had declined considerably after the First World War. The restrictions on immigration introduced by the American government in 1924 in particular had created acute difficulties for many countries in Southern and Eastern Europe where birth rates remained high. Consequently when the Conference met in May 1927 several countries pressed for the removal of legal barriers to migration. Their position was summed up by Mr Belloni of Italy. His country he said was reluctant to pursue a protectionist policy but saw no alternative. 'In densely populated countries, without natural resources', he argued, 'unless there is freedom of circulation all over the world, there is only one means whereby a government can fulfil its duty and provide work, a guarantee of work for its citizens'. Although population pressure had not yet led to social unrest he warned that if a solution were not found rapidly there could be 'serious repercussions on world peace'.[4] The final report recommended as 'one of the essential conditions of economic co-operation between nations' that foreign nationals, firms or companies should be guaranteed equal treatment in the territory of another state.[5] Two years later, however, the depression led to

[1] Preparatory Committee for the International Economic Conference; Report to the Council on the 2nd Session, November 1926 [1926. II. 57]; and International Economic Conference, May 1927: Documentation [1926. II. 61].   [2] Our italics.

[3] International Economic Conference: Documentation, op. cit., 'The Natural Movement of Populations during the first quarter of the 20th Century', [C.E.I. 14 (1)], p. 4

[4] *Report and Proceedings of the International Economic Conference, Geneva, 1927*, vol. I, p. 136. [1927. II. 52.]   [5] Ibid., pp. 35–6.

ever greater restrictions on the movement of men, money and materials.

Interest in some kind of international machinery to regulate population movements revived in 1936 when the Conference of American States of the ILO adopted a resolution calling on the Governing Body to 'have special enquiries made in connection with migration from Europe to America'.[1] This initiative raised hopes that Latin American countries might replace North America as the outlet for 'surplus' European population. In February 1938 the ILO convened a conference of experts from interested European and Latin American countries to discuss the technical and financial aspects of migration for settlement. The conference called on the ILO to investigate the possibility of creating a 'Permanent International Committee on Migration for Settlement'.[2]

In 1937 the International Studies Conference discussed demographic problems in connection with German, Italian and Japanese demands for a revision of the 'status quo.'[3] Two ILO officials participated in the conference and put forward suggestions for international action to facilitate migration. One of the contributions, by Imre Ferenczi, served as a background paper to the discussion. It outlined a set of criteria for determining the optimum population of each country and proposed a series of bilateral and multilateral agreements designed to reduce the inequalities resulting from the uneven distribution of world population.[4]

Meanwhile the question had also been raised in the League of Nations. Italian policy on migration had been reversed when the fascists seized power. In the absence of Germany and Japan, Poland became the spokesman for the countries suffering from 'overpopulation'. In the 1937 Assembly debate on economic and financial questions, the Polish delegate argued eloquently for a return to the era of liberalism that had existed before 1914. Any plans for the promotion of world trade, he said, had to be accompanied by measures to facilitate the free movement of

[1] Governing Body of the ILO, 75th Session, April 1936, Appendix IV, pp. 98–9. Report on the work of the Labour Conference of American States.
[2] Technical and Financial International Co-operation with regard to Migration for Settlement — Technical Conference of Experts—Conclusions. *ILO Studies and Reports, Series O (Migration), no. 7*, Geneva, 1938, pp. 165–6.
[3] *Peaceful Change: Procedures, Population Pressure, the Colonial Question, Raw Materials and Markets*: Proceedings of the Tenth International Studies Conference, Paris, June–July 1937, Paris, International Institute for Intellectual Co-operation, 1938.
[4] Imre Ferenczi: *The Synthetic Optimum of Population: An Outline of an International Demographic Policy*, Paris, International Institute for Intellectual Co-operation, 1938.

capital and people. A small country like Poland could not agree to free trade unless outlets were provided for her overpopulated rural districts. Although he did not wish to deprecate the work done by the ILO to improve the treatment of immigrants, he felt that the time had come to consider the economic and demographic consequences of the restrictions on migration. He proposed 'the appointment of a committee to study demographic problems in their international aspect', and suggested that the question of migration be placed on the agenda for the next session of the Assembly.[1]

The international climate was too heavily charged with mistrust for governments, especially colonial powers, to contemplate a return to the 'era of liberalism' to which the Polish representative had referred. The French delegate, Mr Faure, was quick to reply: 'Certain states had stressed the delicate question of overpopulation and the rise in the birth rate. France did not underestimate the seriousness of the question, and outlets would have to be found for excess population. The fact of having many children did not, however, confer the right to conquer foreign territories, especially when the authorities of the countries which complained most of lack of space for their growing population redoubled their appeals, their grants and their subsidies for the purpose of increasing the birth rate still more.' He quoted Leon Blum, then French Prime Minister: 'What nation is going to agree to co-operate with another . . . by giving it facilities for settlement or colonization . . . if it has the slightest suspicion that the help thus given may one day be used against it?'[2]

The Chinese delegate pointed out that the annexation of Manchuria had not solved Japan's population problems. He warned the Assembly that 'to justify territorial expansion on the grounds of overpopulation would be to create a most dangerous precedent'. To emphasize the danger he reminded the delegates from the British Empire that they had vast expanses of virtually unoccupied territory.[3]

Nevertheless, in its report, the Second Committee referred to the Polish proposal and recommended that the Assembly request the League Council to 'take the necessary steps to draw up a scheme of work for the study of demographic problems'.[4]

The Council endorsed the proposal, but there was little satisfaction for the Polish government in the memorandum on the subject prepared by the League secretariat. As in the Assembly, the major concern was German and Japanese claims to territorial

[1] LN: Records of the 18th Session of the Assembly, 1937. Minutes of the Second Committee, pp. 56–8 and p. 71.   [2] Ibid., pp. 66–7.
[3] Ibid., p. 76.
[4] Ibid., annex 5, Report of the Second Committee, p. 127.

expansion. Arguing that the criteria for deciding whether or not a country was overpopulated was not density but the degree of economic development at any given time, the memorandum concluded that 'solutions other than territorial solutions' were to be preferred, since they prepared the way for 'a natural absorption of future excess population'.[1]

When the question was debated in 1938, the Polish representative recognized, with a hint of regret, that in view of the difficulty in reaching agreement on trade and raw materials, the most valuable service that the League could render was through its studies. Since the problem of 'man in the world economy' was of particular importance, he welcomed the endorsement given to his government's proposal for a committee on demographic problems.[2]

The Assembly adopted a resolution requesting the Council to set up 'a special committee of experts to study demographic problems and especially their connection with the economic, financial and social situation and to submit a report on the subject which may be of value to governments in the determination of policy'.[3]

The Committee was nominated by the Council in January 1939. Its members included Sir Alexander Carr-Saunders, as well as experts from India, Egypt, Argentina, Brazil and Poland.[4] At its first meeting it drew up a work programme covering three areas: the problems facing governments with a rapidly growing population; those facing governments with a diminishing population; and those arising from a population which was small in relation to the productive area or the natural resources of the country. The outbreak of war prevented further meetings of the committee. However, Princeton University offered the services of its Office of Population Research and as a result a series of demographic monographs were issued on various aspects of European population.[5]

[1] LN: 'Preliminary observations on the drawing-up of a scheme of work for the study of demographic problems'. Report of the Economic Committee to the Council on its 48th Session, 1938 [C.233M.132 : 1938.II.B].
[2] LN: Records of the 19th Session of the Assembly, 1938. Minutes of the Second Committee, pp. 33-4.
[3] Ibid., p. 67.
[4] LN: Minutes of the 104th Session of the Council, January 1939, p. 54.
[5] The titles of the studies included *The Future Population of Europe and the Soviet Union, 1940–1970*, by Frank Notestein; *The Population of the Soviet Union* by Frank Lorimer and *Europe's Population in the Inter-War Years* by Dudley Kirk.

3

The League and Birth Control

THE decline in fertility described in Chapter 1 had been brought about by a conscious limitation of family size.[1] The social and economic changes associated with urban living and industrialization had removed many of the advantages of a large family, while reduced mortality meant that fewer births were required to achieve the desired number of children.[2] The most widely used methods of birth control in the nineteenth century were probably 'coitus interruptus' and induced abortion. During the last quarter of the century there was increasing use of contraceptive techniques. The vulcanization of rubber in the 1840s had made possible the mass production of cheap but effective condoms. The development of the diaphragm in Germany in 1882 represented a considerable improvement on the sponges soaked in vinegar or oil which had been previously available.[3]

The subject of birth control however aroused great hostility. The Catholic Church, basing itself on the teaching of St Augustine and St Thomas Aquinas, insisted that birth control was illicit. Protestants had been brought up on the Old Testament with its message of a chosen people and of individual men and women who would be fruitful and multiply. In most other societies, the successful ruler had been the King in whose reign the population had increased; and priests had prayed for human fertility as well as that of lands and of crops. Medical opinion, too, with some notable exceptions, was at first hostile to birth control. Until the 1930s contraception was officially condemned as being not only dangerous to health, but also immoral.[4]

The attitude of the Marxists and socialists was ambivalent. Marx indeed had strongly attacked Malthus, but mainly it seems because of the underlying pessimism of his analysis. Malthus, he believed, had provided the English ruling classes

---

[1] United Nations: *The Determinants and Consequences of Population Trends*, Population Studies, no. 17, New York, 1953, pp. 74–6.

[2] Ibid., pp. 76 ff. See also A. Coale: 'Factors Associated with the Development of Low Fertility: An Historic Summary', *Proceedings of the World Population Conference, Belgrade, 1965*, vol. II.

[3] See N. O. Himes: *The Medical History of Contraception*, Baltimore, 1939, and International Planned Parenthood Federation: *The History of Contraceptives*, London, 1967.

[4] See P. Fryer: *The Birth Controllers*, op. cit., and J. Peel, 'Contraception and the Medical Profession', *Population Studies*, November 1964, pp. 133–46.

with a rationale for opposing assistance to the poor and unemployed. Engels, however, had recognized the abstract possibility 'that the number of people in a Communist country might have to be limited by conscious control' but felt that this was essentially a private matter between husband and wife.[1] Lenin, for whom family planning was a key factor in the emancipation of women, insisted that a distinction be made between what he called on the one hand 'the freedom of dissemination of medical knowledge and the defence of the elementary democratic rights of citizens of both sexes' and neo-Malthusian propaganda on the other hand.[2] Early socialist antagonism to the birth-control movement seems to have been partly due to a feeling that it diverted attention away from the class struggle. The German socialist Bebel, for example, considered that sex was a diversion of the poor and that fertility would be reduced with better nutrition. He and other Social Democrats also wanted to discourage the impression that socialists were libertines. Other socialists, however, supported the birth-control movement on the grounds that large families provided an abundance of cheap labour and cannon-fodder for imperialist wars. Before the First World War Rosa Luxembourg and Anatole France had proposed a 'birth strike' in Germany and France. In Britain the Labour Party and the trade unions favoured birth control. In the USA the anarchists also were, for a time, among the leading advocates of birth control.[3]

In many countries the dissemination of information about contraception or abortion was suppressed under the laws relating to obscenity. In others special laws were introduced prohibiting the sale, distribution and advertising of contraceptive devices.

The opponents of birth control concentrated on the suppression of public discussion of family limitation and of all propaganda in favour of birth control not only from a realization that it would be impracticable to prohibit the practice of contraception, but also from an inability, or unwillingness, to distinguish between pornography and scientific works. In the climate of opinion prevailing in most countries at the time the League of Nations was established, any subject connected with sex, however presented, was liable to be considered pornographic.

Some propaganda was, not unsurprisingly, of a dubious character. The hostility of the medical profession and the initial

---

[1] Letter from Engels to Karl Kautsky, February 1st, 1881. Marx and Engels: *Collected Works*, vol. XXVII.

[2] V. I. Lenin: 'The Working Class and Neo-Malthusianism', *Collected Works*, vol. XIX, pp. 255-7.

[3] See W. Petersen: *The Politics of Population*, London, 1964, Notes on the Socialist Position on Birth Control, pp. 90-102.

unwillingness of neo-Malthusian organizations to extend their activities beyond economic and social arguments in favour of family limitation left the dissemination of contraceptive advice and services largely in the hands of commercial enterprise. The dominance of commercial interests provided an opportunity for all kinds of 'quacks' and there was a flourishing illicit trade in supposed abortifacients. The neo-Malthusians shared the concern felt about the situation, because of the harm it did to their cause, but argued that the solution was not repression but the involvement of the medical profession and the state.

In 1910 an intergovernmental conference was called to draw up a convention for the suppression of the traffic in obscene publications. The Belgian delegation wanted to include within the scope of the convention publications advocating abortion or the use of means to prevent conception. The question was not placed on the agenda. However, a unanimous declaration was issued at the end of the conference drawing attention to 'the danger with which, by drying up their very sources of life, this vile propaganda threatens all nations'.[1]

At the third Assembly of the League in 1922 it was decided to renew the 1910 agreement, and the French government was entrusted with the organization of a conference. In 1920 a coalition of Roman Catholics and right-wing parties had secured the adoption by the Assemblée Nationale of a law prohibiting the dissemination of contraceptive information. In its memorandum submitted to the conference, the French government took the opportunity to propose an amendment which would have placed a complete ban on all kinds of contraceptive propaganda. The amendment would also have made the dissemination of contraceptive devices illegal.[2]

In the course of the debate on this question, the French delegate, Mr Hennequin, disclaimed any desire to restrict individual freedom regarding the practice of contraception. But, he argued, 'contraceptive propaganda is undoubtedly made the cloak of obscenity and is founded on a desire to make commercial profits of a discreditable nature'. He continued: 'young married couples have even been recommended, on the day of their wedding, to seek their pleasure whilst evading the consequences of sexual relations and the institution of the family. The laws of nature and the sanctity of marriage were thus violated.'[3]

[1] *Records of the International Conference for the Suppression of the Circulation of and Traffic in Obscene Publications, Geneva, August–September 1923*, Annex IV, p. 108.

[2] *Records of the International Conference* ... Annex IV, op. cit. Note by the French government.

[3] *Records of the International Conference*, op. cit., pp. 52–3.

Other delegates, as in 1910, thought that the question did not fall within the competence of the conference. Moreover, they suggested, not all contraceptive propaganda was necessarily obscene. The Greek delegate echoed the thought of many delegates when he argued that the conference could only 'deal with and take measures against contraceptive propaganda in so far as it touches obscenity. If this propaganda is pursued for obscene purposes, or by means of obscene works, it will be covered by our convention: if not we have no jurisdiction in the matter.'[1] Finally, the French, like the Belgians in 1910, had to be satisfied with a declaration recognizing the importance of the question. The British, Indian and Australian delegations dissociated themselves from the hope expressed in the declaration that a time would come 'when circumstances would permit the consideration of an international agreement for the defence of all states against this social menace'.[2]

The conference reflected prevailing attitudes towards birth control. In most continental European countries, national legislation prohibited propaganda in favour of birth control. Although the repressive legislation seems to have had little impact on birth rates, it did succeed in suppressing the birth-control movements which had been set up around the turn of the century. As a result, in the inter-war period, the birth-control movement became a primarily Anglo-Saxon affair. In Britain the birth-control movement had not been handicapped by legal obstacles since 1892. Indeed, it was paradoxically the prosecution of the advocates of birth control which had done most to arouse interest in and promote knowledge of its methods. Thus when Annie Besant and Charles Bradlaugh were prosecuted in 1877 for republishing Charles Knowlton's *Fruits of Philosophy*, 125,000 copies of the book were sold in the three months between the arrest and the trial. In 1887 the publicity given to the removal of Dr H. A. Allbutt's name from the medical register by the General Medical Council for publishing '*The Wives' Handbook*' contributed to the even more remarkable success of his book which sold at least 500,000 copies.[3] In the United States too, the prosecution of Margaret Sanger's sister and the police raid on the Brownsville clinic led to public pressure for the removal of legal restrictions on the dissemination of birth control information.

During the 1920s the birth-control movement in Britain and the United States began to win a grudging acknowledgement of respectability from the medical profession. The turning point

[1] Ibid., pp. 54–6.
[2] *Records of the International Conference*, Final Act, para. 5.
[3] P. Fryer, op. cit., pp. 160–72.

in Britain was a speech in 1921 by Lord Dawson, the King's physician, to an important lay congress of the Church of England. Arguing the case for birth control on medical, social and personal grounds, he called upon the Church, and, by implication, his own profession, to reappraise their attitude in the light of modern knowledge.[1]

Lord Dawson's speech was prompted by the decision of the Church of England's Lambeth Conference in 1920 to uphold its condemnation of all 'artificial' means of family limitation. The evolution of attitudes towards birth control was evident when the 1930 Lambeth Conference authorized, albeit grudgingly, the practice of contraception provided that the motives were not 'selfishness and luxury, or mere convenience'.[2] In the United States a similar evolution occurred in the doctrine of the Protestant Churches and the Jewish Reformed Sect.[3] More significantly, in 1930 Pope Pius XI, while stressing that the primary purpose of marriage was procreation, authorized couples to utilize the 'rhythm method' or periodic abstinence where there were pressing reasons to limit family size.[4]

In America the medical profession seems on the whole to have been less hostile to birth control. However, few doctors were willing to risk prosecution under the Comstock Act.[5] Margaret Sanger became convinced that the medical profession must be involved, and the energies of the American Birth Control League were directed towards changing the laws which prevented doctors from giving advice. They were unsuccessful until 1929 when, after a police raid on Margaret Sanger's Brownsville clinic, the courts upheld the right of doctors to prescribe contraceptives for health reasons. A more important victory was won in 1936 when a New York judge ruled that the Comstock Act did not apply to the medical profession. The court ruling finally changed the attitude of the American Medical Association, whose committee on contraception recommended research into effective methods of birth control and the inclusion of the subject in the curricula of medical schools.[6]

[1] Ibid., pp. 243–5.

[2] The Lambeth Conference, 1930, Encylical letter from the Bishops together with Reports and Resolutions, London, 1930, pp. 43–4.

[3] E. Draper: *Birth Control in the Modern World*, London, 1964, chapter 7; R. M. Fagley: *The Population Explosion and Christian Responsibility*, New York, 1960, pp. 194–7.

[4] 'Casti Conubii . . .' Encyclical letter of Pope Pius XI, 1930.

[5] So called after Anthony Comstock who, as chief special agent of the New York Society for the Suppression of Vice, masterminded the prosecution of advocates of birth control under the Federal law against obscenity which, at his insistence, embraced contraception and abortion.

[6] P. Fryer, op. cit., chapter 19.

The change in the attitude of the medical profession transformed the character of the birth-control movement. Before the
First World War the advocates of birth control had limited
themselves to propaganda stressing the economic and social
reasons for family limitation. It was felt that the provision of
contraceptive advice and services was the responsibility of the
medical profession. Lord Dawson's speech was particularly
opportune, since first Marie Stopes and then the Malthusian
League had decided to follow the example of Dr Aletta Jacobs,
Holland's first woman doctor, and open birth-control clinics.
Encouraged by Lord Dawson's speech, some of the more adven-
turous doctors began to co-operate with the new birth-control
clinics. When the National Birth Control Association was set
up in 1930, Sir Thomas (later Lord) Horder, physician to the
Prince of Wales and subsequently to the King, became its first
president.

The clinics began a new phase in the history of the birth-
control movement. As the movement acquired allies and
respectability its radical origins and revolutionary potential were
pushed into the background. Emphasis was placed on the health
and happiness of the individual couple, particularly the woman.
Spacing of children, rather than limitation, was recommended,
partly in deference to the concern felt about falling birth rates.
The term 'birth control', invented by Margaret Sanger and her
friends in 1914, was replaced by 'family planning' or 'planned
parenthood'.

The index to the proceedings of the League of Nations
Assembly contains a discreet reference under 'Health' to 'Documents published by the Health Organization containing
references to a practice abhorrent to a large section of religious
belief and contrary to the national laws of certain countries:
suspension of distribution'.

This entry refers to a debate in the Second Committee of the
Assembly in 1932 on the report of a committee set up by the
Health Organization to investigate maternal welfare and the
hygiene of infants and children of pre-school age. The committee's report contained a short section entitled 'Abortion and
Birth Control' in which the Committee, emphasizing the
dangers of abortion, recommended that in certain cases of serious
ill health, where pregnancy would endanger the woman's life,
it was preferable to prevent pregnancy from occurring, rather
than to terminate it. The report continued: 'but it is not sufficient
merely to tell a woman suffering from tuberculosis or heart
disease or nephritis that she should not again become pregnant;
it is necessary to explain exactly what steps she and her husband
should take to prevent this from happening. If the private doctor

is not prepared to do this, the information can be given most appropriately at the Health Centre'.[1]

This recommendation was strongly attacked by Catholic medical organizations and in the Vatican newspaper *Osservatore Romano*.[2] It is curious to note that the chairman of the reporting committee, Dame Janet Campbell, had once before found herself at the centre of a similar controversy in Britain. In 1922, following the dismissal of a health visitor who had told women attending a maternal welfare clinic where they could obtain contraceptive advice, Dame Janet, then Senior Medical Officer in the Ministry of Health, had issued instructions to local authorities pointing out that it was not the function of maternity centres to give advice on birth control. This ruling had precipitated a campaign for the inclusion of contraceptive advice as a part of government maternal and child welfare services. In 1930 the Ministry of Health issued a circular authorizing the provision of such advice, on medical grounds alone, as an incidental part of the normal work of the centres.[3]

Finding herself once again under attack, but from a different quarter, Dame Janet, at the suggestion of the Secretariat, circulated a note to the members of the Second Committee in which she rejected suggestions that the League intended to 'use this indirect means of encouraging propaganda in favour of indiscriminate birth control'. She explained that the Committee had explicitly limited itself to the medical aspects of the question.[4] Meanwhile the Secretariat replied to the many Catholic organizations who had written to protest against the report that there was nothing in it which might not be deemed to refer to the approved Catholic practice of limiting intercourse to the 'safe period'.

These attempts to dispel what Dame Janet called a 'misunderstanding' failed, and the Irish representative in the Assembly demanded that the document be withdrawn and the offending passages omitted, and that the Health Organization be requested to refrain in future from dealing with or publishing documents concerned with the practice mentioned. He was supported by the representatives of Italy, the Netherlands and Luxembourg. The question was referred to a subcommittee, which suggested that the Health Committee should be asked to reconsider its report.

[1] Report on maternal welfare and the hygiene of infants and children of pre-school age by the committee appointed to deal with the question, October 1931 [1931, III 13], p. 25.

[2] Minutes of the 19th session of the Health Committee, LN Archives, p. 16.   [3] P. Fryer, op. cit., pp. 257–63.

[4] Statement by the Chairman of the Reporting Committee on Maternal Welfare . . . regarding a paragraph that has given rise to misunderstanding, 1931. [M(CH 1060 (a)].

The Italian delegate indeed wanted the report to take into account different national legislation on the question of birth control, since, as he pointed out, Italy had a policy of encouraging births. The distribution of the document was suspended, and the Health Committee was asked to reconsider it in the light of these observations.[1]

When the Health Committee next met, Dr Rajchman, the director of the League Health Section, argued strongly against removing the references to which objection had been taken.[2] Rajchman, though an energetic and forceful international official who did much to enhance the League's reputation in the social field, was suspect in some quarters as a 'leftist'. Indeed in a speech to the Health Committee on its 10th Anniversary in 1934 he expressed the belief: 'que pour qu'une organisation technique de la Société puisse réussir et répondre à l'essence même de son existence, il faut qu'elle n'ait pas peur d'être considérée comme une organisation d'avant garde'.[3] He claimed that the report had been rejected for political reasons. Dame Janet agreed with Dr Rajchman, and reminded the committee of the need to uphold its independence. The majority of the members supported a firm stand, but, in the interests of harmony, decided to make certain modifications. The heading of the section became 'Pre-Natal Welfare', and the amended text suggested that advice on birth control should take account of the individual's religious beliefs and moral principles as well as of national legislation. At the same time, however, the committee affirmed 'its right to full liberty and complete independence of opinion on all technical subjects coming within its competence'.[4]

The debate on the report in the League Council was adjourned in order to enable the amended report to obtain the approval of the Papal representative in Berne. Nevertheless, in the following year, when the Second Committee discussed the report of the Health Committee, the Irish delegate protested with even greater vehemence that it was indefensible that League funds should be used to investigate the use of contraceptives, and that the committee's report would bring health centres into disrepute. He warned that public support would be alienated from the League at a time (1933) when its prestige had already been severely shaken by political events. The Assembly once again refused to

[1] LN: Records of the 13th Ordinary Session of the Assembly, Minutes of the Second Committee, p. 12 and annex 5. Also LN Archives files 8F/23354/1499 and 8F/2363/895.
[2] LN: Minutes of the 19th session of the Health Committee, op. cit., p. 16.
[3] LN: Minutes of the 21st session of the Health Committee, 13 May 1934. LN Archives.
[4] LN: Health Committee: Report to the Council on the work of the 19th session of Committee, October 1932 [C.275 M.344], p. 5.

distribute the report, despite the modifications, and resolved to refer it back to the Health Committee.[1]

The Second Committee reported to the Council on the work of the Health Committee. The Rapporteur at the 14th session was Sean Lester of Ireland, who was to become the League's last Secretary-General. In a fairly obvious reference to the report of the Committee on Maternal and Child Welfare he observed: 'in the best interests of the League as a whole, it is essential that, in the consideration of any question which has not only a technical aspect but which is likely also to involve issues affecting religious beliefs, moral principles or the legislation of serious countries, due regard must necessarily be paid to those wider aspects'.[2] At its twentieth session, the Health Committee, chastened perhaps by a cut in its budget, heeded Mr Lester's advice. The Director of the Health Section was instructed to 'find a text which would give entire satisfaction'.[3] The British member of the committee, Sir George Buchanan, claimed that this would be difficult since the report was already published and had been on sale for two months. However there is no record of the publication of the report in a revised form. The entry in the League catalogue is to the 1931 version, with the note 'out of print' and one must conclude that the report was in fact suppressed in its entirety.

The debate in the League Assembly in 1932 and 1933 was a significant precursor of that which was to develop in the World Health Assembly twenty years later.

It is notable that in the League period its Health Organization took a more advanced position regarding the League's involvement in population and birth-control questions than did the Assembly and Secretary-General. In the United Nations period the converse was to be the case. In the sixties the Secretary-General and ECOSOC were ahead of the World Health Organization in advocating involvement of international organizations in family planning and population questions.

Personalities were relevant. Opposition in the League Assembly came mainly from Catholic countries whose high proportion of the membership gave them greater influence than they were to enjoy in the United Nations. Drummond was a civil servant of conservative temperament and a convert to Catholicism, whereas Rajchman, and indeed Albert Thomas, were radicals. Yet a constitutional point may also be significant. The League Health Organization had no political independence: it was sub-

[1] LN: Records of the 14th session of the Assembly, Minutes of the Second Committee, p. 11.

[2] LN: Records of the 70th session of the Council, p. 223.

[3] LN: Minutes of the 20th session of the Health Committee, Seventh Meeting, 31 October 1933. LN Archives.

ordinate to the Secretary-General and Assembly of the League. Therefore its officials were perhaps not as cautious in relation to political factors as were their successors in WHO who felt a direct responsibility, in an independent organization, to maintain the cohesion of its member states in the World Health Assembly, and who were also more directly exposed to political pressures from governments. The dangers for a dependent functional organization of taking initiatives which are unwelcome to a higher political body were shown however when the services of Rajchman were enthusiastically dispensed with by Secretary-General Avenol in the period of League retrenchment.

Part II

THE INITIATIVE THAT FAILED
(1946–1952)

'Population must be balanced against resources or civilization will perish.'

Julian Huxley, Director-General of UNESCO, 1948

4

The Nature of the Problem

THE world of 1945 differed in many important respects from the world of the League of Nations. The League had been overwhelmingly European both in its membership, and more significantly, in its atmosphere and procedures. Of the original fifty-one members of the United Nations, on the other hand, only two-fifths were from Europe or from areas of European settlement. By 1955 the number of member states from Asia, Africa and the Middle East had increased from twelve to seventeen and, despite the influx of ten new members, Europe represented only a third of total membership. Not only were the non-European members more numerous; they were also more confident and more demanding. Moreover, most of them were desperately poor.

Many of the new member states from the 'Third World' had recently entered or were about to enter what is called the second phase of the 'demographic transition', characterized by falling death rates and high or very high birth rates.[1] The absence of major famines, together with improvements in the standard of living, in public health and in the control of epidemic diseases had begun to affect mortality in the period between the two World Wars. War-time scientific developments, particularly the use of DDT to control malaria, subsequently speeded up the decline in mortality. The results were most dramatic among the populations of small islands. In Ceylon, for example, the death rate fell from 20 per thousand to 14 per thousand in the year 1946–7 alone, while in Mauritius, in the same year, it fell from 30 per thousand to 20. Life expectancy in Ceylon, which had been 44 in 1946, reached 60 by 1954.[2]

Elsewhere the decline in mortality was less precipitous. Nevertheless, throughout the 'Third World' death rates were falling far more rapidly than had been the case in Europe during the corresponding stage of the demographic cycle. Declines in mortality which in Europe had been spread over a century were achieved often in little more than a decade in many less developed

[1] See *The Determinants and Consequences of Population Trends*, op. cit., p. 44; and D. Bogue: *Principles of Demography*, New York, 1969, pp. 55–61.

[2] P. Newman: *Malaria eradication and population growth with special reference to Ceylon and British Guiana*, University of Michigan, Bureau of Public Health Economics Research Series no. 10. Ann Arbor, 1965, p. 14; *World Population and Resources, A PEP Report*, London, 1955, pp. 12–14.

countries.[1] Moreover, since the impact of poor health conditions and of diseases like malaria and smallpox was greatest among young children, the progress made in death control meant that a much larger proportion of the children born survived to the age at which they themselves could have children.

The decline in mortality was occurring so rapidly that its significance was not at first fully appreciated. The first issue of the United Nations Population Bulletin in 1951, for example, stated that 'any expectation of a constant rate of population growth in the future would be unrealistic'. Although a continued reduction in mortality in Asia and the Far East could cause the population to 'shoot up' this was considered unlikely: 'Many observers tend towards the view that . . . a high rate of increase occasioned by low death rates during some years would be checked by periodic catastrophes such as widespread epidemics, failure of the food supply and internal strife'. Latin America was considered to have passed through the period of maximum growth.[2] In 1955, and again in 1957, the estimates of future world population growth had to be revised upwards, since it now seemed 'more certain' that 'current and future mortality declines (would be) substantial'.[3]

To some observers however the situation appeared alarming because the decline in mortality seemed to be occurring independently of improvements in productivity. In Europe and in other parts of the developed world, the fall in the death rate had been spread over many years and had followed, and was indeed mainly the result of, improvements in living standards. Although there was continuing disagreement about the exact contribution of medical science, particularly malaria control, to the decline in mortality in less developed countries, it was clear that 'death control' had created an entirely new situation.[4] Not only was the population growing at an unprecedented rate, but the countries

[1] United Nations, *Demographic Yearbook, 1959*, p. 1.

[2] 'Past and Future Growth of World Population: a Long-range View', *United Nations Population Bulletin*, no. 1, December 1951 (ST/SOA/ ser. N.1), pp. 3–6.

[3] '*Future Growth of World Population*', Population Studies no. 28, 1958 (ST/SOA/ser. A. 28), p. viii.

[4] See P. Newman, op. cit., and R. Titmuss and B. Abel-Smith: *Social Policies and Population Growth in Mauritius*, London, 1961. For a contrary view see H. Frederiksen: 'Malaria Control and Population Pressure in Ceylon', *Public Health Reports*, vol. 75, October 1960, and: 'The Determinants and Consequences of Population Trends', *Public Health Reports*, vol. 81, August 1966. The question was also discussed at the first World Population Conference in 1954. See *Proceedings of the World Population Conference, Rome 1954* Summary Report, meeting 4: 'Mortality trends with special reference to areas of high mortality'. See also *United Nations Population Bulletin*, no. 6, 1962 (ST/SOA/ser. N.6).

of Asia, Africa and Latin America were far poorer and much less well equipped than the now developed countries had been when they had experienced a similar, but less rapid, population explosion. Nor were there the same opportunities for migration and colonization which had played such an important part in European economic prosperity. In many places there was little additional land that could be brought into agricultural use, and even where arable land existed its exploitation required substantial investments of capital and technology.[1]

In Europe and in the other areas of white settlement on the other hand the post-war 'baby-boom' was short-lived and failed to allay the prevailing apprehension regarding low birth rates. In Europe particularly fears of depopulation remained strong, and pro-natalist policies were pursued in many countries.[2] The most strenuous efforts to raise the birth rate were made in France and, to a lesser extent, in the Soviet Union. In the case of the Soviet Union the motivation was primarily the heavy loss of life suffered during the Second World War. In France, on the other hand, where war losses had been less than in 1914–18, this was not the only reason. Successive governments were under considerable pressure to increase family allowances for reasons which had little to do with population policy. At the same time several leading French demographers associated with the government-sponsored Institute for Demographic Studies (INED) argued that a high birth rate was a sign of national vitality. This philosophy of growth was contrasted with what they called the restrictionist approach of Anglo-saxon neo-Malthusianism.[3]

The contrast between the low birth rates in Europe and some other parts of the developed world and the high birth rates in the 'underdeveloped world', as it became known, led to a dichotomized view of the world population situation. This view was reinforced by the linking of the problem of economic development to that of rapid population growth. 'Over-population' and 'runaway' population growth were thought to affect the countries of Asia and, to a lesser extent, parts of Africa and Latin America. In fact the population of the whole world was increasing at a phenomenal rate. For example, between 1920 and 1940 world population had increased by an estimated

[1] See F. Lorimer: 'Essential Standards of Living', *Proceedings of the International Congress on Population and World Resources, Cheltenham, August 1948,* pp. 28 ff.; and Simon Kuznets: 'Underdeveloped Countries and the Pre-industrial Phase in the Advanced Countries: an Attempt at Comparison', *Proceedings of the World Population Conference, Rome 1954,* vol. V, pp. 947–68.

[2] H. T. Eldridge: *Population policies: a survey of recent developments,* IUSSP, Washington, 1954, chapters I and II.

[3] See, for example, A. Sauvy: 'Le neo malthusianisme anglo-saxon', *Population,* avril–juin 1947, pp. 221–42.

433 millions: between 1940 and 1960 over 700 millions were added.

Among the first to draw attention to the exploding growth of world population were conservationists, such as Sir Frank Fraser Darling in Britain and Fairfield Osborn and William Vogt in the United States. They warned, often in tones of deep gloom, of the dangers to the human environment of continued rapid population growth.[1] Others, like the biologist Julian Huxley, expressed concern at the effect of human numbers on the quality of human life.[2] Osborn and Vogt, and those who shared their fears, argued that population was growing so rapidly that it would soon prove impossible to provide enough food to feed the already undernourished world. They advocated that highest priority be given to spreading the practice of birth control in the less-developed world.

Their predictions of widespread famine were discounted by agronomists and nutritionists. The successes achieved during the Second World War in America, Britain and Switzerland had induced a mood of almost unbounded optimism regarding the opportunities provided by science and technology for increasing production. 'Recent discoveries', declared the first report of the Interim Commission of FAO, 'have made it possible for all men and all nations to achieve freedom from hunger ... Indeed, we can now expect to do much more.'[3] Although this optimism had begun to wane towards the end of the 1950s, the majority of agricultural experts and the FAO itself continued to suggest that even with existing technologies it was possible to produce sufficient food to feed a much larger world population.

The idea of a race between people and food reflected the persistence of a Malthusian perspective with regard to population problems. Although many people continued to argue in terms of the Malthusian dilemma, one of the most significant developments of this period was the emergence of a more comprehensive and more sophisticated approach to the population question.

Various influences were at work. A major contribution was made by demographers, especially in America. Demography expanded rapidly after the Second World War in the United

[1] See W. Vogt: *Road to Survival*, New York, 1948, and Fairfield Osborn: *Our Plundered Planet*, Boston, 1948, and *The Limits of the Earth*, Boston, 1953. Vogt was head of the conservation section of the Pan-American Union and later in 1951 became director of the Planned Parenthood Federation of America. His book *Road to Survival* had a considerable impact.

[2] See Julian Huxley: 'Population and Human Destiny' in *World Review*, January and February 1950, and his introduction to R. C. Cook: *Human Fertility, the Modern Dilemma*, New York, 1951. Huxley's role is dealt with more fully in chapter 6.

[3] HMSO, London, Cmd. 6590. *Documents Relating to FAO*, p. 15.

States, and American demographers became the leading exponents of the possibility of engineering a rapid demographic transition in underdeveloped countries. American foundations and universities pioneered research into the economic, social and psychological factors which determined fertility behaviour and led the way in the development of new contraceptive techniques.

The demographers emphasized the dynamic aspects of population, and drew attention to the interrelationships between population growth and economic growth. During the interwar period demographers and economists had sought, without success, to calculate the optimum population of a country on the basis of the ratio of people to resources. By concentrating on the effects of population growth on the various factors which influenced economic development it became possible to arrive at more meaningful conclusions, particularly in relation to the underdeveloped parts of the world. It was shown for example that, given a rate of population growth of 2 % per annum, a rate not unusual in less developed countries, the investment ratio needed to maintain per capita income at the same level implied a rate of savings which few low income countries seemed capable of sustaining. A very influential study carried out between 1955 and 1957 by the Office of Population Research at Princeton concluded that in India 'per capita consumer income would attain a level about 40 % higher by 1986 with reduced fertility than with continued high fertility'.[1]

Some economists, particularly from Eastern Europe opposed this view and argued, on the basis of European experience, that birth rates would fall spontaneously with rising living standards. The answer to the population problem was, therefore, to accelerate economic development. On the other hand the research carried out on the relationship between population growth and economic development suggested that a high rate of population growth was itself a major obstacle to the achievement of a satisfactory rate of economic development. Moreover, it was pointed out that one of the first results of a rise in the standard of living might in some cases be an increase in the birth rate and a further fall in the death rate.

Additional cogent arguments were provided by doctors and public health workers. Margaret Sanger's interest in birth control had been aroused by the desperate plight of mothers of large families. Public health workers from colonial territories and less developed countries drew attention to the serious health problems

[1] A. J. Coale and E. M. Hoover: *Population Growth and Economic Development in Low Income Countries: a Case Study of India's Prospects*, Princeton, 1958, p. 286.

38   THE INITIATIVE THAT FAILED

caused by excessive childbearing in insanitary conditions and against a background of undernourishment and malnutrition. Their own success in reducing mortality was adding to the problem. Fewer babies, as they pointed out, meant healthier babies.

The public health workers soon found themselves in alliance with the advocates of family planning. The planned parenthood movement, as it was now called, argued that family planning was essential, regardless of any economic or neo-Malthusian reasons for limiting the rate of population growth, on individual and health grounds alone. There were doubts as to whether birth control would be acceptable and whether it could be effectively practised by the mass of the population in underdeveloped countries. Moreover, until the development of the 'pill' and the IUD in the 1960s, there were no safe, effective, cheap female contraceptives. Encouragement was, however, derived from the growing evidence, particularly in Asia, of a widespread desire for smaller families and of the high incidence of induced abortion. During the 1950s a network of family-planning clinics sprang up which started by serving the urban middle classes and spread downwards and outwards.

In a few cases, notably in Asia and the Caribbean, family planning activities received government support. Political leaders and officials in planning offices had to cope with the problems caused by their burgeoning populations. Rapid population growth increased the proportion of children and young people in relation to producers. This placed a growing strain on educational and health facilities and on the creation of employment opportunities. Resources which should have gone into capital producing investments had to be diverted into providing more and more hospitals, schools, housing and other facilities for the growing numbers.

In 1951 the Indian government became the first government in the world to declare a national policy aimed at moderating the rate of population growth. Similar policies were adopted in the Peoples Republic of China in 1955 and Pakistan in 1959. Somewhat paradoxically, these countries were not among those with the most rapid rates of population growth. What seems to have aroused public concern more was the immensity of the numbers involved.

Most governments however were slow to realize the significance of the rate of population growth for their prospects of achieving rapid economic development. Knowledge and understanding of demographic phenomena were lacking and there was a severe shortage of trained demographers. The traditional European belief that a growing population was a sign of national vitality was widely shared. Indeed in many developing countries, particularly in Africa and Latin America, low population densities were seen as proof of underpopulation. In addition, there were deep rooted fears that the rich countries sought to place the blame for the poverty of the 'Third World' on 'over-population' and thus avoid making genuine sacrifices to assist poor countries to develop.

The advocates of population control and family planning from western developed countries were aware of the dangers of intervening in this highly sensitive area. Indeed, within their own countries, although attitudes were beginning to change, birth control was still a highly controversial and emotionally charged subject. At the official level it was treated with the utmost caution. The United Nations system, because of its neutrality and its international character, was viewed by the birth control lobby as a key platform for discussion of ways of dealing with the problem.

5

Responsibility for Population in the UN System

THE UNITED NATIONS POPULATION COMMISSION

THE San Francisco conference which established the United Nations authorized the Economic and Social Council to establish 'such commissions as may be required for the performance of its functions'.[1] The initiative for a commission which would deal specifically with population problems came from the United Kingdom in a memorandum to the Executive Committee of the Preparatory Commission.[2] The British were at this time particularly population conscious. Shortly before the outbreak of the Second World War, there had been considerable concern in Britain about an anticipated decrease in the population, and demographic considerations figured prominently in the changes in the social services introduced at the end of the war.[3] The British proposal envisaged 'a clearing house of information' whose terms of reference would cover the factors determining population growth, the effectiveness of policies designed to influence growth rates, the effect of population growth on economic conditions and problems of migration.[4]

[1] United Nations Conference on International Organization, San Francisco, April–June 1945. Conference Proceedings. Texts of Documents Adopted by the Conference, Article 68, London, 1945.

[2] The Preparatory Commission was established at San Francisco to make provisional arrangements for the first sessions of the organs of the United Nations. Each signatory to the Charter nominated one member. An Executive Committee of fourteen was created to expedite the work. The Executive Committee met in London in August and September 1945. The full Commission approved the report in November and December of that year. See Proceedings of the Preparatory Commission of the United Nations, roneod, London, 1945.

[3] Report on Social Insurance and Allied Services, Cmd. 6404 (Beveridge Report). Beveridge was particularly concerned about the dangers of depopulation and recommended a system of family allowances and other measures to improve the economic position of the family as much to arrest the decline in the birth rate as to effect a redistribution of income. A Royal Commission on Population was appointed in March 1944. See Report of the Royal Commission on Population, Cmd. 7695, 1949.

[4] United Nations Preparatory Commission: Documents and Proceedings of the Committees, Document PC/EX/ES.8, p. 5.

40

The Executive Committee of the Preparatory Commission agreed on the necessity of a Demographic Commission, as it was then called, 'it being understood that "demographic" would have to be read in its broadest sense'. The Committee also emphasized that the commission would be an independent body of experts and therefore free to deal with economic and social aspects of population problems.[1]

The final report of the Preparatory Commission recommended the creation of eight functional commissions. Five of these were to be set up at the first session of the Economic and Social Council. The establishment of the remainder, including the Demographic Commission, was considered less urgent, and the Preparatory Commission recommended that the Council consider the possibility of establishing them 'at an early date, and possibly at its first session'.[2]

No decision was reached at the first session of ECOSOC in January 1946 nor at the second session in May. In July, the US government suggested that, since population questions affected all social and economic activities, there should be a small coordinating committee on population comprised of members of the Statistical, Economic and Social Commissions.[3] Concerned at the delay in reaching agreement, and prompted by the American proposal, the British pressed for an early decision, suggesting incidentally a change in title to 'Population Commission'.[4] When the Council met at its third session in September, the British had persuaded the Americans of the desirability of a separate body to deal with population.

The majority of the Council members supported the joint Anglo-American resolution calling for the immediate establishment of a Population Commission. The representatives from USSR and Yugoslavia opposed the resolution. Mr Mates of Yugoslavia argued that it would be inopportune to add to the number of international bodies already created.[5] Mr Feonov, the Soviet delegate, proposed 'as a compromise' that the Commission might take the form of 'a subcommission of the Statistical Commission'.[6] The Soviet proposal was rejected and the Population Commission came officially into existence on

[1] Ibid., PC/EX/ES.15, p. 2.

[2] United Nations Preparatory Commission, Report, London, 1945, chapter III, section 1(a), para. 5.

[3] United States delegation: Proposal for the Establishment of a Population Committee, July 1946. UN Document E/93.

[4] United Kingdom delegation: Proposal on the Establishment of a Demographic (Population) Commission, August 1946. UN Document E/98. (Joint Resolution E.190.)

[5] OR of ECOSOC, 3rd session, Supplement no. 8, p. 104.

[6] Ibid., p. 103.

3 October 1946. Its rules of procedure provided for annual meetings. There were to be twelve members, and the working languages were French and English.[1]

In the course of the discussion, Mr Feonov had raised the question of membership.[2] The membership of functional commissions had already been the source of considerable disagreement at the first session of the Economic and Social Council. The British proposal, which had formed the basis for the discussions of the Executive Committee of the Preparatory Commission, envisaged mixed commissions comprised in part of qualified government officials and in part of 'unofficial' experts chosen by the Council. The official experts, according to the scheme approved by the Committee, 'would usually be the predominating element'.[3] However, when the Council came to discuss the establishment of the first five commissions the debate centred on the question whether members should be 'experts' or 'government representatives'. After much argument it was agreed that the governments represented on the Council would submit for approval the names of suitable experts. The subcommittee set up to make the final selection was requested to bear in mind not only their qualifications but also the need to reflect regional and ideological differences.[4]

The main role of the Population Commission, like that of the Statistical and Fiscal Commissions, was to undertake studies and to make available the best technical knowledge. It was not intended to be a decision-making body. Such a concept implied a body comprised of experts rather than of government representatives. However, apart from a requirement to consult with the Secretary-General to secure 'a balanced representation in the various fields covered by the Commission', member states were given complete freedom in the choice of a representative. The resolution setting up the Commission indicated merely the countries which were to be represented on the Commission.[5]

A second source of disagreement occurred in connection with the Commission's terms of reference. The original version had been drawn up by a drafting committee of the Preparatory Commission, composed of representatives of Australia, France, the

[1] Resolutions of ECOSOC, 3rd session, Resolution 3(III). The size of the Commission was increased from 12 to 15 in 1953, from 15 to 18 in 1963 and from 18 to 27 in 1967 in order to take into account the enlarged membership of the United Nations.
[2] OR of ECOSOC, 3rd session, op. cit., pp. 104–6.
[3] United Nations Preparatory Commission, op. cit., PC/EX/ES.8, p. 7.
[4] OR of ECOSOC, 1st session, pp. 90–7, pp. 110–14.
[5] Resolutions of ECOSOC, op. cit. The countries nominated were Australia, Brazil, Canada, China, France, Netherlands, Peru, Ukraine, USSR, UK, USA and Yugoslavia.

Netherlands, the United Kingdom and the United States. The original draft reflected their preoccupation with population decline. The Commission was to make studies and advise the Council on (a) population growth and the factors determining such growth, (b) the effectiveness of government policies designed to influence these factors and (c) the bearing of population changes on economic and social conditions.[1] However as a result of an amendment suggested by the USA in its July memorandum, the resolution adopted by the Council referred under (a) not to 'growth' but to 'population changes' and to 'the interrelationships of economic and social conditions and population trends'.

In view of the controversy which arose in subsequent years over UN involvement in questions of population policy it was perhaps surprising that the terms of reference approved by the Council were so broad. A possible explanation may be that the countries responsible for the creation of the Population Commission had low birth rates and thus understood population policy to mean measures designed to encourage larger families.

The Commission was authorized to suggest modifications to its terms of reference. At the first session, it was decided to defer the question until further thought had been given to the Commission's work programme and its relations with other commissions, particularly the Statistical Commission.[2] At its second session, in August 1947, the Commission endorsed a proposal by Mr Sauvy of France that the second item be split into two parts: 'the influence of demographic factors on economic and social conditions' and 'the influence of economic and social factors on the state of and changes in population'.[3] Justifying the change before the Economic and Social Council, Mr Marshall, the Commission's spokesman, explained that it was felt that the proposed alteration made the terms of reference 'more specific' and that they provided 'a clearer and more comprehensive definition of the work to be undertaken by the Commission'.[4]

Although the change did not alter the substance of the terms of reference, it was opposed by the USSR, which was becoming increasingly concerned at the direction in which the Commission seemed to be moving. When, at the third session of ECOSOC, Mr Feonov had opposed the creation of a separate Commission for population his objection may not have been, as he claimed, merely a question of personnel and expense. The compromise which he had suggested would have involved the deletion of the

[1] United Nations Preparatory Commission, op. cit., PC/EX/ES.22, p. 2. See also Report, section 4, para. 32.
[2] UN Doc. E/CN.9/SR.2, p. 2.
[3] UN Doc. E/CN.9/SR.17, p. 3.
[4] UN Doc. E/AC.7/SR.31, p. 5.

reference to population policies. At the first session of the Commission the Soviet member Mr Malyshev took exception to the use of the term 'optimum population'.[1] At the same session the Chinese member, Mr Wu, had submitted a resolution calling for a study of areas where the pressure of population on resources presented a major obstacle to the improvement of public health and the attainment of higher standards of living.[2] The member from the Ukraine, Mr Rabichko, objected to the proposed study because he felt that it implied that the population of some countries ought to be reduced. This, he said, was 'contrary to the humanitarian aims of the United Nations'.[3]

Consequently, when the Economic and Social Council met, Mr Arutinian, the head of the USSR delegation, reproached the Commission for 'approaching the very important questions of population, and the economic factors associated with it, according to out of date theories'.[4] The matter was referred to the Council's Social Committee, where the USSR member explained that the proposed change was unacceptable because it separated two aspects of the same question. The other members of the Committee were at a loss to understand the USSR member's objection, and, at the suggestion of the British representative, the matter was referred back to the Population Commission for reconsideration in the light of the views expressed by the USSR delegation.[5]

Mr Malyshev and Mr Rabichko had been absent from the second session when the change in the terms of reference was discussed. At the third session in May 1948, Mr Rabichko returned and the USSR was represented by Mr Ryabushkin. The Commission once again discussed the terms of reference without at first finding a satisfactory wording or sequence. Finally it was a formula suggested by Mr Rabichko which provided the basis for agreement.[6] The Commission was to 'arrange for studies and advise the Council on:

a) the size and structure of population and the changes therein;

b) the interplay of demographic factors and economic and social factors;

c) policies designed to influence the size and structure of population and the changes therein;

d) any other demographic questions on which either the principal or the subsidiary organs of the United Nations or the Specialized Agencies may seek advice'.

Although migration was not mentioned specifically it was under-

[1] UN Doc. E/CN.9/SR.13, p. 2. [2] UN Doc. E/CN.9/SR.9, pp. 2–3.
[3] UN Doc. E/CN.9/SR.13, p. 2. [4] OR of ECOSOC, 6th session, p. 51.
[5] Ibid., E/AC.7/SR. 31, pp. 6–11. [6] UN. Doc. E/CN.9/SR.28, pp. 2–3.

stood that it came within the Commission's terms of reference.[1] The Commission's proposals were approved without discussion when the Council next met, and have remained unchanged ever since.

As was recognized at the first session of the Commission, the terms of reference were closely related to the question of its responsibilities vis-à-vis other commissions. Although the problems with which the Population Commission was concerned impinged upon nearly all the economic and social activities of the Council, the question was particularly important in relation to two fields: migration and statistics. In the case of migration, agreement between the bodies concerned was reached without difficulty. The allocation of responsibilities in the field of statistics proved less easy. The question was not merely one of 'who did what'. In the background there was the more general issue of whether the United Nations should go beyond the collection and improvement of demographic statistics and concern itself with policy questions. In addition, there was disagreement on the scope of demography as a discipline. There were also significant differences in the practices of national administrations regarding the allocation of responsibilities for population questions. Within the UN Secretariat itself cooperation was not facilitated by the location of the Statistical Office within the Economic Affairs Department, while the Population Division was part of the Department of Social Affairs.

The League of Nations had become an important source of statistical information including demographic statistics. The Statistical Commission was one of the five functional commissions which the Preparatory Commission had recommended should be established immediately. The procedure adopted involved the creation of nuclear commissions of nine members selected by the Council. The nuclear commissions were authorized to draw up their own terms of reference and work programmes. Consequently, by the time the Population Commission came into existence, the Statistical Commission had already claimed for itself the central role in the collection, coordination and improvement of statistics.[2]

When Mr Rice attended the first session of the Population Commission as observer for the Statistical Commission, he warned the members of 'the danger of assuming responsibilities which are clearly within the province of other commissions'. He cited the example of the coordination of population census statistics which, he said, was 'clearly the responsibility of the

---

[1] UN Doc. E/CN.9/SR.30, pp. 2–3.
[2] OR of ECOSOC, 2nd session, annex 3. Report of the nuclear statistical commission.

Statistical Commission'. According to Mr Rice the Population Commission had 'a unique responsibility for the formulation of principles of population policy and for advising the Economic and Social Council as to means of solving the pressing demographic problems with which the world (was) faced'.[1] The Commission reacted strongly to what was interpreted as an attempt to reduce the scope of its functions, realizing also, perhaps, that the discussion of population was likely to stir up bitter controversy. Quoting the Statistical Commission's own summary records, the Commission called for 'a policy of collaboration rather than a sharp delineation of functions'. Mr Rice agreed that this was the view of his Commission, and assured the members of the Population Commission that its advice would be sought concerning the preparation and publication of demographic statistics.[2]

The Commission went on to call for a demographic Year Book in addition to the demographic information contained in the regular statistical publications. It also staked out its claim for a leading role in the encouragement and coordination of the population censuses planned in many countries for 1950 or thereabouts.[3] The Statistical Commission acquiesced in the Population Commission's view of its functions, and the two projects became joint undertakings. Despite a certain jealousy, relations between the two Commissions, and between the corresponding sections in the Secretariat improved in subsequent years.

THE SPECIALIZED AGENCIES

Population trends were of vital importance to the work of the Specialized Agencies. The agreements concluded between the United Nations and the Specialized Agencies provided for cooperation in the collection, analysis and dissemination of statistical information, including population statistics. Each agency retained the right to collect statistics which were of relevance to its field of operations. At the same time, it was accepted that, as far as possible, statistical work should be coordinated by the United Nations itself, in order to ensure comparability, to prevent duplication, and to keep to a minimum the demands made on governments.[4]

[1] UN Doc. E/CN.9/SR.3, p. 2.
[2] UN Doc. E/CN.9/SR.4, pp. 3–4.
[3] Report of the Population Commission its first session. OR of ECOSOC 4th session, supplement 5, pp. 7–8.
[4] See L. M. Goodrich and E. Hambro: *Charter of the United Nations*, Boston, 1949, pp. 344–59. The text of the agreement between the United Nations and the FAO is given p. 626 ff. See particularly article XII dealing with statistical services.

Under the arrangements for reciprocal representation, the agencies were invited to participate, as observers, in the work of the Population Commission and to make known their needs and their own plans. As the representative of the FAO pointed out at the first session of the Commission, the agencies were 'consumers rather than producers' of demographic statistics and analytical studies.[1] The importance of reliable population estimates and forecasts to the forward planning of the Specialized Agencies reinforced the Commission's decision to concentrate on statistical work and basic research.

Although none of the Specialized Agencies which were set up at the end of the Second World War were given specific responsibilities in the field of population, as we shall see in the next chapter, FAO, UNESCO and WHO became involved in the early fifties in a keen debate over their role with regard to the population question. Before turning to this debate mention should be made of the ILO and migration, since for many migration represented a means of relieving population pressure.

THE INTERNATIONAL LABOUR ORGANIZATION

During the interwar period migration had been seen by some governments as a way to relieve underemployment and rural overpopulation and by others as a means of making good manpower shortages. After the war there was renewed interest in international cooperation to promote migration. The immediate postwar problem was the resettlement of people displaced by the war and its after effects. The International Refugee Organization which was set up in 1946 to deal with this problem was unable to find new homes for all the European refugees before it was dissolved in 1951. Moreover, its terms of reference excluded certain groups of displaced persons and it inevitably left untouched the much wider problem of those people who wished to emigrate for economic reasons.

The Declaration of Philadelphia signed in 1944 laid on the ILO an obligation to 'further ... the provision ... of facilities for the training and transfer of labour, including migration for employment and settlement'.[2] Negotiations were begun with the United Nations, and agreement on a working arrangement reached in November 1947. The creation of a separate Specialized Agency to deal with migration problems was rejected in favour of a coordinated multi-agency approach. There was to be

[1] UN Doc. E/CN.9/SR.4, p. 4.
[2] *Declaration of Philadelphia*, article III(c), June 1944.

a consultative committee composed of representatives of the
United Nations and the interested Specialized Agencies. Under
the terms of the agreement the United Nations retained responsibility for 'the migratory problem from the population point
of view'.[1]

Since the Population Commission was authorized to advise the
Council on policy questions as well as carry out research, it
might logically have replaced the ILO as the forum for the
discussion of population redistribution. The Commission, however, for reasons which will be discussed shortly, was at that time
unwilling to involve itself in questions of population policy. Its
work programme in the field of migration covered the improvement of migration statistics and the promotion of research into
the demographic consequences of migration.[2]

Two factors encouraged ILO in 1950 to take the initiative. The
first was the receipt from the Organization for European
Economic Cooperation of funds for technical assistance to
promote migration. The second was the interest shown in
migration by European and Latin American governments. The
Preliminary Conference on Migration, convened by the ILO
in April 1950, expressed the view that 'the Office should become
a sort of clearing house where offers of, and applications for manpower would be assembled'.[3] At the next session of the Governing
Body, the Director General of ILO, David Morse, referred to the
'tragic paradox of the present epoch . . . the simultaneous existence of countries with too many hands and brains and of countries where those hands and brains could contribute to the
development of unexploited resources'. The ILO he said was
already active through its special migration fund but more
needed to be done. 'Where national action failed or was in-
appropriate', he concluded, 'international action might be
effective'.[4]

When the governments who had attended the Preliminary
Migration Conference met at Naples in October 1951, once
again under ILO auspices, the Office presented an ambitious
scheme for the creation of an international migration administration. The plan involved the setting up of a migration aid fund
and an international secretariat, with its own director and
governing council, composed of representatives of interested

[1] UN Doc. E/CN.5/40, Annex II.
[2] Report on the third session of the Population Commission, May 1948,
chapter III. OR of ECOSOC, 7th session, Supplement no. 7.
[3] See 'Migration and Economic Development: Report of the Preliminary
Conference on Migration, April–May 1950' in *International Labour Review*,
vol. LXII, no. 2, p. 110.
[4] ILO, Minutes of the 114th session of the Governing Body, November
1950, pp. 50–1.

governments. The aim was to move 1,700,000 people over a
period of five years.[1] Although the Office insisted that its scheme
was intended only to 'supplement national efforts', the conference
virtually collapsed when the United States delegate said that his
government could not subscribe to the proposed plan.[2] It is
possible that the Americans were concerned that subversive
elements might be able to infiltrate the western hemisphere as
settlers. The Mutual Security Act of 1951, under which funds
had been made available to the IRO specified that funds were
not to be given to any international organization which had
Communist members. Other delegations, notably those of
Australia and New Zealand, were equally unwilling to allow the
ILO an independent role in the movement of population from
one country to another.

Henceforth the migration of Europeans to North America and
to Latin America was kept within the framework of the western
alliance system. Immediately after the Naples Conference, the
American government organized a conference in Brussels at
which it was decided to set up an intergovernmental committee
to deal with the remaining refugees and with other potential
migrants.[3] The committee, which became the Intergovernmental
Committee for European Migration in 1953, had powers not
unlike those envisaged in the plan drawn up by the ILO. Its
functions were 'to make arrangements for the transport of
migrants for whom existing facilities were inadequate' and 'to
promote an increase in the volume of migration from Europe by
providing, at the request of and in agreement with the governments concerned, services in the processing, reception, first
placement and settlement of migrants. . . .'[4]

The ILO was made responsible for the co-ordination of the
migration activities of the United Nations agencies through the
Administrative Committee on Coordination. It was but small
comfort. For a variety of reasons few governments were willing
to remove the stringent restrictions placed on immigration,
except in the case of short term movements to remedy specific
manpower shortage. Of the countries who had pressed for an
increase in international migration during the League period
only Italy continued to show any real interest. Poland and the

[1] See 'The ILO and Migration', *International Labour Review*, vol. LXV,
no. 2, pp. 172–6. This article is the only published record of the conference.
See also E. B. Haas: *Beyond the Nation State*, Stanford, 1964, pp. 172–3; and
A. Alcock: *The History of the ILO*, London 1971, pp. 226–35.
[2] 'The ILO and Migration', op. cit., pp. 176–8.
[3] See Migration Conference, Brussels, 1951: Documents and Summary
Records, Geneva, 1951–2.
[4] Intergovernmental Committee for European Migration. Constitution,
Venice, October 1953. HMSO, London, Cmd. 1706.

other countries of Eastern Europe, who had also been prominent, were now within the Soviet sphere of influence. Emigration was extremely difficult, and considerable efforts were made to secure the return of those emigrants whom it was felt had been enticed away by the West. Elsewhere in Europe, economic recovery removed much of the urgency to emigrate.[1]

A very evident gap in the international machinery set up after the war was the absence of arrangements to facilitate migration from Asia. The countries of immigration argued that the numbers involved were so great that such an international machinery could not be effective and that anyway the high birth rate would rapidly fill the gap left by emigration. Much was made also of the problem of assimilating immigrants from very different cultures.[2] The Asian countries themselves seem to have shown little interest in migration except in relation to the question of racial discrimination. Japan was not admitted to the United Nations until 1956, and not unnaturally felt a certain reluctance to reopen the question of outlets for surplus population. Moreover, the Japanese birth rate was declining rapidly, and the economy was beginning to recover from the devastation of the war. India was represented on the ILO Permanent Migration Committee but apparently did not use this opportunity to press the question of emigration as a means of relieving population pressure.

From a demographic point of view the question was somewhat academic. The enormous number of people involved and the rate at which they were multiplying made population redistribution an unrealistic proposition. Only in a few isolated cases, for example the West Indies, could emigration provide relief from 'population pressure'. This fact had been underlined by the League Secretariat in a report on demographic problems prepared at the request of the Economic Committee in 1938. The report concluded that 'solutions other than territorial solutions' were preferable since they prepared the way for 'a natural absorption of excess population'. The Secretariat recommended instead international cooperation to raise the living standards in less privileged areas.[3] A similar recommendation was made by

[1] See ILO: International Migration 1947–57, *Studies and Reports, new series, no. 54*, Geneva, 1959.

[2] See for example A. Sauvy: 'Some Aspects of the International Migration Problem', *International Labour Review*, vol. LVIII, no. 2, July 1948; and W. S. Thompson: *Population Problems*, New York, 1953, p. 282 ff.; and his *Danger Spots in World Population*, New York, 1930, in which he argues that migration can be an 'effective' solution to over-population: see pp. 332–3.

[3] LN Report of the Economic Committee, 48th session, July 1938, Annex, p. 13. [C. 233 M.132 1938 II B;] and Report of Coordination Committee on Economic and Financial Questions, July 1938, pp. 9–10, [A.16 1938 II.]

the Coordination Committee on Economic and Financial Questions in 1938. Whilst this was widely regarded as the solution to the problems facing the poor, heavily populated countries of Asia not all observers believed that it would be possible to achieve any substantial improvement in living standards without at the same time taking steps to slow down the rate of population growth.

6

The Refusal of Action Programmes

WITH the creation of the Population Commission a potential focus existed within the UN system for the consideration of population problems and for the promotion of a coordinated policy. The Population Division as well as several members of the Commission wished the United Nations to play a leading role. Frank Notestein, the first head of the Population Division and former Director of the Princeton Office of Population Research, was one of the leading American population specialists. Like his successor, Pascal Whelpton, also an American, Notestein was a member of a group of committed demographers, economists and public health experts brought together after the Second World War by the Milbank Memorial Fund.[1] The group became the main protagonists of the view that economic development alone would not bring about a spontaneous fall in the birth rate in less developed countries, and that ways would therefore have to be found of inducing social changes which would encourage smaller families. Birth control was seen as the means whereby couples would achieve their desire for smaller families. Mass family-planning campaigns were not at first envisaged since there was, as yet, little indication that people in less developed countries would adopt contraception on a wide scale.

At the same time it was feared that discussion of policy questions, in the absence of agreement on the size and nature of the problem, might split the Commission. Mr Arca Parro, chairman of the Commission, explained the dilemma in his report to ECOSOC in 1947. Population problems, he said were 'too delicate to discuss in the abstract ... the Commission realized that its real work was to formulate population policies; for the moment, however, the emphasis should be placed on

---

[1] The meetings were organized by Frank Boudreau and Claude Kiser. The topics included 'International approaches to problems of underdeveloped areas' in 1947; 'Modernization programmes in relation to human resources and population problems' in 1949; and 'Interrelations of social economic and demographic problems in selected underdeveloped areas' in 1953. UN officials participated regularly in the discussions. Other members of the group included Kingsley Davis, Philip Hauser, Ronald Freedman, Frank Lorimer and Warren Thompson. Summaries of these discussions can be found in the Milbank Fund Quarterly and in the Proceedings of the Round Tables held at the Fund's annual meetings.

laying the necessary factual foundations.'[1] The work programme recommended by the Commission thus covered activities, such as the improvement of demographic statistics and the coordination of national population censuses, on which all could agree. As a result, the Commission played a peripheral role in the controversy over the population question which developed between 1948 and 1952.

HUXLEY'S INITIATIVE

The controversy arose as a result of a forceful initiative by the first Director-General of UNESCO. Julian Huxley was a biologist with a remarkable flair for popular exposition and an enjoyment of controversy. He was a keen exponent of the need to control the rapid expansion of population because of the lasting damage which it was causing to both man's environment and to the quality of human life. As early as 1926, he had been reprimanded by Sir John Reith, Director of the BBC, for mentioning birth control in a broadcast, a reference which was explained by the BBC in a letter of apology to *The Times* as 'entirely inadvertent and at variance with our policy'.[2] In 1927 he had played a leading role in Margaret Sanger's World Population Conference.

Brilliant, versatile and undiplomatic, sparking a dozen new ideas a day, Huxley inspired affection in most of his staff but distrust in some of UNESCO's more influential member Governments. The latter were estranged from the very beginning by the publication by Huxley of a pamphlet which outlined his own ideas for a UNESCO philosophy of scientific humanism, including a reference to the population question, before he had submitted his policies for discussion by Governments.[3] Nevertheless, the UNESCO General Conference agreed at its first session in 1946 to a study of the cultural problems caused by excessive population increase or decrease and by migratory movements, as part of its concern with international tensions which were likely to lead to war.[4]

In his second Annual Report as Director-General in 1948, Huxley emphasized that overpopulation could drastically affect

---

[1] OR of ECOSOC, 4th session, 1947, pp. 162–3.

[2] R. W. Clark: *The Huxleys*, London, 1968, p. 330.

[3] J. Huxley: *UNESCO, its Purposes and its Philosophy*, London, Preparatory Commission of UNESCO, 1946. Regarding the population question he said: 'The recognition of the idea of an optimum population size (of course relative to technological and social conditions) is an indispensable first step towards that planned control of populations which is necessary if man's blind reproductive urges are not to wreck his ideals and his plans for material and spiritual betterment', p. 45.

[4] UNESCO General Conference, 1st session, Paris, 1946, pp. 234–5.

the type of civilization possible and its rate of advance. He was particularly concerned by the undernourishment of much of the world's population and with the problems of erosion and of natural resources. 'Somehow or other', he wrote, 'population must be balanced against resources or civilization will perish. War is a less inevitable threat to civilization than is population increase.' One of UNESCO's duties, as he saw it, was to educate people as to the dangers of the situation. He did not believe however that the problem of world population should be brought onto the international stage unless it were previously made a matter of public world concern. This, he thought, could best be done by means of a conference of private individuals, free to arrive at any conclusions they liked without being tied by official instructions or by national interests. Such a conference, he suggested, should be sponsored by ECOSOC, with the co-operation of WHO, FAO and ILO as well as UNESCO.[1]

Huxley obtained a limited response from his Conference to his interest in the population question and indeed to his proposed philosophy for UNESCO. He was suspect in some quarters as an agnostic and in others, quite erroneously, as a communist. His Director-Generalship lasted only two years. Nor was the response of the other agencies to his initiative any more enthusiastic. The Population Commission recommended that the question of a population conference be postponed until the results of the 1950 census were known,[2] a view shared by the majority of experts and interested bodies consulted by the UN Secretariat.[3] When the first World Population Conference was finally held under UN auspices in 1954 it was, as will be seen, very different in form and in spirit from the one envisaged by Huxley.

Within UNESCO his initiative had one important result. The UNESCO Conference shared his desire to educate the public to the extent that it proposed 'Food and Population' as the chief subject for group discussions in member states in 1949. A series of background studies was sponsored by UNESCO for this purpose. The most striking of these pamphlets consisted of an essay entitled 'The Double Crisis' by Aldous Huxley and a rejoinder by Sir John Russell, a noted agronomist.[4] Aldous Huxley maintained that whilst atomic energy could destroy

[1] Report of the Director-General on the activities of the Organization in 1948, UNESCO Paris, 1948, pp. 28 ff. Huxley referred his proposal to the United Nations for discussion by the Population Commission. See UN Doc. E/CN.9/26 and E/CN.9/SR.29, pp. 2–3.
[2] UN Doc. E/CN.9/SR.29–30 and Report of the 4th session of the Population Commission, OR of ECOSOC, 9th session, Supplement no. 7.
[3] UN Doc. E/CN.9/W.28.
[4] *Food and People*, London, Bureau of Current Affairs, 1949. A. Huxley: *The Double Crisis* and Sir J. Russell: *The Way Out*.

one particular civilization, soil erosion could put an end to the very possibility of any civilization: whilst population went up, the fertility of the soil was declining and minerals were being worked out. He estimated that by 1970 the population of France and of Great Britain would have declined by about four million, whilst that of the underdeveloped countries would continue to rise, and in a startling apocalyptic vision predicted that 'military leaders of countries with low birth rates will come to believe that their only chance of survival consists in using, before it is too late, their technical superiority in atomic and biological weapons in order to offset the effects of the big battalions'. The world's underlying population crisis, he concluded, could only be relieved through the adoption by all the nations of a world policy aiming at the stabilization of a population at a figure at which the relationship between numbers and resources, between numbers and the amenities of life, would be most favourable.

Sir John Russell disagreed completely with most of Aldous Huxley's conclusions, considering that the union of science and technology was so recent that no one could foresee what improvements might be possible in food production, just as Malthus had not foreseen the consequences of the opening up of North America.[1]

UNESCO's sponsorship of the series of background papers on Food and Population as well as the tone of some of these papers, involved Julian Huxley in discussions with FAO late in 1948. By this time Boyd-Orr, FAO's first Director-General, had resigned when his World Food Board was not approved. It is interesting to speculate what FAO's reaction would have been if Boyd-Orr, a character as visionary and bold as Huxley himself, had remained Director-General. Boyd-Orr indeed believed that 'modern science (had) the answer to Malthus'.[2] Shortly after his resignation, however, he was the main guest speaker at the International Conference on Population and World Resources, organized by the British FPA. In the course of the discussion

---

[1] It is interesting to note that by 1954 the situation was such that Sir John was less confident of the ability of the world to feed itself. Although he still believed that production could be increased considerably he felt that 'a sound population policy must be adopted to ensure that the numbers do not outstrip the food resources'. See Sir J. Russell: *World Population and World Food Supplies*, London, 1954.

[2] J. Boyd-Orr, *The White Man's Dilemma*, London, 1953, pp. 71–81. In a speech to the London International Assembly Conference on world food problems in July 1943 he had pointed out that improvements in nutrition would 'add more man years of life to the world population within the life of our children than have been lost in all the wars of modern history'. As a result, he said, 'there would need to be a great increase in food production'. See *Freedom from Want of Food*, London International Assembly Report, London, 1944, p. 32.

Boyd-Orr said that he supported efforts to spread birth control in poor countries although he felt that these efforts would have little impact until there were substantial improvements in educational levels and living standards.[1]

His successor as Director-General, Norris Dodd, proved unenthusiastic. Dodd, a former official of the US Department of Agriculture, was disturbed at the 'propaganda that the world's present resources are not sufficient to feed the present population, let alone any increased population. If this is true FAO might as well fold up'.[2] He asked Frank McDougall, the veteran Counsellor to the Director-General, to explain the FAO attitude to UNESCO. McDougall did so in no uncertain terms, informing UNESCO that 'it would be intolerable pessimism to maintain that the world cannot produce enough food . . . and that any concentration of attention upon population control would be dangerous and unsuitable for an international organization'.[3]

Of all the senior officials in FAO in this period, McDougall, who is generally regarded as its principal Founding Father, probably gave the most attention to population: demographic charts covered the walls of his office. But another of his constant preoccupations was FAO's relationship with the Vatican which he believed could considerably influence American support for FAO and the level of American financial contributions. The importance of FAO's work was indeed eventually recognized handsomely in the Papal encyclical 'Mater et Magistra'. It is possible that this preoccupation may have been in McDougall's mind in his discussions with UNESCO. Later, perhaps in light of the results of the 1950 censuses, he moderated his earlier view and wrote in 1955 that 'our line ought, I suggest, to be that we are not concerned with birth control but are not opposed to it. In so far as other people urge it, we should not discourage their activities.'[4]

By 1955 it had become increasingly apparent that food production was not keeping up with the growth of population. In most less-developed countries food consumption was only just above the already inadequate levels which had prevailed before the Second World War. In the Far East the amount of food available for each person was actually less in the 1950s than in the 1930s.

[1] *Proceedings of the International Congress on Population and World Resources in Relation to the Family, Cheltenham, August 1948*, pp. 8–26.
[2] Dodd to McDougall, 8 November 1938, FAO Archives.
[3] McDougall to Dodd, 10 November 1948, FAO Archives.
[4] McDougall to F. T. Wahlen, 28 November 1955, FAO Archives. See also F. D. McDougall: 'Food and Population', *International Conciliation*, December 1952, no. 486.

As it became clear that population was increasing more rapidly than had been expected in the less-developed countries, the hopes placed in the application of modern techniques began to fade. The change of emphasis is clearly reflected in the annual survey of FAO, *The State of Food and Agriculture*. At first, although it was clear that production was not keeping abreast of population growth, the survey continued to find the prospects encouraging. The reports stressed the importance of increased efforts by governments and the potentially valuable role of technical assistance. The first sign of lessening confidence appeared in 1951. 'After five years of FAO's existence', the Director-General commented in his introduction, 'we had hoped there would be much progress to report . . . especially in the areas of greatest difficulties and shortages'. But, he explained, a combination of factors, including population growth, had 'limited actual progress to much less than had been hoped'.[1] In the same year the sixth session of the FAO Conference expressed concern that 'food production . . . was not keeping pace with the growth of population' and that 'the expansion planned for the next two years, even if fully achieved, would be insufficient to remedy this situation'. The final report noted that there seemed 'little prospect of achieving by 1960 the levels of production and consumption hoped for at the time of the founding of the FAO'.[2] The good harvests of 1952–53 gave renewed hope but, as the 1954 survey pointed out, expansion was unevenly distributed. Surpluses had reappeared in North America while in most parts of the less developed world there was 'little improvement in the diets of millions of inadequately fed people'.[3] The report of the eighth session of the Conference in 1955 concluded: 'The slow progress made over the last few years was due neither to lack of human needs nor lack of agricultural resources—[but]—to the failure under existing national and international social and economic conditions to expand the effective demand for farm products'.[4]

Huxley's initiative found a brief echo in ILO. The report of the Director-General, David Morse, to the organization's second Asian Regional Conference, held in Ceylon in 1950, referred to population as one of the most important obstacles to the work of reconstruction in the region. In a section of the report entitled 'The need for a Positive Population Policy', Morse argued 'only if population growth can be checked will the workers in Asian

[1] FAO: *State of Food and Agriculture, 1951*, p. 1.
[2] FAO: Report of the Sixth Session of the Conference, 1951, p. 11, and Resolution no. 6, pp. 17–18.
[3] FAO: *State of Food and Agriculture, 1954*, p. 1.
[4] FAO: Report of the Eighth Session of the Conference, 1955, p. 6.

countries be able to obtain substantial and lasting gains from programmes of economic and social development'.[1]

In the debate on the report, the government adviser of Ceylon welcomed the attention paid to population and suggested that the problem was so important that the ILO should appoint a special committee to study it.[2] Mr Tessier, workers' delegate of France, found the passage offensive. He said it gave the impression of materialism and pessimism which was not in keeping with the traditions of the ILO. 'Our social duty,' he concluded 'is to have confidence in life, not to place artificial barriers in its way'.[3]

Two years later the *International Labour Review* published an article by the Australian agricultural economist Colin Clark. Clark argued that the world could support a very much larger population and condemned the disciples of Malthus for their lack of faith in human achievement.[4] The article provoked strongly worded rejoinders from a colleague of Clark's, Derek Healey, another from a Norwegian demographer, Sten Nilson, and a third from the Indian economist-demographer, S. Chandrasekhar.[5] There the debate ended. In subsequent years the official reports of the ILO contained occasional allusions to population growth, but the emphasis was entirely on measures to spread industrialization and increase productivity in order to meet the demands of the growing population.

WHO AND FAMILY PLANNING

It was however to WHO that many looked for the principal initiative on the population question, since it had been from Health Ministries that national responsibility for family planning had cautiously emerged in some member states. But just as on the national scene the medical profession had furnished both the leaders and the most ardent opponents of the birth control movement, so this division was to be reflected at the international level in debates in WHO.

At the International Health Conference in 1946 the Polish delegation had suggested that the functions of the proposed United Nations health organization should be as broad as

[1] ILO: Asian Regional Conference, Ceylon, January 1950: Report of the Director-General, ILO, Geneva, 1949, pp. 57–9.
[2] ILO: Asian Regional Conference, op. cit., Record of Proceedings, p. 105.
[3] Ibid., p. 95.
[4] Colin Clark: 'Population Growth and Living Standards', *International Labour Review*, August 1953, pp. 99–117.
[5] D. T. Healey: 'The Problems of Population Growth'; and S. S. Nilson: 'Childbearing and the Standard of Life', *International Labour Review*, January 1954, pp. 68–76; S. Chandrasekhar: 'Population Growth, Socio-economic Development and Living Standards', *International Labour Review*, June 1954, pp. 527–46.

possible and should include, among other things, 'the important
subject of population problems and vital statistics'.[1] However,
the Committee set up to report on the scope and functions of the
new organization decided that demographic problems were the
responsibility of the United Nations.[2]

The question might have come up in a more controversial
fashion had it not been for the fact that the representative of
Transjordan, Dr Tutunji, enjoyed only observer status. On the
final day of the conference, after an anguished night, Dr Tutunji
took the floor to declare his belief in the need for 'worldwide
birth control as a prophylaxis against overpopulation and war'.
He explained that his observer status had prevented him from
presenting his proposal for inclusion in the constitution and
expressed his dismay that no other delegation had been willing to
'defend the noble cause'. He commented sadly: 'the neglect of
this question at a time when one-third of the world's population
was threatened by famine and 300,000 infants under one year
died annually in the USA—the richest country in the world—
because of large families and consequent inadequate infant care
was heartbreaking indeed'.[3]

Although the constitution of WHO contained no specific
reference to population or family planning, despite Dr Tutunji's
plea, there appeared to be nothing which would prevent WHO
from considering either family planning or the health aspects of
population problems. This seems, indeed, to have been the
interpretation of the first Director-General, Dr Brock Chisholm.
Chisholm, who had practised as a gynaecologist before turning
to psychiatry, believed that unwanted pregnancies could affect
the mental as well as the physical health of women.[4] As he
frequently pointed out, the preamble to the Constitution defined
the objective of the organization as 'complete mental and
physical well-being'. He felt that this imposed an obligation on
WHO to respond to all requests for assistance in the field of health
and that governments were the appropriate judges of whether
population growth constituted a health problem.

At the same time, Chisholm, like others who felt that WHO
should concern itself with family planning, believed that the first
priority was to ensure the future of the organization. Several
governments, including the British and the American, were
unwilling to see WHO go beyond the restricted range of tasks
which had been performed by the League Health Organization.
In the circumstances, it seemed rash to jeopardize the chances of

[1] Official Records of WHO, no. 2, p. 39.
[2] Ibid., p. 44.　　　　　　　　　　　[3] Ibid., p. 91.
[4] Dorothy Henderson: *Will Mankind Listen: a Tribute to Dr Brock Chisholm*,
Vancouver, 1970, pp. 58–60.

extending the scope of the new organization by raising what was likely to be a highly controversial issue and one which, at that time, was viewed by many members as one of no great urgency.

Some member states, however, did feel that the question was urgent. Although Transjordan (subsequently Jordan) did not participate in the work of WHO until 1959, the issue was raised almost immediately after the Organization came into existence by the representative of another small, newly independent country. At the second World Health Assembly in 1949, S.W.R.D. Bandaranaike of Ceylon, then Minister of Health and later Prime Minister, argued that there was 'a growing need for consideration of the problem of birth control on an international plane', and proposed that a start be made through the collection of the necessary data and statistics.[1] The representative of the United Kingdom, Dr Melville Mackenzie, opposed the inclusion of the question in the programme on the grounds that population problems were not within the competence of WHO, and should be dealt with by the UN Population Commission. Moreover, he added, 'two of the largest religions in the world were firmly opposed to any kind of birth control'. Dr Bandaranaike agreed to withdraw his proposal but reserved the right to submit the question for consideration by the next session of the Executive Board.[2]

Ceylon was not a member of the Executive Board. However, a loosely worded resolution adopted at the fifth session of the Board in January 1950 provided Bandaranaike with a further opportunity. The Executive Board resolution requested the Director-General 'to cooperate on a wide basis with the United Nations and the Specialized Agencies on questions concerned with population problems'.[3] Three months later at the third World Health Assembly, Bandaranaike called for the creation of an 'expert committee to investigate the problem, particularly those aspects of it which are of especial concern to WHO'.[4] The Irish representative warned that 'the advocacy of such practices (eugenics and birth control) by WHO would cause resentment in many countries and might weaken the position of WHO as a leader in the field of health'. Other delegations repeated the argument raised the previous year that this was not a medical matter and should be left to the Population Commission. Dr Chisholm pointed out that studies were already being carried out by the IUSSP, by national institutes, by the UN Population Commission and by UNESCO. The proposal was overwhelmingly defeated, receiving only one affirmative vote, with thirty against and five abstentions.[5]

[1] OR of WHO, no. 21, p. 84.   [2] Ibid., p. 139.
[3] Report of the Executive Board, 5th session, Resolution 3.1, OR of WHO, no. 25, p. 9.   [4] OR of WHO, no. 28, p. 233.   [5] Ibid., p. 234.

The Regional Committee for South-east Asia, however, held its annual meeting in 1950 in Kandy. Mr Bandaranaike, as Minister of Health of the host country, presided. He informed the Committee that the population problem in his country would soon become alarming if nothing were done to check its growth; and on his initiative the Committee passed a resolution recommending that 'the Regional Director, in cooperation with the other international agencies dealing with the problem of over-population and its effect on employment, food production, and the standard of living, should obtain from member states of the region all possible demographic data, which should thereafter be circulated to member governments for any action which the governments may consider necessary'.[1]

When this resolution came before the Executive Board of WHO in June 1951, Dr Hojer of Sweden pointed out that as medical science was now saving the lives of millions of people by the prevention and cure of disease, the problem of controlling the size of populations was becoming increasingly urgent. It might well be that another international organization or a member state of WHO might ask the Organization for advice on the medical problems of birth control, and it was essential that consideration should be given now or in the near future to the policy of WHO regarding such advice. He therefore proposed that the Board should request the Director-General to prepare a paper on this question for discussion at its next (ninth) session. He was supported by Dr Karunaratne of Ceylon and Dr Jafar of Pakistan;[2] and without opposition the Board requested the Director-General 'within the limits of budgetary resources to carry out studies on the health aspects of this question, and to prepare a paper for the next session'. He was also requested to consult with the United Nations in order to define the respective responsibilities of the two organizations.[3] The Director-General explained that at present either experts could be sent to individual countries, or alternatively WHO could study the problem in the Secretariat or through an Expert Committee and formulate advice to all member states.[4]

In November 1951, a WHO Expert Committee on Maternity Care submitted a report in which it recommended that family planning advice should be included in maternity care programmes 'in areas in which some degree of family limitation

[1] WHO Regional Office for South East Asia, *Handbook of Resolutions*, New Delhi, 1968, p. 10. See also Minutes of the Executive Board, 7th session WHO Doc. EB.7/49.
[2] WHO: Minutes of the Executive Board, 8th session EB.8/Min/10/Rev.1, pp. 10–14.
[3] For the text of the resolution see OR of WHO, no. 36, p. 19.
[4] WHO: Minutes of the Executive Board, 8th session, op. cit., p. 12.

is considered desirable because of population policies, or because the well-being of the mother and child is being affected by excessive childbearing, or because of social or economic reasons'.[1] Unlike the recommendations which had been submitted by the League of Nations Committee on Maternal Care twenty years earlier the proposal did not lead to the suppression of the Committee's report, which was approved by the Executive Board at its ninth session.[2]

It was at this stage that the Roman Catholic Church appears to have become alarmed at the direction which WHO policy was taking and that the Vatican began to intervene diplomatically on the question with Catholic governments which were members of WHO.[3] The results were dramatic in 1952.

The Executive Board when it met in January had three questions to consider. Firstly there was the response of WHO to the resolutions of its South-east Regional Committee and to the Report which the Director-General had prepared at its own request; secondly there was the relationship of its programmes with those of the United Nations; thirdly there was the degree of sponsorship which WHO should accord to the World Population Conference. All three questions were linked in a heated debate.[4]

The Director-General's paper contained two elements which may have contributed to the intensity of the opposition. Annexed to it was a document emanating from a report by Dr M. G. Balfour of the Rockefeller Foundation. Dr Balfour suggested that no more important contribution could be made to Asia and the world's problem of human welfare than research in contraception. 'The East', his report asserted, 'unlike the West cannot afford to await the automatic processes of change . . . in order to complete its transition to an efficient system of population replacement and *we think the main reliance must be placed in contraception.*' (Report's italics). Perhaps even more disturbing to Roman Catholic members was the statement in the Regional Committee's own report that at the eighth session of the WHO Executive Board 'there was general agreement that the or-

[1] Report of the Expert Committee on Maternity Care, 1951, WHO, Technical Report Series, no. 515, para. 6.4.

[2] Resolution 51, ninth session of Executive Board, OR of WHO, no. 40.

[3] Three important speeches concerning population problems and birth control were made by Pius XII in the early fifties: see Speech to the Italian Midwives, 29 October 1951; Speech to the Italian League of Family Organizations, 26 November 1951; Christmas Message, 1952. According to Fagley a 'fertility cult' existed within the Vatican during this period. See R. M. Fagley: *The Population Explosion and Christian Responsibility*, New York, 1960, pp. 184–6.

[4] The debate is reported in WHO Docs. EB.9/Min/15/Rev. 1, pp. 16–27, EB.9/Min/18/Rev. 1, pp. 3–19 and EB.9/Min/19/Rev. 1, pp. 6–7.

ganization should be prepared to give advice on the medical problems relating to controlling the size of population'.[1]

The other item in the Director-General's report on which attention was focused was the information that Dr Abraham Stone of New York had been sent to India, at the request of the Indian Government, as a WHO expert to advise on an experiment in the use of the 'safe period'.[2]

The representative of the United Nations, Halvor Gille, in a statement to the Board suggested that it was WHO's responsibility to give technical assistance in establishing and conducting clinics which would provide contraceptive information and advice whilst the United Nations would be responsible for the more general question of population policy. He also referred to the collaboration between UN and WHO in the technical assistance project which was being carried out in India.[3]

Leading the attack, Dr Alivisatos of Greece stated that 'to introduce contraceptive methods to underdeveloped peoples was tantamount to giving them weapons with which to commit suicide'. Dr Hayek of Lebanon believed 'that sterilization and contraception should be rejected as harmful to the health of the woman and contrary to the laws of nature'. Dr Canaperia of Italy observed that it was 'strange' that WHO was engaged in a pilot project in India in spite of the decision of the World Health Assembly not to set up an expert committee. Dr Hurtado of Cuba indicated that birth control was not the answer to the problems of countries which were overpopulated: the answer was to be found in universal brotherhood and the redistribution of the resources of the world.

Dr Melville McKenzie of Britain made several interventions. He had been a League of Nations official, and his influence seems to have been exerted above all to preserve the unity of WHO. It was not the responsibility of WHO as a technical body, he suggested, to determine whether family planning was right or wrong. The economic, social, religious and moral aspects of the questions were outside its scope, though it was right to give technical advice if required. He suggested that WHO should co-sponsor

[1] WHO Doc. SEA/RC.4/14, annexed to EB.9/16. See particularly p. 8. Also contained in OR of WHO, no. 40, pp. 136–8.

[2] WHO Doc. EB.9/96. Pilot study on the voluntary limitation of families in India. In fact it seems that Dr Stone did not hesitate to point out during his time in India that there were other methods of birth control which couples could use and which were more effective than reliance on the so-called safe period. See for example his talk to All-India Conference on Family Planning: Report of the first All-India Conference on Family Planning, Bombay, November–December 1951, p. 78.

[3] Mr Gille's statement is contained in WHO Doc. EB.9/Min/15/Rev.1, op. cit., pp. 16–21. Also contained in OR of WHO, no. 40, p. 141.

the World Population Conference, but must avoid sole responsibility for a conference which would deal with delicate questions on which there was strong feeling. In his last intervention, he said that birth control was not a medical question and that discussion of it in the World Health Assembly would arouse bitter feelings.

The Board requested the Director-General to report to the Assembly. It decided however to not circulate the statement of the UN representative, and by seventeen votes to one 'took note' of the documents and 'welcomed exclusively technical collaboration with the United Nations in demographic problems'.[1]

The debate became general at the fifth World Health Assembly in May 1952. Whereas in previous years, Bandaranaike had been alone in his attempts to interest the Assembly in population problems, several representatives now indicated their support for the WHO initiative in sending a mission to India, and their belief that population presented a health problem for many countries. An important contribution also came from Sir Herbert Broadley, the Deputy Director of FAO, who, in presenting his organization's fraternal greetings, observed that more mouths meant less food, and what WHO's success in lowering the death rate was making FAO's task of seeing that the world was fed more difficult. The current rate of population growth, he said, was such that we could no longer allow 'nature to take its course'. He felt that it was the responsibility of international bodies like the World Health Assembly to discuss such problems.[2]

Dr Evang of Norway, a noted radical who had played a leading role in the spread of family planning in Norway before becoming Director of Health Services, seized the occasion to propose that the 1953 programme should include the creation of an expert committee on the health aspects of the population situation. Dr Evang suggested that this could form part of WHO's contribution to the forthcoming World Population Conference.[3] Other delegations, particularly those from Roman Catholic countries, interpreted the move as proof of the existence of a conspiracy to involve WHO actively in government programmes to reduce the birth rate. Commenting on the debate, the *Osservatore Romano* claimed that: 'behind a curtain of anodine and apparently inoffensive resolutions, the United Nations has over the last few years been gradually building up a population policy' and warned that no one should be taken in by Dr Evang's resolution. What Dr Evang really wanted, the article claimed, was to establish the principle that WHO was competent to deal with the question of birth control.[4]

1 For the text of the resolution see OR of WHO, no. 40, p. 30.
2 OR of WHO, no. 42, pp. 61–2.   3 Ibid., pp. 204–7 and pp. 230–1.
4 See 'Politica demografica all "ONU",' in *Osservatore Romano*, 8 June 1952.

It might have proved possible to secure approval of the Indian mission on the basis of WHO's constitutional obligation to respond to requests for assistance from member governments particularly since the experiment was restricted to a method of birth control approved by the Catholic Church. Dr Evang's proposal, however, provided an opportunity for those who were opposed to any action in this field to attempt to obtain an official embargo on similar initiatives in the future. Thus a rival resolution submitted by the representatives of Italy and the Lebanon affirmed that 'from a medical standpoint population problems (did) not require any particular action on the part of WHO'.[1] Supported by the delegates of several other Roman Catholic countries, they protested against the provision of expert services to India. They argued that this was an economic not a medical question and that the solution was to raise productivity, not to reduce the birth rate. Several of them, led by Ireland and Belgium, hinted at resignation if WHO were to involve itself in family planning activities. Other delegations, which had previously opposed or had reservations about involvement on the grounds that the question was the responsibility of the Population Committee, now argued that they should await the findings of the proposed population conference before deciding whether to take any initiative.[2]

There seemed a strong possibility that the resolution submitted by Italy, Belgium and the Lebanon would obtain a majority. Dr Pandit of India sought to have the discussion postponed to a later session. Dr Mudaliar, head of the Indian delegation and one of the most respected members of the Assembly, also intervened in an attempt to avert the danger. The Chairman, Dr Romero of Chile, was under strong pressure from the Catholic countries to put the joint resolution to an immediate vote. A short break was accorded to permit consultations. It was agreed, at the suggestion of Dr Wickremsinghe of Ceylon, to withdraw all three resolutions and to note in the records the views expressed in the course of the discussion. Dr van de Calseyde of Belgium requested the inclusion of the following statement setting out his interpretation of what had happened:

'. . . it must be made clear that we in this committee are agreed that although the problem of overpopulation in certain regions may call for WHO's advice and assistance for the protection of the health of these peoples—advice and assistance already being given—there can be no question of our organization . . . becoming the advocate of, still less the means of implementing, certain

[1] OR of WHO, no. 42, op. cit., p. 233.
[2] Ibid., pp. 231–40.

economic and social theories which are far from receiving universal approval'.[1]

A few days later a report in the *New York Times* quoted a 'high official' of WHO to the effect that the discussion had confirmed the right of the organization to give advice on request in the field of family planning. Dr van de Calseyde immediately raised the matter in the Plenary Session, and reminded the Director-General of the statement which he had asked to be included in the records of the Committee on Programme and Budget. For Chisholm the situation was delicate. Tactfully he assured Dr van de Calseyde that he would take the wishes of member states into account whether or not they were expressed in a formal resolution.[2]

The debate in the fifth WHA had a traumatic effect. In subsequent years the representatives of India, Ceylon and the UAR continued to insist on the relevance of the 'population explosion' to the work of WHO, but to no avail. The majority of member states continued to feel that WHO should not become involved in family planning. In the circumstances it was hardly surprising that the Secretariat felt unable to take the initiative. Under the Director-Generalship of Dr Candau of Brazil, who succeeded Chisholm in 1953, governments which enquired about the possibility of obtaining help from WHO on family planning were informed that such assistance did not come within the mandate of the organization. The belief thus grew up, both inside and outside the organization, that WHO did not have the right to respond to requests for assistance in this field. The position was made very clear in 1960 when Dr Engel of Sweden suggested that provision should be made in the programme and budget for 'some preparatory measures for the introduction of family planning into WHO's work' in order to be in a position to meet government requests for assistance. Dr Hourihane of Ireland and Dr Canaperia of Italy protested. Dr Canaperia pointed out that birth control had already been discussed twice in WHO. On both occasions, he said, the Assembly had decided against doing anything about the subject, which was, moreover, covered by the terms of reference of other organizations more competent to discuss it. He was immediately challenged by Dr Evang, who accused the two representatives of using terms which had little to do with medicine. To the surprise of some and the consternation of others he produced the records of the fifth Assembly and asked whether Dr Canaperia contended that WHO should be prevented from responding to requests for assistance from member states. He got no reply.[3]

[1] OR of WHO, no. 42, op. cit., p. 242.   [2] Ibid., p. 131.
[3] OR of WHO, no. 101, pp. 228–9.

Part III

THE PERIOD OF QUIESCENCE
(1953–1961)

'It is not the task of the Population Commission to suggest policies that any Government of any Member State should pursue.'

Report of the UN Population Commission, 1959

7

The Population Commission and the United Nations Secretariat

THE period between 1953 and 1961 was one in which the Specialized Agencies gave little attention to population problems, except for their involvement in the World Population Conference in 1954. Within the United Nations itself, whilst little was done to organize action programmes, except through the establishment of regional demographic training centres, studies were undertaken whose impact was subsequently to have a notable impact in illuminating public opinion on the facts of the population situation. At the same time, although the Commission proved unable to reach agreement on the key question of the relationship of population trends to economic development, towards the end of the 1950's there were signs that a change in attitudes was underway.

CONTROVERSIES IN THE POPULATION COMMISSION

The Population Commission had wisely insisted on the need for a sound basis of factual information and an understanding of the implications of demographic phenomena before there could be any meaningful discussion of population policies. It was, however, no easy task to achieve agreement on the nature of the problem or on its significance. Indeed, until 1960, several members of the Commission disputed the very existence of a 'population explosion' and refused even to entertain the idea that governments might feel obliged to introduce measures to slow down the rate of population growth for economic reasons.

At the fifth session of the Commission, in 1950, a confrontation had occurred over the allegedly 'Malthusian' conclusions of a survey prepared by the Population Division on the interrelationships between population trends and economic and social factors. Interest in this question had begun at the first session of the Commission. A French proposal to investigate 'the most favourable rate of population change from the economic point of view' had been combined with a controversial suggestion from the Chinese representative for a study of the areas where population pressure constituted an obstacle to the achievement of higher standards of living.[1] The arrangements for the study were making slow progress when the question acquired a new significance as a result of the decision to expand United Nations technical assistance to less-developed countries. The Commission was anxious that demographic factors should not be neglected in technical assistance activities and encouraged the Secretariat to begin preparation for the project immediately. Meanwhile, the Secretariat was asked to undertake 'a survey of existing studies concerning the relationship between population trends and economic and social factors'.[2]

The survey, which eventually became the *Determinants and Consequences of Population Trends*, a major reference book for demographers, contained three parts.[3] The first discussed the influence of social and economic factors on changes in mortality and fertility and on migratory movements. It described the demographic transition of the developed countries and pointed out the part played by contraception in bringing about a fall in the birth rate. Part two, covering the effects of population changes on economic conditions, emphasized the economic difficulties caused by rapid population growth resulting from high birth rates and falling death rates. The third section was devoted to the relevance of the findings to the economic development of underdeveloped areas. It was argued that on the basis of the available evidence, mortality would continue to decline as living standards rose but that fertility would respond only slowly. Migration was unlikely to make a significant impact on population trends. Since less developed countries seemed likely to experience rapid rates of population growth, 'it is essential' the report stated 'that economic development be planned . . . on a sufficient scale to meet the needs of the growing population. . . .' However, 'where it is thought to be difficult or impossible to achieve economic development on a scale large enough to provide the desired standard of living for a rapidly growing population, some governments may consider it advantageous to adopt policies to curb population growth'. Family planning was not mentioned: 'the measures adopted will probably be mainly in social fields such as education, public health and the status of women'.[4] As regards the

[1] For the discussion of these proposals see UN Doc. E/CN.9/SR.7, 9, 13 and 14, and Report of the 1st session of the Population Commission, OR of ECOSOC, 4th session, supplement no. 5. The plan drawn up by the Population Division is contained in E/CN.9/W.6.

[2] Report of the 4th session of the Population Commission, OR of ECOSOC, 9th session, supplement no. 7, paras. 30–1.

[3] UN Doc. E/CN.9/55 and Add. 1 and 2, 'Findings of Studies on the Relationship between Population Trends and Economic and Social Factors'. Report of the Secretary-General.

[4] UN Doc. E/CN.9/55/Add. 2, paras. 10–18.

relationship between population growth and the prospects for economic development, the survey concluded: 'The results of research have not yet supplied complete and unequivocal answers to these questions. However, it seems well established that an early curtailment of the population growth that is now occurring in most of the underdeveloped countries would in many cases be advantageous in improving the material welfare of the people'.[1] It was part three which aroused the most severe criticisms when the Commission met in May 1950.

In the absence of the USSR and the Ukraine over the question of Chinese representation, the main attack on the report came from Mr Vogelnick of Yugoslavia. There were, he said, two conflicting theories concerning the relationship between population and living standards. The first held that low standards of living, high mortality and agrarian overpopulation were the result of imperialism. Countries were underdeveloped because they were colonies or near colonies, valued merely as a source of raw materials. The other theory alleged that overpopulation was the cause of poverty and the major obstacle to economic development. He claimed that the latter views, whose validity was disproved by the experience of socialist countries, were given 'undue emphasis' in the survey. 'The Secretariat', he said, 'gave the impression of endorsing them by failing to include more than the briefest critical comment or statement of opposite views.'[2]

Alfred Sauvy, of France, Chairman of the Commission and one of its leading personalities, also criticized the Secretariat's survey. He agreed that 'the predominant trend of the document was Malthusian'. Nor was it only Marxist theories and authors who had been ignored. The Secretariat had failed to make sufficient use of French sources. While not doubting the impartiality of the Secretariat, he felt that it had allowed itself to become too greatly influenced by one particular culture and environment. He proposed that the survey be withdrawn pending further research and considerable revision.[3]

Replying to the criticism, John Durand, acting Director of the Population Division since the departure of Frank Notestein, agreed that more space would be accorded to Marxist views. But, he pointed out, Marx's theory of population was almost a century old while contemporary writings by Marxist authors 'were not supported by any detailed exposition of the reasons on which they were based, much less by statistical facts'.[4] He also rejected a claim by Professor Mahalanobis of India, representing

[1] Ibid., para. 29.
[2] UN Doc. E/CN.9/AC.3/SR.1, pp. 3–7.
[3] UN Doc. E/CN.9/SR.57, pp. 3–4 and E/CN.9/L.2.
[4] UN Doc. E/CN.9/AC.3/SR.2, pp. 2–6.

the Statistical Commission, that certain statements in the report 'might be construed as an implied advocacy of the curtailment of population growth as the best, if not the only, means of bringing about economic development'.[1] There was, said Mr Durand, nothing in the survey to indicate that the UN saw population control as a precondition for economic development.[2] He was supported by the representatives of the USA and the UK who said that the fears expressed by Mr Mahalanobis and Mr Vogelnick were unfounded. David Glass, of the UK, suggested that 'the real question was whether levels of living might not in some cases be raised more quickly if the rate of population growth were not so high'.[3]

It was finally agreed that 'substantial changes should be made . . . principally in the form of additions to fields which have been incompletely explored and by the use of sources which were not, or not sufficiently, utilized'.[4]

The Commission also had before it a paper setting out the Secretariat's ideas on the kinds of technical assistance which the United Nations might provide in the field of population.[5] Their suspicions aroused by the previous item, Sauvy and Vogelnick scrutinized the Secretariat's proposals for any trace of 'Malthusianism'.

The original introduction had stated: 'it is to be expected that governments of underdeveloped countries will realize the importance of taking demographic factors into account when planning economic development measures' particularly since, in many less developed countries, population growth and age structure 'may be an important factor tending to hinder the achievement of permanent advances in the level of living'.[6] This was replaced by a Yugoslav text stating, on the contrary, that substantial improvements in the unfavourable demographic situation of less developed countries could be achieved by raising living standards, improving health and medical conditions, and by increasing production.[7]

The substantive sections, dealing with the fields in which assistance might be provided, suffered only minor alterations. A paragraph referring to 'legislative and administrative mea-

[1] UN Doc E/CN.9/AC.3/SR.1, p. 11.
[2] UN Doc. E/CN.9/AC.3/SR.2, p. 5.
[3] UN Doc. E/CN.9/AC.3/SR.1, pp. 10–11.
[4] Report of the 5th session of the Population Commission, OR of ECOSOC, 11th session supplement no. 7, para. 12.
[5] UN Doc. E/CN.9/52. 'Demographic Aspects of Technical Assistance for Economic Development.' Memorandum submitted by the Secretariat. See also E/CN.9/L.1–4.   [6] UN Doc. E/CN.9/52, op. cit., pp. 6–7.
[7] Report of the 5th session of the Population Commission, op. cit., Annex 1, para. 4.

sures', the Secretariat's circumlocution for population policy, was retained with a small but illuminating amendment. The text originally read 'legislative and administrative measures . . . may have an important influence upon populations and thereby upon economic development'. The Commission deleted the words 'and thereby upon economic development'.[1]

Family planning was not mentioned in the report, but neither was assistance in this field excluded. However, it is significant that in its report to the Economic and Social Council the Commission spoke merely of the demographic *consequences* of economic development programmes'.[2]

The Population Division became a branch of the Bureau of Social Affairs in the course of Hammarskjöld's administrative reorganization of the UN Secretariat in 1955. Hammarskjöld believed that it was preferable for research to be subcontracted to universities and national institutions, rather than to be undertaken by the Secretariat. As a result of the downgrading the number of professional staff was reduced from 30 to 18, a reduction proportionately much greater than that suffered by other sections of the Secretariat. Announcing the decision to the eighth session of the Commission, the representative of the Secretary-General stated bluntly: 'it must be emphasized that the Secretariat's capacity to undertake studies would be smaller in future. . . . Governments, the Specialized Agencies and other units of the UN would therefore have to limit their demands on the Branch'.[3]

It seems generally agreed in retrospect that the new approach to research was not successful, and that in the demographic field the United Nations had advantages when conducting research which were not enjoyed by national institutions. On the other hand, within the Bureau of Social Affairs, under a Director, Julia Henderson, who was interested in the possibilities of action programmes, the demographers were brought into closer contact with housing and other social experts, and perhaps became more conscious of the social implications of demographic trends.

In these somewhat unfavourable circumstances, John Durand, another American, took charge of the Population Branch. Durand, a distinguished demographer who had been deputy to both Notestein and Whelpton, was all too well aware of the difficulties he would face. In 1950, while acting director, he had found himself at the centre of the controversy over the allegedly Malthusian tone of a Secretariat study. It is possible that this experience impressed upon him the need for patience in so far as involvement in family planning was concerned.

[1] UN Doc. E/CN.9/SR.57, p. 16.
[2] Report of the 5th session of the Population Commission, op. cit., para. 11.
[3] UN Doc. E/CN.9/SR.93, pp. 4–5.

In addition, two of the members of the Commission most interested in action programmes, Philip Hauser of America and David Glass of the UK, ceased to attend. The Commission fell increasingly under the influence of Alfred Sauvy, a member of the Commission at every session and Director of the highly respected Institut National d'Etudes Demographiques in Paris. His competence extended well beyond the confines of demography but he remained firmly wedded to the French pronatalist tradition. He was, as much as any of the delegates from Communist countries, an implacable opponent of what he called 'le malthusianisme anglo-saxon'.[1]

In 1951, Belgium, elected in place of the Netherlands, appointed Jacques Mertens de Wilmars as its representative on the Population Commission. De Wilmars, who was Professor of Economics at Louvain and a staunch Catholic, remained a member of the Commission until the twelfth session in 1963 and was twice its chairman. His attitude reflected the official Catholic position. He accepted that the rate of population growth in many underdeveloped countries was a serious problem, but felt that it could be solved without recourse to birth control if the rich countries were prepared to make the necessary sacrifices. Birth control was, he said, 'a solution of abandon and weakness'; its advocacy even directly by international bodies was unacceptable.[2]

Latin American countries have been among the foremost opponents of birth control and have frequently distinguished themselves by their tenacity in international discussions on the question. During the 1950s both Brazil (1946–61) and Argentina (1955–61) were members of the Commission. However, like the other Latin American countries represented on the Commission, they rarely took part in the discussions on population policy or on the implications of the world population situation. Indeed the most striking Latin American contribution during this period was made not against but in favour of birth control by the representative of Costa Rica. 'Many countries', he said, 'would double

---

[1] See for example 'Le Malthusianisme anglo-saxon', *Population*, avril–juin 1947, pp. 221–42, and 'Le faux-problème de la population mondiale', *Population*, juillet–septembre 1949, pp. 447–63. The evolution in his thinking about the population question may be seen in two later books, *De Malthus à Mao-Tse-Tung: le problème de la population dans le monde*, Paris, 1958, and *Malthus et les Deux Marx: le problème de la faim et la guerre dans le monde*, Paris, 1963.

[2] See J. Mertens de Wilmars: 'Les problèmes demographiques des pays sous-developpés' quoted in *Migration News*, no. 3, December 1952, p. 6. While Chairman at the 10th session in 1959 he gave every opportunity to the representatives of Catholic non-governmental organizations to present their views: see E/CN.9/SR.129 ff. His own account of this session appears in *Migration News*, March–April 1959, pp. 1–8.

their population in the next 25 or 30 years, and their governments would do well to devise a policy of limitation of births or
other measures to meet the challenge.'[1]

After 1950 the members from the Communist countries
seemed more aggressive in their opposition to what they saw as
the Malthusian tendencies within the Commission. The 'Cold
War' undoubtedly exacerbated the differences which already
existed over the interpretation of demographic phenomena. At
the fifth session of the Commission the USSR member had
walked out as a protest against the seating of the representative
of Nationalist China.[2] His absence may, incidentally, have saved
the Secretariat from even greater embarrassment in the discussion of the Population Division's report on population trends
and economic and social conditions. In 1951 the USSR and the
Ukrainian representatives returned and the next three sessions
opened with a Soviet attempt to unseat 'the representative of the
Kuomintang group'. At the 6th and 7th sessions the Communist
members refused to approve the final report.

At the World Population Conference in Rome in 1954 there
were forceful exchanges between demographers from the USSR,
Poland and the Ukraine and those from western non-Catholic
countries.[3] At the eighth session of the Commission in March
1955 Mr Ryabushkin said that the Conference had demonstrated
the existence of 'two diametrically opposed trends, one towards
progressive consideration of the problem from the points of view
of economic development, solution of social problems and improvement of international relations, and the other towards
reactionary neo-Malthusianism and the prevention of the growth
of populations'.[4] At the ninth session the Communist members
challenged the projections prepared by the Population Division
and argued that the report on the world demographic situation
presented a one-sided and pessimistic view.[5]

The election of Sweden in 1951 and of India in 1955 did little
to redress the balance within the Commission. The Indian
government did not send an expert but contented itself with
representation by a member of the Indian Permanent Mission
in New York. At the eighth session in 1955, Mr Hyrenius of
Sweden suggested that the Commission should submit recommendations to governments based on the findings of the World
Population Conference. The most to which the Commission
would agree was that governments should be invited to 'arrange

[1] UN Doc. E/CN.9/SR.123, pp. 4–5.
[2] UN Doc. E/CN.9/SR.52.
[3] *Proceedings of the WPC, Rome, 1954*: Summary Report. See especially
meetings 11 and 26.　　　　　　　　　　[4] UN Doc. E/CN.9/SR.93, p. 9.
[5] UN Doc. E/CN.9/SR.136, pp. 6–7.

for the findings of the Conference to be studied in relation to the needs of their own countries'.[1] Sweden was not re-elected to membership of the Commission. Although the British and American members of the Commission continued to be concerned about the implications of the world population situation, they did not appear to consider it opportune to press the issue. The governments of western countries seemed generally more concerned to avoid controversy, not only at the international level but also at home where, particularly in the United States, birth control was still a very live issue.

TECHNICAL ASSISTANCE

The Commission's terms of reference provided for three kinds of action: the provision of demographic information; the explanation of demographic phenomena; and advice on matters of policy. The Commission saw these as consecutive, rather than complementary, aspects in an overall strategy. As a result of the growing concern within the UN system for the promotion of economic and social development, emphasis was increasingly placed on activities which were felt to be of direct relevance for policy making. However, apart from recommendations of a general nature that governments should take demographic factors into account in their programmes and plans for economic development, the Commission was slow to come to grips with the question of population policy.

Apart from the Economic Commission for Asia and the Far East, none of the other organs of the UN showed any great interest in population problems either. In 1957 the General Assembly passed without serious debate a resolution introduced by Peru, Brazil, Italy, Mexico and Pakistan on 'demographic questions'. The resolution affirmed the importance of demographic factors in economic development, but limited itself to requesting ECOSOC to include information on this subject in the reports to the Second Committee. Previously such information had been sent only to the Assembly's Social Committee.[2]

The United Nations clearly had the right, and, it might be argued, the obligation to take the lead. There were various ways in which this could have been done. The most direct contribution which the UN could make was through the provision of technical assistance to member states. Resolution 222(IX) of ECOSOC, the basic charter of UN technical assistance programmes adopted

[1] UN Doc. E/CN.9/SR.94, p. 5.
[2] OR of the General Assembly, 12th session, 1957, SR of the second Committee, pp. 231–2, 258–60 and 279. See also A/C.2/L.355 and Rev. 1 and Rev. 2.

in 1949, authorized the UN to provide, on request, advice and assistance in all economic and social fields. The Population Commission itself had submitted to ECOSOC a resolution drawing attention to the importance of the demographic aspects of technical assistance activities, and had drawn up guidelines for such assistance.[1]

The officials of the Population Division and of the United Nations Technical Assistance Administration, which was responsible for the technical assistance operations of the UN itself, were anxious for the UN to acquire an operational role. Few requests, however, were received from governments. Moreover, the majority of these were for advice on census taking and on vital statistics programmes. A small number of governments sought help on the demographic aspects of their programmes for economic development. Thus, in 1957, a demographer was assigned to assist in the preparation of a report on a demographic and economic survey in Thailand; and between 1953 and 1960 demographers were assigned to the Indonesian State Planning Bureau to advise on research into urbanization and inter-island migration as part of the government's policy of population redistribution.[2]

Even among the governments who were alive to the importance of the population factor few had as yet reached the stage where rapid population growth was seen as a sufficiently serious impediment to improvement in standards of living as to warrant government intervention in order to reduce fertility. A few requests for help with action programmes were received. In 1952 India requested assistance from the UN with the statistical evaluation of the 'rhythm method' experiment for which WHO had provided technical advice.[3] Expert advice was discreetly given to Barbados in 1953 and again in 1957 on ways of dealing with the island's population problems. In addition, in 1953, an expert in medical statistics, Dr Christopher Tietze, was sent to advise on the development of a system of records for use in the island's family planning clinics.[4] Expert advice was also given to the Egyptian government in 1955 in evaluating the country's demographic situation in relation to prospects for economic development, including the formulation of population policy measures.[5]

[1] Report of the 5th session of the Population Commission, OR of ECOSOC, 11th session, 1950, supplement no, 7, para. 11 and Annex.
[2] UN Doc. E/CN.9/158, 'Objectives and Accomplishments of the UN in the Field of Population', pp. 15–16. See also E/CN.9/94; E/CN.9/130 and E/CN.9/149, part III.
[3] Final Report on Pilot Studies in Family Planning, WHO, S.E. Asia Regional Office, New Delhi, 1954. Introduction.
[4] UN Doc. TAA/BAR.2 and TAA/BAR.4.
[5] UN Doc. E/CN.9/149 and 158, op. cit.

The lack of interest shown by governments in obtaining assistance in population policies placed the Secretariat in a difficult position. It should be remembered that in other fields, governments often became interested in obtaining assistance in response to initiatives taken by visiting officials of the UN agencies, sometimes rudely described as 'travelling salesmen'. No such initiatives seem to have been taken in the field of population policy or family planning. The conservatism of the Population Commission undoubtedly influenced the Secretariat's attitude and served to hinder the development of an operational role in relation to population policy.

The most important contribution made by the UN during this period was thus indirect, through the preparation of population projections, and through demographic training and research activities.

POPULATION PROJECTIONS

From 1951 onwards the statistical work of the UN was complemented by a series of demographic projections. Projections were presented in 1954 to the World Population Conference and published in a revised version in 1957.[1] On each occasion new data, notably information concerning mainland China, or improved methodology, led to substantial upward revisions of population size and rate of growth. The feeling in 1957 moreover was that the future growth was more likely to conform to the 'high' rather than the 'low' variant. This is in striking contrast to the expectations in 1951 when the first projections were made. It was stated then that 'any expectations of a constant rate of population growth in the future would be unrealistic'. Although in South-East Asia rapid growth was thought possible as a result of continued decline in mortality, it was felt that famines, epidemics, and internal strife would check any long-term expansions.[2]

The projections were prepared ostensibly as an aid to member states and to the Specialized Agencies in their forward planning, and as exercises in methodology. The main result of the publication of the projections, however, was to dramatize the increase in world population, especially in those parts of the world where overcrowding and poverty were already a problem, and to make

[1] 'The Past and Future Growth of World Population—a Long-range View', *UN Population Bulletin*, December 1951, pp. 1–13; 'Past and Future Population of the World and its Continents', *Proceedings of the World Population Conference, Rome, 1954*, vol. III; and *The Future Growth of World Population*, Population Studies, no. 28, 1958 (ST/SOA/Ser. A, no. 28).

[2] See chapter 4, p. 34.

it more difficult for the Commission and member states to avoid discussion of the implications. Moreover, the further the projections were carried, the more alarming they became. In 1954 the 'high' estimate for world population in the year 1980 was 3,990,000,000. In 1957 this had jumped to 4,820,000,000 and the figure for the year 2000 was 6,900,000,000. This implied that the population of the world would more than double between 1960 and 2000. Increases in Asia, Africa and Latin America were expected to be even greater.[1]

At the Rome World Population Conference the projections presented by the UN Secretariat were criticized, notably by Soviet participants, on the grounds that past experience in population forecasting had shown the unreliability of projections. Similar objections were heard in the Population Commission at the ninth and tenth sessions, during the discussion of the estimates prepared in 1957. Some delegates felt that there was a danger that the general public would misunderstand the nature and purpose of the projections and might take the figures literally. 'The Commission', said the Chairman, Mr Mertens de Wilmars, 'should avoid unnecessarily alarming the public by putting out sensational figures.'[2] However, the publication of results of the censuses carried out in 1960–1 were soon to show that population growth in the period 1950–60 had in fact been higher than the 'high' estimates issued during the period.[3] The implications of the need for upward revision each time new information became available could not easily be dismissed.

RESEARCH AND STUDIES

Several of the studies carried out by the UN in the nineteen-fifties also helped to awaken interest in and deepen understanding of population problems. The most influential of these was undoubtedly *Determinants and Consequences of Population Trends*,[4] the survey whose first version had caused such controversy in the Commission in 1950. *Determinants and Consequences* became a major source of reference for demographers, important not only for the information which it contained but also because it drew attention to the gaps in contemporary knowledge concerning human fertility behaviour. A group of experts was convened in 1955 to discuss these lacunae. They prepared a list of topics

[1] *The Future Growth of World Population*, 1958, op. cit.
[2] UN Doc. E/CN.9/SR.122 and E/CN.9/SR.136.
[3] H. Gille, 'What the Asian Censuses Reveal', *Far Eastern Economic Review*, 29 June 1961, pp. 635–41.
[4] *Determinants and Consequences of Population Trends*, op. cit.

which acted as a spur to further research and discussion, especially in the field of family planning.[1]

Another influential study was the *Mysore Population Study* carried out by the United Nations between 1950 and 1951 in cooperation with the Indian Government.[2] The Mysore study was the result of the proposals made at the first and second sessions of the Commission for an investigation of the interplay between population trends and economic and social conditions in a large, densely populated poor country. The study was primarily intended as an experiment in ways of obtaining and processing information. In fact it became a key document, both inside and outside India, in the development of population action programmes. Despite objections from some members of the Commission, the study included a survey of contraceptive knowledge, attitude and practice. It revealed a crucial fact in the development of family planning strategy—the existence of a widespread desire for smaller families among rural semi-literate populations. Hitherto there had been little evidence that the practice of birth control would be acceptable to the populations of less developed countries, even if other national and international obstacles to action could be overcome.[3]

Various other publications also deserve mention, notably the technical manuals, on such topics as census taking, vital statistics and population projections, and the chapter on population in the 1957 *Report on the World Social Situation*. The latter contained an unambiguous statement of the difficulties facing less developed countries, and ended: '. . . what measures for dealing with problems of population should be included in programmes of economic and social development? The UN Population Commission considering this question at its 9th session recommended that each country should study this question and decide its own policy'.[4]

DEMOGRAPHIC TRAINING

Training was seen as one of the most valuable forms of assistance which the UN could provide. There was in most developing countries a serious shortage of trained demographers and statisticians. Attention was drawn to the problem in 1950 by a

[1] UN Doc. E/CN.9/116.

[2] *The Mysore Population Study: Report of a field survey in selected areas of Mysore State, India*, Population Studies, no. 31, 1961 (ST/SOA/Ser. A, no. 31).

[3] S. N. Agarwala: 'Population Control in India: Progress and Prospects', *Law and Contemporary Problems*, Summer 1960, pp. 582–4.

[4] *1957 Report on the World Social Situation*, United Nations, Department of Economic and Social Affairs, 1958, p. 27.

UNESCO expert committee.[1] The Population Commission at its
fifth and sixth sessions recommended the provision of fellowships
for training in demographic techniques and analysis and the
holding of regional seminars.[2] The first of such seminars was held
at Bandung in 1955[3] and the second in Brazil later in the same
year.[4] The Bandung seminar, directed by Whelpton, was
attended by officials from eleven countries in Asia and the Far
East. Speakers included Philip Hauser and John Durand.
Dr Abraham Stone was present as an 'observer'. The seminar
gave a considerable impetus to the development of population
policies in the region. In 1956 its recommendations were endorsed by ECAFE. The Commission noted 'with concern that
the rate of economic development was not much faster than the
rate of population growth . . . it was thought that a slowing down
in the fertility rate might help alleviate the pressure of population
on available resources'.[5]

A development of more far-reaching consequences was the
creation of regional demographic training and research centres.
The decision was a consequence of Hammarskjold's policy that
the United Nations should not carry out its own research but
should cooperate with universities and other national and international research institutions. In 1955, the Commission requested the Secretary-General 'to explore the possibility of
establishing . . . relations with qualified institutions in each of the
major underdeveloped regions of the world which could serve as
centres for studies on population problems in the region and for
the training of personnel . . .'[6]

Meanwhile the Indian Government, encouraged by the
Population Council and the Rockefeller Foundation, was con-
templating the creation of its own training centre. Agreement
was reached in 1956 for the establishment of a centre at Chembur
near Bombay to be financed jointly by the United Nations and
the Indian Government.[7] A second centre, CELADE, was set
up, along the same lines in 1957, at Santiago in Chile to serve the

[1] UNESCO meeting of experts on population problems, July 1950:
International Social Science Bulletin, vol. II, no. 3, August 1950, pp. 402–7.
[2] Report of the 5th session of the Population Commission, Annex, para. 13,
OR of ECOSOC, 11th session, 1950, supplement no. 7; Report of the 6th
session, paras. 22–25, OR of ECOSOC, 13th session, 1951, supplement no. 11.
[3] Report of the Asia and Far East Seminar on Population, Bandung,
November 1955. UN Doc. ST/TAA/Ser. C, no. 26.
[4] Report of the Latin American Seminar on population, Rio de Janeiro,
December 1955. UN Doc. ST/TAA/Ser.C, no. 33.
[5] Report of the 12th session of ECAFE, OR of ECOSOC, 22nd session,
1956, supplement no. 2, p. 24.
[6] Report of the 8th session of the Population Commission, Appendix, OR
of ECOSOC, 19th session, 1955, Supplement no, 5, p. 11.
[7] UN Doc. E/CN.9/131.

Latin American region.[1] Awareness of the importance of demographic factors and population problems was less developed in
Latin America than in Asia. The creation of CELADE was thus
particularly opportune, since it helped prepare the way for the
debate on the population question which was sparked off by the
1960 censuses. A third centre was set up in Cairo in 1963 to
cover the African region.

THE 1954 WORLD POPULATION CONFERENCE

In 1951 the Population Commission had shelved Huxley's
proposal for a world population conference on the grounds that
it would be better to wait until after the results of the 1950 round
of censuses had become available.[2] In fact, several members were
suspicious of Huxley's scheme and were anxious to prevent the
discussion of policy questions for fear that the conference would
be used to propagate birth control. They insisted that any conference which was held should be a scientific gathering of demographers and should limit itself to the exchange of information.[3]

The idea of a world conference was nonetheless tempting. The
Population Division favoured the idea and, in order to prevent
the question being shelved indefinitely, the Assistant Secretary-
General for Social Affairs, Henri Laugier, hinted privately to the
IUSSP that an initiative by them would be welcome. Accordingly, in 1951, the IUSSP formally proposed the holding of a world
population conference at the earliest possible opportunity.[4]

The Commission at its 6th session in 1951 affirmed its belief
in the 'scientific' value of holding a conference in 1953 or 1954,
the majority taking the view that the participants should be
experts attending in their private capacity and not, as the USSR
would have preferred, representatives of governments. The
majority view was shared by most member states whose views on
the question of a population conference were solicited by the
Secretary-General at the request of ECOSOC.

In June 1952 the Economic and Social Council decided that
the conference would be held in 1954 under the auspices of the
UN and in collaboration with the IUSSP and interested Specialized Agencies. The FAO, ILO and UNESCO had already
indicated their support for a conference. WHO was in the midst
of the crisis over the question of the organization's involvement
in population matters and its response was far from enthusiastic.

[1] UN Doc. E/CN.9/148.
[2] See Chapter 6.
[3] UN Doc. E/CN.9/SR.29 and E/CN.9/SR.41, pp. 7–10.
[4] UN Doc. E/CN.9/NGO2.

The resolution confirmed that the conference would be a purely scientific gathering. It would therefore pass no resolutions nor make recommendations to governments. On the question of participation, the Secretary-General was instructed 'to invite, in their individual capacity, experts nominated by (a) governments, (b) non-governmental scientific organizations concerned and (c) the interested Specialized Agencies and, in addition, to invite a small number of experts with a scientific interest in population questions'.[1]

Detailed arrangements were entrusted to a preparatory committee to be made up of individual experts and representatives of the organizations involved in the sponsorship of the conference.

Although it had not been explicitly stated, the decision to hold a scientific conference reflected the determination on the part of some governments and individuals involved to prevent discussion of the need for population control. Almost twenty-five years had passed since Margaret Sanger had found herself excluded from her own world population conference because of the hostility aroused by the subject of birth control.[2] The rules laid down for the 1954 conference showed that there had been but little change of attitude in the meantime. In the words of the Secretariat's circular, issued after the first meeting of the preparatory committee, 'the term "non-governmental scientific organization" is interpreted as meaning an autonomous organization which has the advancement of science as its aim. It therefore excludes any organization or the subsidiary organ of any organization concerned with the promotion of any particular theory or policy or any special social or religious interest.'[3]

However, the chairman of the preparatory committee was Pascal Whelpton and the secretary of the sub-committee in charge of arrangements was Frank Lorimer of the IUSSP. Thanks to their influence family planning did find a place at the conference. To the delight of some, to the indignation of others and to the amazement of many, Dr Abraham Stone was invited to present a paper on modern contraceptive techniques. In addition, several of the papers submitted for the same session discussed the effects of contraceptive practice on fertility levels.[4]

Provision had been made for the nomination of individuals to attend the conference at the invitation of the UN or the Specialized Agencies. In this way twelve associates of the newly formed

[1] Resolution 435 (XIV), OR of ECOSOC, 14th session, 1952, supplement no. 1, pp. 27–8.
[2] See Chapter 2
[3] Plans for the World Population Conference, UN Doc. E/CONF.13/INF.1, p. 2.
[4] Programme for the World Population Conference, UN Doc. E/CONF.13/INF.2, meeting 8, pp. 19–20.

International Planned Parenthood Federation attended the conference as participants, nine of whom presented papers. To its surprise IPPF itself was invited to send two observers.[1]

A session on legislative and administrative measures affecting population was included in the programme. Although several of the papers described national policies, the main emphasis was explicitly on the role of research in the formulation of population policies.[2] However, included in the documentation provided for participants was a survey of national population policies. The initiative had come from UNESCO, which had asked the IUSSP to prepare a report on recent developments in order to make good the gap in the conference programme.[3]

The first World Population Conference met in Rome from 31 August until 10 September 1954. Over four hundred delegates attended from eighty countries and colonies. Thirty working sessions were held and over four hundred papers presented. Both in terms of size and scope the conference was by far the most important international conference on population held until that time.[4]

The summary of the conference proceedings published by the United Nations contains only the reports written by the rapporteurs of each session. Consequently they give little impression of the atmosphere at the conference, nor is there any detailed account of the debates which took place. However, it is possible to piece together from this and from other sources a fairly clear picture of what happened.[5]

The point which emerges most strongly is that the fears which had been felt in many quarters that the conference would be torn apart over the question of birth control proved exaggerated. The conference was dominated by the professional demographers from France and the USA. The participants from the Communist bloc submitted few papers and, apart from Mr Vogelnick of Yugoslavia who was chairman of the final session, they played a relatively minor role in the conference proceedings. The only real

[1] *News of Population and Birth Control*, no. 28, October, 1954.

[2] Programme for the WPC, op. cit., meeting 11, pp. 23–4.

[3] H. T. Eldridge: *Population Policies, a Survey of Recent Developments*, op. cit. See especially the foreword by David Glass.

[4] *Proceedings of the World Population Conference, Rome, 1954*, United Nations, New York, 1955.

[5] The most comprehensive survey of the conference is to be found in *Population*, octobre–decembre 1954, pp. 699–710 and avril–juin 1955, pp. 217–38. The first article deals with the preparations for the conference, the second with the results obtained. A brief summary appeared in *Population Index*, October 1954, by Frank Notestein. See also *News of Population and Birth Control*, no. 28, October 1954, op. cit., and *Eugenics Review*, October 1955, pp. 205–11.

confrontation between western and Marxist demographers occurred at the session devoted to the interrelations of population, economic development and social change. Speakers from Poland and the Soviet Union argued that the experience of Communist countries showed that the real problem facing underdeveloped countries was not rapid rates of population growth but their economic and social structure. They were challenged by the American demographers who questioned not only their conclusions but also the figures on which they were based.[1]

For the most part, however, the participants from the Communist countries were content to reaffirm their belief that present rates of population growth were not excessive and their opposition to restrictionist policies.[2] At the final session, at which the conference discussed the economic and social implications of population trends, Mr Ryabushkin claimed that the conference had made a positive contribution because it had demonstrated the lack of realism in neo-Malthusian theories. These theories he said were 'incompatible with the scientific principles of demography, economics and sociology and contrary to the basic principles of humanitarianism'.[3]

The meeting on fertility trends in areas of high fertility, at which Abraham Stone presented his paper, passed off remarkably smoothly, much to the surprise of the small group of family planners attending the conference.[4] Participants from Catholic countries were for the most part more interested in the technical meetings. Their main contribution was made in the sessions dealing with migration, a contention of the Catholic Church at this time being that emigration could provide a solution to population pressure.

Despite the presence of well-known advocates of family planning and the participation of Communist countries, the Pope received the conference. His address was remarkable for its tact. He commended the participants for their concern with what he said was a most important problem and one which greatly preoccupied the Church. He trusted that, in their deliberations, they would not forget the moral and human aspects of the problem.[5]

The lack of controversy was to a large extent due to the careful selection of topics for discussion. The main emphasis was on demographic research, case studies and the identification of gaps in knowledge. This was particularly noticeable in the questions

[1] *Proceedings of the WPC*, op. cit., pp. 130–1.
[2] Ibid., p. 63.   [3] Ibid., p. 178.
[4] *News of Population and Birth Control*, no. 28, op. cit.
[5] *L'Osservatore Romano*, 17 September 1954. The text of the address is translated in *Eugenics Review*, April 1955, p. 6.

drawn up for meeting 11 on population policies. The questions asked were: (1) on what basis are population policies formulated; (2) how far is demographic research used, and how far could it be used in formulating specific policy measures; and (3) how far is demographic research used to ascertain the effectiveness of general or specific policy measures.[1]

Consequently it was the professional demographers who benefited most from the conference. In the words of Frank Notestein 'the conference was immensely useful in stimulating the interest of both scholars and governments . . . in the scientific study of population'.[2]

In Julian Huxley's original vision the conference was to have been the first step in a concerted attack on the world population problem. The decision to hold a scientific conference had ruled out from the start such a possibility. For those interested in finding practical solutions to world population problems the conference was a disappointment. They need not, however, have found the balance sheet entirely negative. The mere fact that it had proved possible to hold a world population conference, under UN auspices, and with the participation of experts nominated by fifty-eight governments, was an event of considerable significance. Moreover, as the conference progressed, family planning moved more and more into the open. Speakers, notably from India, Egypt and Japan, described efforts that were being made in their countries to spread birth control. The respectful attention with which their contributions were received was an indication of the changing climate of opinion with respect to the gravity of the world population situation.

THE COMMISSION AND POPULATION POLICIES

Towards the end of the 1950s there were signs that the Population Commission was becoming more ready to face the problems of rapid population growth.

At the ninth session in 1957, the agenda for the first time included an item entitled 'The world demographic situation'. The report prepared by the Secretariat emphasized that in underdeveloped countries population was growing at rates never before experienced in human history. Many governments, it stated, did not seem to recognize the importance of the economic and social consequences of this situation. The report concluded with a brief survey of some of the more important implications

[1] *Proceedings of the WPC*, op. cit., pp. 61–3.
[2] *Population Index*, op. cit., p. 248.

of rapid population growth, but the Secretariat was careful not to draw any conclusions regarding the possibility of achieving economic development or the need to seek ways to slow down the rate of population increase.[1] In the discussion Alfred Sauvy claimed that it was a matter for satisfaction that the world's population was increasing at an unprecedented rate. 'No-one', he said, 'could advocate a decline in the birth rate.'[2] Mr Ryabushkin of the USSR also found the situation encouraging. He argued that the policies which governments should follow in the light of their own analysis of demographic changes would depend on the specific conditions of each country. The Commission, he suggested, could not formulate any general policy rules.[3]

Two years later at the tenth session in 1959, the Commission once again discussed the world population situation. The basis for the discussion was the latest set of projections prepared by the UN for major regions up to the year 2000. The estimates for each region had been revised upwards and it was pointed out that future growth seemed more likely to conform to the 'high' rather than the 'low' variant.[4] The Commission showed a greater sense of urgency than at the ninth session. The Chairman, Mr Mertens de Wilmars, said that 'while the Commission should avoid unnecessarily alarming the public by putting out sensational figures . . . it was duty bound to call attention to the rapid growth of the world's population as an indisputable fact'.[5] The final report contained, for the first time, a recognition that rapid population growth could jeopardize hopes for economic progress: 'the question must frankly be raised as to whether, in certain of these nations (the less developed countries), population growth has reached such a point as to make economic development more difficult or slower in its progress, or to make it dependent on special kinds of measures'.[6]

The Commission still hesitated to accept the implications of its analysis of the situation. Under its terms of reference the Commission was expected to advise ECOSOC on measures designed to influence population trends. Nevertheless, Mr Marshall of Canada felt that 'the political implications of demographic changes should not be stressed', while Mr Mertens de Wilmars stated that the Commission 'should not attempt to propose a solution to what was a serious problem, and least of all suggest

[1] UN Doc. E/CN.9/139. 'Background Facts on World Population and Population Trends'.
[2] UN Doc. E/CN.9/SR.122, p. 4.
[3] Ibid., p. 7, and SR.123, p. 5.
[4] *The Future Growth of World Population*, op. cit.
[5] UN Doc. E/CN.9/SR.136, p. 9.
[6] Report of the 10th session of the Population Commission, para. 12. OR of ECOSOC, 27th session, supplement no. 3.

that it advocated curbing or stopping demographic expansion'. Mr Ryabushkin said he would oppose 'any suggestion that the Commission should recommend action which would lower the birth rate.'[1]

Mr Benjamin of the UK, on the other hand, argued that the Commission was not adopting 'a sufficiently constructive attitude'. He was disappointed, he said, to hear the same remarks as had been heard at the World Population Conference five years earlier. Although it was clearly not up to the Commission to tell governments what policy they should adopt, it could not avoid consideration of the measures that might be needed to resolve the problems resulting from population growth. 'All members could agree', he said, 'that, particularly in the Far East, some families were even at present too large for the health of the mother and of the children, and in relation to the food and other resources available'.[2] He was supported by Mr Bjerve of Norway, who said that it was not enough merely to call for increased output to absorb the increase in population.[3]

Agreement was finally reached on the basis of a text produced by Kingsley Davis of the USA, rapporteur for the session.[4] It recognized that 'it is not the task of the Population Commission to suggest policies that any Government of any member state should pursue'. At the same time it was emphasized that each government should study the interrelations between population growth and economic and social progress as fully as possible and should take them into account when formulating and implementing its policies.[5] The affirmation of the right of each government to decide upon its own policy implied that governments should have a population policy, although this policy would not necessarily aim at reducing the birth rate. The role of the UN was to ensure that decisions were made in the light of all the relevant knowledge. As we shall see in Part III, the facts were becoming increasingly eloquent.

[1] UN Doc. E/CN.9/SR.136, p. 6 ff.
[2] Ibid., p. 9.   [3] Ibid., p. 10.
[4] UN Doc. E/CN.9/SR.137.
[5] Report of the 10th session of the Population Commission, op. cit., para. 14.

8

Changing Attitudes in Rich Countries

THE World Population Conference and the discussions in the Population Commission had indicated growing awareness that traditional attitudes towards population growth might need to be questioned in the light of the unprecedented increase in world population. There was still little agreement as to whether rapid rates of population growth constituted an obstacle to the economic development of poor countries, and even less as to what kinds of government action might be required. Meanwhile, however, behind the scenes and outside the formal framework of the UN, important developments were under way which helped to prepare the ground for the breakthrough at the international level which occurred in the mid-sixties.

ROMAN CATHOLICS

First, the apparent inflexibility in the attitude of the Roman Catholic Church concealed a significant change of emphasis in the Catholic position. Although Catholic spokesmen continued to denounce as pessimists those who advocated birth control and to insist that the world could support a very much larger population, they were more and more willing to accept the reality of the 'population explosion'. In his address to the World Population Conference, Pius XII declared: 'the Church is not unaware of these problems; she is not indifferent to their anguishing aspects . . .' And he went on to urge Catholics to take 'an active part in research and in the efforts (being) made in this domain'.[1] Migration, which had received considerable encouragement in the early fifties, was mentioned less and less, as it became clear that 'the lack of solidarity among people and nations',[2] which the Pope had condemned in 1952, was unlikely to change. By 1960, therefore, although Catholic representatives were still likely to question some estimates of future world population growth, it was generally agreed that the present situation was exceptional and that it posed serious problems, especially for poor countries.

The change in emphasis narrowed the area of disagreement between Catholics and non-Catholics, which was now increasingly centred on the strategy to be adopted to solve the

[1] *L'Osservatore Romano*, 17 September 1954, op. cit.
[2] Pius XII, Christmas Message, 1952, op. cit.

problem. The Catholics maintained that higher standards of living would bring about a spontaneous fall in the birth rate and that, consequently, the solution was to increase the assistance given to poor countries in order to further their economic development. The condemnation of all 'artificial' means of family limitation and of all policies based on 'a formula that the number of inhabitants should be regulated according to the public economy'[1] remained absolute. Nevertheless, in 1951, Pius XII had confirmed that, in certain very limited circumstances, the regulation of births was compatible with the teaching of the Church. Moreover, in the same speech, the Pope had urged scientists to seek ways of making the 'rhythm method' more effective.[2] Slight though these changes were they tended to weaken the philosophical basis of the Catholic position.

Even within the Church itself the logic of this position was, for the first time, being questioned.[3] Many Catholics appeared to be interpreting the 'serious reasons' for regulating family size in a very wide sense. Family planning surveys, notably in the United States, showed that many Catholics practised contraception in defiance of the teaching of their Church.[4] Although the pressure for a revision of Catholic doctrine came from the laity, within the Vatican itself there were those who argued that the Church should pronounce itself in favour of 'responsible parenthood'.[5]

PROTESTANTS

The success of the Roman Catholic 'lobby' in preventing WHO from becoming involved in family planning in the early fifties prompted a counter-offensive on the part of the Protestant Churches. By the early 1950s the grudging approval given to the practice of contraception at the Lambeth Conference in 1930

[1] Pius XII, Christmas Message, 1952.
[2] Pius XII, Address to the Italian 'Fronte della Famiglia', 26 November 1951.
[3] See, for example, articles by Rev. J. O'Brien and by John Rock reprinted in *Population Bulletin*, November 1961, 'New Trends in Roman Catholic Opinion', and R. P. S. de Lestapis: *La Limitation des Naissances*, Paris, 1959.
[4] The Growth of American Families survey in 1955 for example revealed that half the fertile Catholic couples married in the previous ten years had used a prohibited method. See C. F. Westoff et al.: *Family Growth in Metropolitan America*, Princeton, 1956, p. 183. These findings were confirmed in a follow-up study in 1960 and in surveys carried out in Europe. See R. Freedman et al.: *Family Planning, Sterility and Population Growth*, New York, 1959; and D. V. Glass: 'Family Limitation in Europe, a Survey of Recent Studies' in C. Kiser (ed.) *Research in Family Planning*, Princeton, 1962, pp. 251–3.
[5] See R. M. Fagley: *The Population Explosion and Christian Responsibility*, op. cit., pp. 184–6.

was evolving into a doctrine of 'responsible parenthood'.[1] The initiative for discussion of the wider problems raised by the 'population explosion' came from the Commission of the Churches for International Affairs. Rev. Richard Fagley, Executive Secretary of the Commission and its main animator on the population question, was convinced that 'a clear lead from the Churches of the Reformation (would) help to overcome the neglect of the demographic problem in Western and UN policy more rapidly than any other factor'.[2] At Evanston in 1954 the World Council of Churches had made a brief reference to population and birth control. The final report urged the Churches to give guidance on what it called 'these burning questions'.[3]

At this stage the Churches were unwilling to take up a position, and limited themselves to stressing the urgency of the problem and the seriousness of the ethical questions which it raised.[4] The efforts of Fagley and his colleagues, however, were finally rewarded in 1958, when the American Conference of the World Council of Churches adopted a firm resolution on the question, affirming that 'few problems have a greater bearing on the welfare of our fellow men and on world peace than responsible control of population growth' and calling on Protestant Churches to make a 'courageous and forthright judgement on this issue'.[5]

Meanwhile the 1958 Lambeth Conference of Anglican Bishops had adopted a historic statement of Protestant doctrine on marriage and parenthood.[6] A resolution on 'the family in contemporary society' declared: 'The responsibility for deciding upon the number and frequency of children has been laid by God on the consciences of parents everywhere . . . such responsibility requires . . . thoughtful consideration of the varying population needs and problems of society . . .'[7] The final report emphasized 'the duty of the better developed countries to help (poor) countries become self supporting in food supplies and health measures through technical and other aids' and concluded: 'population control has become a necessity'.[8]

[1] Ibid., pp. 194 ff. [2] Ibid., p. 210.
[3] Second Assembly of the World Council of Churches, Evanston, 1954, p. 125.
[4] See, for example, WCC: Minutes and Reports of the 9th meeting of the Central Committee, Hungary, 1956, p. 36; and Second Statement on the Issues in the Study of Rapid Social Change, Herrenhalb, Germany, 1956, p. 10.
[5] Quoted in R. M. Fagley, op. cit., pp. 214–15.
[6] See the Report of the Committee on The Family in Contemporary Society, Lambeth Conference, 1958: Report and Encyclical letter of the Bishops, pp. 142–71.
[7] Lambeth Conference, 1958, p. 57 (Resolution 115).
[8] Ibid., p. 23.

The conference was described by Fagley as a 'watershed'. Shortly afterwards the joint committee of the WCC and the International Missionary Council convened a study group to prepare a report on 'responsible parenthood and the population problem'. The study group met at Mansfield College, Oxford, in April 1959. Participants included churchmen from India, Nigeria and the Philippines. Their report welcomed the decision of the Lambeth Conference and urged Christians in rich coun-tries 'to help their fellows in less developed lands towards condi-tions in which they can enjoy the freedom to ... exercise responsible parenthood'. The group sanctioned the use of all methods of contraception provided that they were 'acceptable to both husband and wife in Christian conscience' and caused 'neither physical nor emotional harm'.[1] Two years later at New Delhi, the Assembly of the WCC gave its official blessing. The committee on economic development endorsed 'the need to control the growth of population, especially in developing countries' and called on the developed countries to provide the necessary technical knowledge and assistance if requested to do so.[2]

THE UNITED STATES

Prominent among those who pressed for a clear statement of the Protestant position on the population question were churchmen from the USA and Scandinavia. Their interest reflected a grow-ing sense of alarm among informed opinion in western countries about the world population situation, and, in particular, the problem of Asia's 'teeming millions'.

American interest in Asian population growth had been aroused during the 1920s by the Japanese challenge to American hegemony in the Pacific. The writings of Warren Thompson and others, who argued that the basic cause was population pressure, made a considerable impact.[3] The defeat of Japan removed this source of anxiety. It was replaced by the fear that the poor densely populated countries of Asia would provide a breeding ground for Communism. Malthusian writers claimed that over-population produced discontent and increased the scope for

[1] See Report of a Study Group on Responsible Parenthood and the Population Problem, Oxford, April 1959.
[2] Third Assembly of the WCC, New Delhi, 1961, p. 276.
[3] See W. T. Thompson: *Danger Spots in World Population*, New York, 1930, and *Population Problems* for many years the basic text in demography. The first edition appeared in 1930 and a second in 1935. See also by the same author *Population and Peace in the Pacific*, New York, 1946. Warren Thompson was director of the Scripps Memorial Foundation for Population Research from its creation in 1922 until 1953 when he was succeeded by Pascal Whelpton.

CHANGING ATTITUDES IN RICH COUNTRIES 93

Communist propaganda. The introduction of modern medicine had served merely to worsen the situation by accelerating the rate of population growth. Death control, they argued, must be balanced by birth control. However much foreign aid was given, it would achieve nothing unless accompanied by measures to limit population growth.[1]

These fears were shared, to some extent, by many American demographers, although in a less apocalyptic fashion. They pointed out that the rates of population growth which many underdeveloped countries were experiencing constituted an obstacle to rapid economic development. Although industrialization and higher standards of living would probably lead to a fall in the birth rate, as in Europe, there was no guarantee that this would happen quickly enough. They argued that ways could and should be found to speed up the 'demographic transition'.[2]

Development economists and others involved in the aid programme, on the other hand, did not, on the whole, come to share the pessimistic outlook of the Malthusian propagandists nor even the more restrained arguments put forward by the demographers until the early sixties. The success of the Marshall Plan in Europe, coupled with the enthusiasm that accompanies new ventures, conspired to prevent thoughts of failure in the new global attack on poverty .The problem was seen quite simply as one of ensuring that economic growth kept ahead of population growth. Some argued that population pressure itself would provide an incentive for increased effort and innovation. Most ignored population and emphasized the importance of other factors, particularly capital.[3]

The American government carefully avoided taking up a position. In the early 1950s the depletion of natural resources had caused considerable concern, prompted in large part by William Vogt's *Road to Survival*, but this had not been linked in official discussion to the population problem. The main reason for the official silence was the controversiality of birth control within the USA.

In 1958 a storm had erupted in New York over the right of

[1] See notably G. Burch and Elmer Pendell: *Population Roads to Peace or War*, Washington, Population Reference Bureau, 1945; Elmer Pendell: *Population on the Loose*, New York, 1951; and R. C. Cook: *Human Fertility: the Modern Dilemma*, New York, 1951. See also the *Population Bulletin* of the Population Reference Bureau, Inc., Washington, eight issues a year and *The Population Bomb*, Hugh Moore Fund, New York, 1958(?).

[2] See, for example, the reports of the Round Table Conferences organized at the Annual Conferences of the Milbank Memorial Fund, particularly 'Modernization Programmes in Relation to Human Resources', and 'The Interrelations of Demographic, Economic and Social Problems in Selected Underdeveloped Areas', op. cit.

[3] See J. J. Spengler: 'The Economist and the Population Question', *American Economic Review*, March 1966.

doctors to give contraceptive advice to patients of municipal hospitals.[1] A year later the report of a Presidential committee on the American foreign aid programme added to the controversy. The committee, which was chaired by General William Draper Jr., devoted a chapter of its report to the 'population question'. Pointing out the difficulties which rapid population growth was causing in underdeveloped countries, the report recommended that the government should 'assist . . . countries . . . on request in the formulation of . . . plans designed to deal with the problem of rapid population growth', and that it should support research, within the United Nations and elsewhere, on the question.[2]

President Eisenhower passed the report to the Senate Foreign Relations Committee 'without comment' in an attempt to have it quietly buried. The Committee on Foreign Relations had however come to the same conclusions as the Draper Committee. In March 1957, William Vogt had spoken before the Senate's Special Committee on the Foreign Aid Programme of the need for research to find a satisfactory oral contraceptive for use in underdeveloped countries.[3] Although this proposal was not commented on at the time, the Senate included population within the terms of reference of a study on foreign aid which the Stanford Research Institute was asked to undertake. The Stanford report came to similar conclusions as the Draper Committee and recommended that the government explore 'the possibility of providing research funds to certain foreign agencies (for example in India and Japan) for the large scale human testing of devices'.[4] The Committee on Foreign Relations released both reports with the recommendation that they be given urgent consideration.

The debate continued with even greater intensity. Roman Catholic bishops, meeting in November 1958, declared their total opposition to the use of public money to 'promote artificial birth prevention for economically underdeveloped countries' and talked darkly of a Malthusian scare campaign.[5] Pressed for his

[1] See A. W. Sulloway: 'The Legal and Political Aspects of Population Control in the United States', Law and Contemporary Problems, Summer 1960, pp. 605–7; and Dr. J. Rock: The Time Has Come: A Catholic doctor's proposals to end the battle over birth control, New York, 1963, pp. 181–8.

[2] President's Committee to Study the United States Military Assistance Program. Third Interim Report: Economic Assistance Programmes and Administration, Washington, July 1959, pp. 42–3.

[3] US Senate. Hearings of the Special Committee to Study the Foreign Aid Program, March–April 1957, pp. 680–5.

[4] Possible Non-military Scientific Developments and their Potential Impact on Foreign Policy Programs of the US, Stanford Research Institute, 1959. Chapter 3, 'Population, Food and Science'.

[5] 'Explosion or Backfire?' Statement signed by the Administrative Board of the National Catholic Welfare Conference, 26 November 1959.

opinion, President Eisenhower declared: 'I cannot imagine anything more emphatically a subject that is not a proper political
or governmental activity or function or responsibility.' He went
on 'as long as I am here this government will not have a positive
political doctrine on birth control'.[1] Some leading Democrats,
including Hubert Humphrey and Adlai Stevenson, on the other
hand, stated that the government should not refuse to provide
information or assistance if less-developed countries considered
it essential for their national welfare.[2]

The question quickly became an election issue. John F.
Kennedy, leading Presidential Democratic contender and a
Catholic, surprised many by the independence of his views from
those of the Catholic hierarchy. Although he felt that 'it would
be a mistake for the US government to advocate the limitation
of the population of underdeveloped countries', he agreed that it
would not be 'wise to deny aid to a country just because it had a
birth control programme'. Asked what he would do if elected
President in the event of a request for assistance or a Con-
gressional bill calling for assistance, he said he would make his
own 'personal judgement' according to what would be in the
interests of the United States.[3]

Meanwhile public opinion was becoming increasingly restless
at Roman Catholic attempts to dictate domestic and international attitudes with respect to birth control and population
policies. In New York in 1958 the Catholics had eventually failed
in their attempt to prevent doctors who were not Catholics from
giving contraceptive advice.[4] Although several states retained
laws on the statute book prohibiting the sale or advertisement of
contraceptives or the giving of information on ways of preventing
conception, it was only in Massachusetts and Connecticut that
legislation constituted an effective barrier to the provision of
family planning services.[5] A Gallup Poll in 1960 showed that
72% of those questioned were of the opinion that birth control
information should be available to anyone who wanted it.[6]

After his inauguration, President Kennedy, perhaps because
he was a Catholic, was able to maintain his independent attitude
towards the Roman Catholic hierarchy on the population
question. In his first message to Congress on the US foreign aid
programme he referred to the difficulties facing less developed

[1] *New York Times*, 3 December 1959. Quoted in John Rock, op. cit., p. 163.
[2] *New York Times*, 29 November 1959.
[3] *New York Times*, 28 November 1959. Quoted in Rock, op. cit., see
pp. 161–2. See also A. M. Schlesinger: *A Thousand Days*, London, 1965, pp.
478–80, for an account of Kennedy's attitude towards the population question.
[4] See Rock, op. cit., pp. 187–8.
[5] Sulloway, op. cit., pp. 600–5.
[6] *New York Herald Tribune*, 17 February 1960.

countries as a result of rapid population growth.[1] In response to repeated appeals, notably from the Indian ambassador to the United States, Mr Chagla, a spokesman for the State Department revealed that US missions abroad had been discreetly informed that the US government was willing to consider requests for assistance in the collection and analysis of demographic statistics.[2] The Deputy US Ambassador to the United Nations, Francis Plimpton, in an address to the annual dinner of the Planned Parenthood Federation of America, expressed the view that the role of the United States should be to help the governments of less-developed countries to understand their population problems.[3] Meanwhile requests for assistance with action programmes were quietly referred to non-governmental bodies such as the Planned Parenthood—World Population and the Population Council.

BRITAIN

There were no legal obstacles in Britain to the dissemination of contraceptive information or services. In 1944 the government had accepted responsibility for the provision of family planning advice for medical reasons through government-sponsored health services. As in the United States, however, the official attitude was highly cautious. No attempt was made to persuade or encourage doctors or local health authorities to provide satisfactory services, and the main burden continued to fall on voluntary agencies.

The Royal Commission on Population pointed out in 1946 that the decline of the population of the West in relation to that of Asia 'might be decisive in its effects on the prestige and influence of the West ... The question is not merely one of military strength and security: it merges into more fundamental issues of the maintenance and extension of western views and culture.'[4] Since 1940 the British government had accepted financial responsibility for the development and welfare of colonial territories. A report, in 1955, by the influential private research organization PEP argued that the ever-increasing rate of population growth caused by improvements in health threatened to nullify these efforts.[5]

[1] Presidential Message on the US Foreign Aid Programme, *Department of State Bulletin*, 10 April 1961, p. 507.

[2] William Nunley, Special Assistant to the Under-Secretary of State for Economic Affairs in an address to the National Conference on International Economic and Social Development, Washington, DC, 30 November 1961, quoted in John Rock: *The Time Has Come*, op. cit., p. 169.

[3] Quoted in John Rock, op. cit., p. 169.

[4] UK Royal Commission on Population, op. cit., p. 134.

[5] *Population and World Resources: A PEP Report*, op. cit., pp. 42–3 and pp. 299 ff.

In April 1954 the House of Lords debated the question of world population and resources. The debate was precipitated by a preview of the PEP report which recommended, inter alia, that the British government and the UN should provide technical assistance for birth control, and that countries seeking aid should be asked 'to indicate the anticipated increases in resources in comparison with the anticipated increases in local population.' This was seen not as a condition for giving aid but as a way of inducing governments 'to face their population problems realistically'.[1]

Many of the members of the House of Lords shared the misgivings expressed in the PEP study. However, Lord de la Warr, replying for the government, explained that he did not intend to deal with the question of birth control 'not because it is a difficult one, or one to be hushed up, but simply because it is primarily a question first for the countries concerned and then for the individuals concerned. I cannot see India thanking us or the UN for venturing to go into India to teach these people methods of birth control'.[2] It is possible that Lord de la Warr was not aware that in 1951 the Indian Government had sought just this kind of assistance from WHO and that the British representative to the World Health Assembly had adopted an ambiguous attitude on that occasion.

Despite growing concern among informed opinion, the government continued to defend itself against charges of inaction by arguing that it would be dangerous for a colonial power to recommend birth control. Considerable importance, though less than in the USA, was also attached to the views of the Roman Catholic minority.

OTHER WESTERN EUROPEAN COUNTRIES

The inhibitions which hampered public discussion and government action in the United States and, to a lesser extent, in Britain did not exist in Sweden. The first Swedish Royal Commission on Population in 1935 had pioneered an enlightened approach towards population policy based on a balance between the interests of the community and the rights of the individual.[3] A second Royal Commission, which reported in 1946, had confirmed this policy.[4] It was therefore not surprising that Sweden

[1] Ibid., pp. 324–9.
[2] UK *Parliamentary Debates*, House of Lords, vol. 187, col. 194. The debate is reported cols. 108 ff.
[3] See Chapter 1, p. 5.
[4] See H. Gille, 'Recent Developments in Swedish Population Policy', *Population Studies*, June 1948, pp. 3–10; and September 1948, pp. 129–84.

became the first country to provide assistance for family planning as part of its official foreign aid programme. In 1958 the Swedish government approved a request from the Ceylon government for help in incorporating family planning into the public health services.[1] The initiative for the request came as a result of contacts between Swedish planned parenthood groups and the Ceylon Family Planning Association.[2] In 1961 assistance was provided to Pakistan on a much larger scale; whereas only one doctor had been sent to Ceylon, the Pakistan project comprised three medical teams.[3]

In the late fifties the decision was taken to raise the question in the United Nations, despite hints from the Secretariat that it would be preferable to leave the initiative to the less developed countries. At the General Assembly in 1960, Mrs Lindstrom, Swedish Minister of State, informed the Second Committee that her government would in due time seek to have the population question placed on the agenda of the Assembly. Drawing attention to what she saw as the failure of the Population Commission to tackle questions of population policy and the refusal of WHO to accept its responsibilities in the field of family planning, she said that the time had come for the General Assembly to discuss the problems seriously and without bias. She hoped that 'narrow conventions and prejudices would be overcome everywhere and the principle of voluntary parenthood internationally accepted'.[4]

Elsewhere in Western Europe birth control was still illegal. Despite this, family planning organizations were set up in France, Belgium, Holland, West Germany and Italy.[5] Advantage was taken of the fact that the main target of the legislation introduced in the inter-war period was propaganda in favour of birth control. Although the organizations were thus unable to advertise their activities, advice and services provided privately to members did not come within the definition of propaganda. Where the legislation condemned the practice of birth control itself doctors relied on their oath of professional secrecy as a protection against prosecution. Nevertheless, the number of people who received advice and services in this way was necessarily limited.

[1] See D. S. Greenberg: 'Birth Control: Swedish Help to Underdeveloped Nations', *Science*, vol. 137, September 1962, pp. 1038–9.
[2] Ibid. See also *Proceedings of the 5th International Conference on Planned Parenthood, Tokyo, 1955*, London, IPPF, 1956, p. 294. According to this report the request was made in 1955.
[3] *Swedish Activities in the Field of Family Planning*, SIDA, Stockholm, 1967.
[4] OR of the General Assembly, 15th session, 1960, SR of the second Committee, p. 155.
[5] D. V. Glass: 'Western Europe' in B. Berelson *et al.*: *Family Planning and Population Programmes*, Chicago, 1966, pp. 190–205.

EASTERN EUROPE

In 1955, in response to the growing popular demand for means of family limitation, the Soviet government removed the restrictions on induced abortion introduced in 1936.[1] Shortly afterwards, other Eastern European countries also liberalized their abortion laws.[2] In Poland planned parenthood societies were set up in 1957 and their agitation seems to have convinced the government to discount the opposition of the Roman Catholic Church in Poland to birth control. The death of Stalin in 1953 may have opened the way for the Soviet decision. On the other hand, there are indications that economic factors may have also been influential.[3]

At the international level, on the other hand, there was little apparent change in the Communist position. Marx and Engels had denied that the working class could improve its situation through limiting family size. Similarly, contemporary Marxist observers argued that population control would not solve the economic difficulties faced by underdeveloped countries. They pointed out that insistence on the problems caused by population growth was liable to divert attention away from the need for profound changes in the economic and social structures of poor countries. Lenin had drawn a distinction between 'neo-Malthusianism' and the provision of contraceptive advice and services. Communist spokesmen, however, failed to apply this distinction in relation to the western interest in family planning programmes in less developed countries. Western advocates of birth control were accused of favouring 'cannibalistic theories' and of seeking to divert attention from what were considered to be the real causes of world poverty. The tone of some of the western literature on the population problem was partly responsible for this reaction. However, it is significant that the Communists were noticeably less vociferous when the less developed countries themselves argued the case for family planning either on health or economic grounds.

[1] Code of Laws of the USSR, 1938–61, Moscow, 1961, p. 174. See also A. Inkeles: 'The Family and the Church in the Post-war USSR', *Annals of the American Academy*, May 1949, pp. 35–6.

[2] See K. H. Mehlan: 'The Socialist Countries of Europe', in Berelson, op. cit., pp. 207–26.

[3] See W. P. Mauldin: 'Fertility Control in Communist Countries: Policy and Practice', *Population Trends in Eastern Europe, the USSR and Mainland China*, New York, Milbank Memorial Fund, 1960.

9

Evolving Policies in Poor Countries

THE SPREAD OF FAMILY PLANNING

AS has been seen in Chapter 1, a few family planning clinics
had been opened in Asia before the Second World War.
These were mainly in India but also in Hong Kong, China and,
for a short while, in Japan.[1] In 1949 a Family Planning Association was formed in India. Two years later, at the first All India
Family Planning Conference, it was reported that there were
clinics in most of the major cities.[2] Meanwhile associations had
been set up in Singapore in 1949 and in Hong Kong in 1950. In
1953 national family planning associations were formed in
Ceylon, Pakistan and Japan. In Malaysia and Thailand local
associations were set up in the mid-fifties and came together to
form national federations in 1958, in 1955 an association was set
up in Taiwan.[3]

In the Caribbean the lead was taken by Puerto Rico. Attempts
had been made since 1925 to open clinics but had failed because
of Roman Catholic opposition. In 1937 the island legislature
authorized the provision of contraceptive advice and services in
government hospitals and health centres. There were strong
protests by the Catholic hierarchy and by Roman Catholic
organizations. The Acting Governor who had signed the bill
found himself excommunicated. Nevertheless, by 1939 over a
hundred clinics were in operation.[4]

The 1937 law authorized doctors to perform sterilization and
the operation soon became very popular with women of all
classes. Propaganda in favour of birth control was not allowed.
However Roman Catholic pressure to prevent doctors carrying
out 'the operation', as it was called, had the opposite effect to

---

[1] See Chapter 1, pp. 7–10.

[2] Report of the First All India Family Planning Conference, Bombay
1951, p. 29.

[3] For details see: *Proceedings of the 3rd International Conference on Planned
Parenthood, Bombay, 1952*, Bombay, FPAI, 1953. Appendix I, pp. 204 ff.;
Proceedings of the 5th International Conference . . ., Tokyo, 1955, op. cit., Appendix
II, pp. 281 ff.; and B. Berelson *et al.: Family Planning and Population Pro-
grammes*, op. cit., chapters 1, 4, 6, 7, 8 and 10.

[4] C. R. Alvaredo and C. Tietze: 'Birth Control in Puerto Rico' in *Human
Fertility*, March 1947, pp. 15–18.

that desired. As the word spread, demand for sterilization increased dramatically.[1] There was renewed controversy after 1957 over field trials of the pill and other contraceptives. The opposition played on religious and nationalist feelings in an attempt to reverse the Government's policy. The attempt failed but in subsequent years government support for family planning cooled noticeably.[2]

In the English-speaking Caribbean family planning developed rapidly in the 1950s. In 1954 the Government of Barbados endorsed a recommendation from a parliamentary committee set up in 1952 that it should accept responsibility for the provision of family planning services and entrusted the operation of clinics to the newly formed family planning association. In Jamaica interest in family planning had been aroused as a result of a visit, in 1939, by Mrs Howe-Martin of the Birth Control International Information Centre, and a clinic was opened in Kingston. After the war clinics were opened in other parts of the island and in 1957 they joined together to form the Jamaica FPA.[3]

Interest in family planning was not confined to Asia and the Caribbean. Family planning associations were formed in Rhodesia in 1955, in Uganda in 1956, and in Kenya and Mauritius in 1957. Clinics were opened in Nigeria and Sierra Leone in 1958.[4] In Iran several maternal and child health centres began to provide family planning education after 1953 although it was not until 1957, with assistance from the IPPF, that they began to supply contraceptives. In the UAR some doctors and intellectuals had advocated family planning during the 1930s, but it was not until after the revolution of 1952 that public family planning facilities began to be made available.[5]

In Latin America and areas under French influence, on the other hand, little interest was shown in either population or family planning. Latin America was traditionally regarded as under-populated. The implications of the distinction between population growth and population size were not understood.[6] Public discussion of birth control was inhibited more by traditional pro-natalist attitudes and the predominant position

[1] C. Senior: 'Women, Democracy and Birth Control', *The Humanist*, no. 5, 1952, pp. 221–4.
[2] J. Mayone Stycos: *Human Fertility in Latin America*, Cornell, 1968, pp. 108–15: 'Bishops, Politics and Birth Control'.
[3] G. Cadbury: 'Outlook for Government Action in Family Planning in the West Indies', in C. V. Kiser (ed.), *Research in Family Planning*, Princeton, 1962, pp. 322–9.
[4] J. C. Caldwell: 'Africa', in B. Berelson, op. cit., pp. 163–82.
[5] Hanna Rizk: 'Population Policies in Egypt', *Proceedings of the 5th International Conference . . .*, op. cit., pp. 37–41.
[6] J. Mayone Stycos, op. cit., pp. 32–5, 'Latin American Intellectuals and the Population Problem'.

of the Catholic Church than by repressive legislation against birth control.

THE INTERNATIONAL PLANNED PARENTHOOD FEDERATION

One of the first moves of the newly formed family planning associations was to seek membership of the International Planned Parenthood Federation. The initiative for the creation of a permanent organization to link national bodies came from the Swedish League for Sex Education. A conference was convened in Stockholm in August 1946. This was followed by a second, much larger conference, organized by the British FPA at Cheltenham in 1948.[1] Over 140 participants attended from seventeen countries. Speakers included Margaret Sanger, Abraham Stone, Pascal Whelpton, Frank Lorimer and Sir John Boyd-Orr. At the final session it was decided to set up an international committee consisting of representatives from Holland, Sweden, Britain and the United States. The committee's tasks were to organize further conferences and to work for the establishment of a permanent international body.[2]

The creation of the Family Planning Association of India and the interest shown by the government encouraged the committee to suggest that the next conference be held in India. The Bombay conference, held in November 1952, was attended by 487 participants from fourteen countries.[3] The conference enthusiastically endorsed the creation of a permanent organization to be known as the International Planned Parenthood Federation. Regional offices were established in India, London and New York. The national associations of West Germany, India, Japan, Hong Kong, and Singapore were invited to become members.[4] By 1955 membership had increased to fourteen, and in 1959 affiliated bodies existed in twenty-two countries.[5]

Agreement on the constitution was not reached until the fifth conference at Tokyo in 1955. There were two quite distinct views regarding the aims and character of the new organization. The

---

[1] *Proceedings of the International Conference on Population and World Resources, Cheltenham, August 1948.* London, FPA, 1948.   [2] Ibid., pp. 244–5.

[3] *Proceedings of the 3rd International Conference on Planned Parenthood, Bombay, 1952,* op. cit.   [4] Ibid., 202.

[5] In Europe: Belgium, Denmark, Italy, Netherlands, Sweden, United Kingdom, West Germany and the Canton of Vaud, Switzerland; in Asia: Ceylon, Hong Kong, India, Japan, Pakistan and Singapore; in the Caribbean: Barbados, Bermuda, Jamaica and Puerto Rico; and the United States, Australia, New Zealand and South Africa. See *Proceedings of the 6th International Conference on Planned Parenthood, New Delhi, February 1959,* London, IPPF, 1959, p. xii.

first drew its inspiration essentially from the neo-Malthusian origins of the birth control movement. Its advocates, mainly American, stressed the global aspects of the problem, the relationship between over-population and war and between over-population and poverty, and argued that the organization's goal should be to promote the control of world population. The second envisaged an organization concerned mainly with individual and family welfare. According to this view, the emphasis should be on voluntary parenthood as a human right, irrespective of any economic, social or political imperatives. The two viewpoints were not necessarily exclusive. Margaret Sanger, for example, shared both points of view, although in her later years she moved towards the former. The question was, essentially, one of emphasis.

The tone of the Cheltenham conference of 1948 was markedly neo-Malthusian. The theme of the conference was population and world resources. Although several working sessions were given over to such questions as sex education and infertility, the main debate centred on the need for birth control to avert a world food crisis. Commenting on the implications of the conference, Dr Joseph Needham said that any organization which was set up should proclaim that 'its fundamental aim was the conscious world control of population by man . . . because it would be very restrictive to consider only family welfare or matters of relatively individual or restricted import.'[1] The final resolution endorsed this view. It began:

> In view of the present world food crisis due, in part, to the growing pressure of global population on food and other resources, control of population increases is one of the essential measures by which real progress towards peace and prosperity may be made . . .

and concluded that:

> . . . all national governments and all international organizations should make every effort to initiate positive population policies . . .[2]

At the Bombay conference in 1952, a major part of the proceedings were once again devoted to the discussion of 'the population problem'. Speakers included William Vogt and Elmer Pendell. Nehru, however, sounded a cautionary note in his message of welcome:

> Some people imagine that almost all the ills of India are due to over-population and therefore the basic remedy for those

[1] *Proceedings of the International Conference . . . Cheltenham, 1948,* op. cit., p. 226. [2] Ibid., p. 244.

ills is to try to limit the growth of this population . . . While I am convinced that it would be desirable to limit the growth of India's population, by proper methods, I do not think that social and economic problems are solved merely by this approach.[1]

The question was discussed at some length at the Stockholm conference in 1953. Finally, a draft constitution drawn up by the international committee was provisionally approved. It declared that the basic aim of the federation was to 'bring about the universal acceptance of planned parenthood in the interests of family welfare, social well-being and international goodwill'. This was to be achieved principally through the establishment and support of national family planning associations in all countries and through the promotion of scientific research.[2] A new paragraph was added at the Tokyo conference in 1955 which spelt out the different motivations. Article 1 stated:

In the belief that a favourable balance between the population and natural resources of the world is an indispensable condition of a lasting world peace; that such a balance is unattainable unless knowledge of planned parenthood is extended; and that this knowledge is a fundamental human right the International Planned Parenthood Federation has set itself the following aims:

a) to advance through education and scientific research the universal acceptance of family planning and responsible parenthood in the interests of family welfare, community wellbeing and international goodwill . . .[3]

The conferences meanwhile were becoming increasingly oriented towards family planning. Although the theme of the Tokyo conference was 'over-population and family planning', most of the topics fell into the latter category. The majority of the participants were doctors or family planning clinicians. This pattern was confirmed at the sixth conference in New Delhi in 1959. The theme of the conference was 'family planning: motivation and methods'. The programme was almost entirely devoted to a discussion of new methods of contraception, particularly the 'pill'.[4] The changing character of the organization was acknowledged in 1963 when the governing body amended the constitution. The original wording was retained but a judicious

[1] *Proceedings of the 3rd International Conference*, op. cit., p. 2.
[2] *Proceedings of the 4th International Conference on Planned Parenthood, Stockholm, August 1953*, Resolutions.
[3] *Proceedings of the 5th International Conference*, op. cit., p. 259.
[4] *Proceedings of the 6th International Conference on Planned Parenthood, New Delhi, February 1959*, op. cit.

re-ordering placed the emphasis clearly on family planning as a fundamental human right.[1]

The difficulties encountered in the framing of a constitution made little difference to the work of the federation. There was general agreement that existing contraceptive methods were unsatisfactory in one way or another. Priority was therefore given to the development of a safe, effective and acceptable contraceptive. Apart from the promotion of research and the organization of conferences, the main task was to provide support to the newer members of the federation in the establishment and running of family planning clinics.[2]

AMERICAN FOUNDATIONS

American foundations also contributed significantly to the spread of family planning in less developed countries. The most important was the Population Council of New York set up as a result of an initiative by John D. Rockefeller III. In the summer of 1952, Rockefeller called a conference of specialists in demography, economics, public health, biology, nutrition and conservation to 'consider available facts and conflicting views about the effects of population growth on human welfare'. It was decided to set up a body 'to stimulate, encourage, promote, conduct and support significant activites in the broad field of population'. The Board of Trustees included Rockefeller himself, Frank Notestein, and Frank Boudreau of the Milbank Fund. Frederick Osborn, the eugenicist, was nominated Vice-President.[3] In 1959 Frank Notestein became President.

Conscious of the dangers of intervention in such a delicate and highly sensitive field, the Council concentrated initially on training and research activites, the latter notably into the biological and medical aspects of human reproduction. Research grants were mainly to American universities and research institutes. In 1955 a large grant was made to the All India Institute of Hygiene and Public Health for 'a field study of population control in West Bengal'. Three years later the Indian Ministry of Health sought assistance with the development of family planning education units. The grant included the provision of the services of an expert. A further step was taken in 1959 when the Council became closely involved in the elaboration of the national family planning programme in Pakistan. The

---

[1] Constitution and rules of the IPPF (as amended at Singapore by the IPPF Governing Body during February 1963), p. 1.

[2] Annual Reports of the IPPF.

[3] *Report of the Population Council, Inc.*, November 1952–December 1955, pp. 5–6.

Population Council also gave considerable financial support to the UN Demographic Training and Research Centres in Chembur and Santiago and for the United Nations seminars in Bandung and Rio de Janeiro.[1]

One of the main contributors to the Population Council's funds after 1954 was the Ford Foundation. Ford had begun to make grants in the field of population on a modest scale two years earlier. Most of the grants were for contraceptive research and went to American institutions. Towards the end of the 1950s the Ford Foundation also began to seek more direct involvement in underdeveloped countries. The first grant specifically for family planning was made in 1959 to India. In the following year arrangements were completed for a large grant to the Government of Pakistan to assist the development of a national programme. The grant was administered by the Population Council.[2]

Alongside these foundations, whose activities covered research, training and conferences as well as technical advice, there existed a very small but highly active organization devoted entirely to the setting up of family planning services in less developed countries. The organization, known after 1958 as the Pathfinder Fund, was the creation of an American doctor, Clarence Gamble, who had begun to campaign for birth control in the US in 1929. His method was simple. Gamble and his associates, working through the National Committee on Maternal Health, toured the country persuading, encouraging and helping local groups to form associations and open clinics. Where necessary, funds or supplies were provided by Gamble. In 1936 a field worker was sent to Puerto Rico to give help to local groups in overcoming Catholic opposition and legal obstacles. In 1949 Gamble was invited to Japan where he agreed to provide financial support for three pilot projects in Japanese villages. Increasingly, emphasis shifted to underdeveloped countries. Between 1953 and 1961 Gamble and his co-workers visited fifty-one countries in Asia, the Middle East, Africa and Latin America. They were ignored by official and semi-official bodies, including the International Planned Parenthood Federation and the Population Council. The reason may have been partly institutional jealousy and partly professional disagreement with Gamble's methods and his forward strategy. There was some feeling that local populations would resent the presence of foreign advocates of birth control. However, both in Africa and Latin

[1] See *Annual Reports of the Population Council* 1956–1961; and F. W. Notestein: 'The Population Council and the Demographic Crisis of the Less-developed World', *Demography*, vol. 5, no. 2, 1968, pp. 553–60.

[2] O. Harkavy *et. al.*: 'An Overview of the Ford Foundation Strategy for Population Work', *Demography*, vol. 5, no. 2, op. cit., pp. 541–2.

America where they were pioneers, Gamble's field workers found doctors and local groups anxious to start family planning activities and grateful for outside assistance. Family planning associations were started with Pathfinder's help in Pakistan, Ceylon, Malaysia, Thailand and in many parts of British Africa. Once associations were set up, the Fund helped with the provision of contraceptive supplies. Gamble was convinced of the need to develop simple methods of birth control for use in less developed countries. Although he could not match the research sponsored by American foundations, such as Ford and Rockefeller, he made a small contribution through his support of field trials of various contraceptive methods including the oral pill.[1]

The importance of the work of these organizations went beyond the formal assistance —fellowships, research grants and funds—which they gave. Their staff members spent much of their time in the field making contacts, giving advice and encouragement and gathering much needed information and expertise. A network of specialists rapidly came into existence, ready when needed to help governments or private groups either formally or informally. They were able to fill, to some extent, the void left by the UN, WHO and UNESCO.

GOVERNMENT POLICIES

The ultimate aim of the family planning movement was to persuade governments to accept responsibility for the provision of family planning advice and services. Before 1950 family planning services were available through government health facilities in the Scandinavian countries and in Britain, Puerto Rico and Japan.[2] Except in the case of Sweden and, to a lesser extent, Britain, these governments had no stated policy with regard to population growth. In Japan the Eugenic Protection law, enacted in 1948 and further liberalized in 1949 and 1952, was not officially aimed at lowering the birth rate. Although its adoption had been accompanied by vigorous discussion of the need to control population growth, the stated purpose of the measure was to improve the quality of the population from the eugenic point of view and to protect the life and health of the mother.[3] In 1952 the government began to encourage the

---

[1] *The Pathfinder Fund: Pioneer in Family Planning*, Boston, April 1966. For a description of the methods used, see C. Gamble: 'The Initiation of Contraceptive Services' in S. Mudd (ed.), *The Population Crisis and the Use of World Resources*, WAAS, 1964, chapter 30.

[2] Hope T. Eldridge: *Population Policies, a Survey of Recent Developments*, op. cit., pp. 99–101 and pp. 104–5.

[3] T. Terao: *Outline of the Birth Control Movement in Japan*, op. cit., pp. 15 ff.; and M. Muramatsu (ed.): *Japan's Experience in Family Planning— Past and Present*, Tokyo, 1967, p. 107.

practice of contraception as a substitute for abortion. However at no stage did it declare an official population policy.[1]

During the nineteen fifties several governments took steps to promote family planning activities, some of them explicitly as part of a deliberate attempt to limit the rate of population growth. Although in the past governments and rulers had frequently intervened to alter population trends, they had almost always sought to increase population size for military or economic reasons.[2] Government measures to slow down population growth were an entirely new departure.

The earliest and most explicit commitment to population control was made by the Indian Government. As early as 1937 the Congress National Planning Committee had recommended limiting the number of children 'in the interests of social economy, family happiness and national planning.[3] The need for a national programme was subsequently endorsed in several official reports and by the Planning Commission.[4] The government, however, proceeded cautiously, partly through inexperience and fears of an adverse public reaction and partly because of the lack of enthusiasm shown by some ministers.[5] Although the long term aim as laid down in the First Five Year Plan, was 'to stabilize the population at a level consistent with the requirements of national economy', the need for family planning was presented principally in terms of concern for individual health and family happiness. Main reliance was placed on the rhythm method, ostensibly on the grounds of cost and acceptability.[6] It seems probable, however, that this decision was prompted by the legacy of Gandhi's opposition to artificial contraceptives. The first Minister of Health of independent India, Rajkumari Amrit Kaur, who was both a Catholic and a former member of Gandhi's *ashram*, is reported to have said, 'Any widespread knowledge of the artificial method of birth control is bound to be misused and will result in moral degradation'.[7]

The Indian Second Five Year Plan gave greater prominence

[1] M. Muramatsu, 'Japan', in B. Berelson, op. cit., pp. 7–10.

[2] D. V. Glass, *Population Policies and Movements in Europe*, op. cit. pp. 86–98.

[3] Report of the National Planning Committee; 'Population', Bombay, 1947, op. cit., p. 145.

[4] See T. J. Samuel, 'The Development of India's Policy of Population Control', *Milbank Memorial Fund Quarterly*, January 1966, pp. 51–5.

[5] Ibid., pp. 56–64. See also Gunnar Myrdal: *Asian Drama*, vol. III, Appendix 12, 'Family Planning Policy in India', pp. 2152–3.

[6] Government of India Planning Commission: First Five Year Plan, New Delhi, 1951, pp. 522–4.

[7] Cited in N. V. Sovani: 'The Problems of Fertility Control in India', *Approaches to Problems of High Fertility in Agrarian Societies*, Milbank Memorial Fund, 1952, p. 68.

to population, which was referred to as one of the 'key factors' in development. The programme nevertheless remained essentially experimental.[1] Although the funds allotted to family planning activities were increased from 6·5 million to 50 million rupees, actual expenditures under both plans were considerably less. It was not until preparations began for the Third Plan that official circles became fully convinced of the need to control population growth in the interests of economic development. In 1959 the Government declared its support for all methods of family limitation, including sterilization.[2] Estimates of future population growth were increased from the annual rate of 1·25 per cent, assumed in the First and Second Plans, to over 2 per cent.[3] The Third Five Year Plan declared that 'the objective of stabilizing population growth over a reasonable period must . . . be at the very centre of planned development'. Much greater emphasis was placed on motivation and on extending services to a larger proportion of the population.[4]

The First Five Year Plan of Pakistan published in 1955 contained a chapter on the subject of population and manpower.[5] Noting the serious population problem which the country was facing, it endorsed the provision of financial support by the Government to the newly formed family planning association. As in India, the report stressed the contribution of planned parenthood to the health of the mother and to the care and upbringing of children.

The new regime of Ayub Khan attached much greater importance to family planning. In a broadcast in 1959 he said:

> planning for a sensible size of family is . . . a vital condition of progress to prosperity. Without widespread acceptance and support family planning may well fail. We must not let it fail.[6]

Plans for a national programme were worked out during 1959. The Second Five Year Plan in 1960 stressed the need for a conscious population policy and made provision for a large programme of training and educational activities, including the

[1] Government of India Planning Commission: Second Five Year Plan, New Delhi, 1956, p. 651.

[2] R. A. Gopalaswami: 'Family Planning; Outlook for Government Action in India', in C. V. Kiser, Research in Family Planning, op. cit., p. 80.

[3] Government of India Planning Commission: Third Five Year Plan; a Draft Outline, June 1960, pp. 4–5.

[4] Government of India Planning Commission: Third Five Year Plan, New Delhi, 1961, p. 25 and pp. 675–8.

[5] Government of Pakistan National Planning Board: First Five Year Plan, 1955–60, Karachi, 1957, chapter 13, pp. 189–196.

[6] Quoted in News of Population and Birth Control, no. 86, June 1960.

creation of a network of clinics. It was hoped to reach ten per cent of all women of childbearing age.[1]

In Egypt, after the overthrow of King Faroukh, it seemed as if the new government would declare a population policy. In 1953 a National Commission on Population Questions was set up 'to outline a population policy for the country'. Its tasks were to clarify the demographic situation, to assess the effects of population growth on the prospects for economic development and to draw up a scheme for the introduction of birth control.[2] The Commission's Economic Committee reported in 1955. After considering the opportunities offered by emigration, improvements in agriculture and rapid industrialization, the report concluded that 'population growth at its present rate within the coming ten years will cancel the effect of the increase in national income and will impede the hoped-for rise in per capita real income'.[3] Following the proposals made by the Commission's medical committee, several family planning clinics were opened. some in government child welfare centres and others in private maternal welfare clinics.[4] In the years that followed government support wavered. No publicity was given to the clinics, and in 1957 responsibility for their management was transferred to a non-governmental body. The government's concern at the rate of population growth re-awakened in the early 1960s, but it was not, in fact, until 1965 that an official policy was declared.[5]

Although India and Pakistan were the only governments to declare official policies aimed at reducing the birth rate during this period, other governments also encouraged family planning activities for similar reasons without any explicit public commitment to population control. Mention has already been made of Japan. In Puerto Rico, too, official support for family planning was an indication of the seriousness with which the government viewed the island's population situation. In Barbados a parliamentary committee was set up in 1952 'to examine the question of over-population and to make recommendations for dealing with this problem'. After careful consideration the Committee

[1] Government of Pakistan National Planning Board: Second Five Year Plan, 1960–65, Karachi, 1960, pp. 335 and 360. See also M. Sharif: 'Outlook for Government Action in FP in Pakistan' in C. V. Kiser, op. cit., pp. 141–6; and see M.L. Qureshi (ed.): *Population Growth and Economic Development with Special Reference to Pakistan.* Summary report of a seminar held September 1959, Institute of Development Economics, Karachi, 1960.
[2] Government of Egypt, Permanent Council for Public Welfare Services: *The Permanent Council for Public Welfare Services,* Cairo, 1955, p. 104.
[3] Idem., National Population Commission. Economic Sub-Committee, *The Population Problem in Egypt,* Cairo, 1955, pp. 19–23.
[4] Hanna Rizk, 'Population Policies in Egypt', op. cit., pp. 39–41.
[5] See Population Council; *Country Profiles,* Egypt, August 1969.

reported that 'a system of family planning under the aegis of the Government is a solution that offers some hope' and recommended that 'clinics should be set up and operated directly by the Department of Medical Services'.[1] In 1954 the legislature approved a government proposal that financial support be given to the newly formed Barbados FPA to run family planning clinics in government premises.[2]

In several other countries the government provided financial assistance to voluntary family planning bodies. In Asia there were even exceptions to the general British practice of not giving official support to birth control in dependent territories. In Singapore, for example, the government was the major source of funds for the FPA formed in 1949.[3] The first clinics opened in Hong Kong were allowed free use of government premises. In 1955 the government made a grant towards the budget of the Hong Kong FPA. The first subsidy was purely nominal but in subsequent years the amounts were increased considerably.[4]

Although in most cases to which reference has been made grants were channelled through the budgets of the health ministries, it seems fairly clear that demographic considerations were important. In many instances the subsidy preceded, as in Pakistan, the declaration of an official policy.

In 1957 a public controversy over the allegedly 'Malthusian' tendencies of certain prominent intellectuals drew attention to the existence of a campaign in favour of planned parenthood in the People's Republic of China.[5] Since 1953 the Ministry of Health had provided family planning advice and services. In 1956 educational activities were intensified with the aim of encouraging later marriages, smaller families and the spacing of children.[6] Chou-en-lai, addressing the Eighth National Congress of the Communist Party in 1956, declared that family planning was necessary 'to protect women and children and bring up and educate our younger generation in a way conducive to the health and prosperity of the nation'.[7] The 'great leap forward' in 1958 temporarily ended the public campaign in favour of birth

---

[1] Barbados. Report of the Joint Committee appointed by the two Houses to examine the question of overpopulation . . ., 20 July 1954, op. cit.

[2] See G. Cadbury: 'Outlook for Government Action in Family Planning in the West Indies', in C. V. Kiser, op. cit., pp. 327–9.

[3] Berelson, op. cit., p. 91.

[4] Ibid., pp. 73–6.

[5] R. C. North: 'Communist China and the Population Problem' in S. Mudd (ed.), *The Population Crisis and the Use of World Resources*, op. cit., pp. 179–85.

[6] M. Freeberne, 'Birth Control in China', *Population Studies*, July 1964, pp. 6–7.

[7] People's Republic of China. Report on the Proposals for the Development of the National Economy, Peking, 1956, p. 99.

control. Party leaders argued that China's large population was a positive asset and denied the need for population control. Nevertheless family planning services continued to be freely available and, in 1962, the campaign began openly once again.[1]

[1] See Freeberne, op. cit., p. 7.

Part IV

THE DEBATE RESUMED
(1961–1964)

'Can we any more turn our faces away from the concept of family planning when the alternative is starvation and death?'

B. R. Sen, Director-General of FAO, to the International Eucharistic Congress in Bombay, *1964*

10

The Scandinavian Initiative

I N 1960 Dr Evang of Norway reminded the 13th World Health Assembly that WHO had not in fact taken any decision with regard to birth control in 1952 and was not precluded from giving technical assistance if member states requested it.[1] The silence of WHO on this subject was, in the words of Mr Karmarkar, Indian Minister of Health, 'a convention'.[2] Encouraged by the growing support for family planning, those who wished to see the organization involved decided that the time had come to break the convention. The *Daily Telegraph* correspondent at the 13th World Health Assembly reported: 'A showdown cannot long be avoided. When it comes the countries favouring family planning programmes are likely to win the day.'[3]

The 14th World Health Assembly was held in New Delhi in 1961. In his inaugural address, Premier Nehru referred to the 'rather overwhelming situation' created by the success of 'all our good efforts' to reduce mortality.[4] In the general debate several speakers drew attention to the problems their countries were facing as a result of rapid population growth. The representative of the FAO, in an intervention reminiscent of that of Sir Herbert Broadley at the 5th WHA, pointed out the relevance of WHO's work to FAO's task. Success in lowering death rates, he said, meant that the population of the world would double in the next forty years. He asked how it would be possible to feed these 6,000 million people when more than half the present world population was underfed and suffering from malnutrition.[5]

The circumstances seemed favourable. Accordingly Norway and Ceylon, the two leaders of the earlier struggles in WHO, tabled a resolution entitled 'Planned parenthood as a preventive health measure'. Introducing the proposal, Dr Gunaratne of Ceylon quoted WHO's constitution which placed on the Organization the responsibility for promoting maternal and child health. The main purpose of the resolution, he said, was to discover to what extent child spacing was encouraged as a preventive health measure.[6] Discussion was cut short by the

---

[1] See chapter 6, p. 66.
[2] OR of WHO, no. 101, p. 80.
[3] *Daily Telegraph* (London), 16 May 1960.
[4] OR of WHO, no. 111, p. 27.
[5] Ibid. .p. 121.   [6] Ibid., p. 273.

Belgian representative, Dr Kivits, who successfully raised a procedural objection on the grounds that the item had not appeared on the adopted agenda.[1] Victory, it was clear, was not to be won as easily as the *Daily Telegraph*'s correspondent imagined.

Meanwhile, in the United Nations, a new confrontation appeared imminent. In November 1960 at the 15th Session of the General Assembly Mrs Lindstrom of Sweden had indicated her Government's intention to request that the population question be placed on the agenda of the General Assembly. A few days later the Secretary-General circulated a 'Statement of Conviction' signed by distinguished persons from nineteen countries, among whom were thirty-nine Nobel prize winners and over a hundred leading scientists including Julian Huxley. The statement called on the UN to 'take the lead in establishing and implementing a policy designed to limit population the world over' on health, social and economic grounds.[2]

In February 1961 the Population Commission took a further step towards grasping the nettle of population policy. Under a Catholic chairman, Mertens de Wilmars, but with an American rapporteur, the Commission embarked upon a review of its own role and that of the United Nations in the population field. It recommended the convening of an ad hoc group of experts to advise on a long range programme of work. Paragraph 15 of the Commission's report stated that, while it was 'the responsibility of each government to decide its own policies and devise its own programmes of action . . . it was in the interests of the UN that decisions on national policy should be planned in the light of knowledge of the relevant facts and that the programme should be adequate to assure satisfactory economic and social progress'. The report continued: 'it is also considered appropriate for the UN to give technical assistance as requested by Governments for national projects of research, experimentation and action for dealing with problems of population.'[3]

The documents prepared by the Secretariat contained references to the assistance already given by the UN in the field of family planning.[4] In the discussion, Mr Tachi of Japan said that the time had come for the UN to intensify its studies of population policy and that it should expect an increase in requests for assistance in the formulation and implementation of national

[1] OR of WHO, no. 111, pp. 273–4.
[2] Quoted in *News of Population and Birth Control*, no. 91, January 1961.
[3] Report of the 11th session of the Population Commission, OR of ECOSOC, 31st session, supplement no. 3, p. 3.
[4] UN Doc. E/CN.9/158 and Corr. 1, 'Objectives and Accomplishments of the UN in the Field of Population'. Report by the Secretary-General.

population programmes.[1] Since no member of the Commission objected to the assistance already given to India, Barbados and UAR, or indeed to Mr Tachi's remarks, it appeared that the Commission was endorsing the right of the UN to provide technical assistance for policies aimed at affecting population trends, including family planning programmes. In the General Assembly debates in 1961 and 1962 Sweden and Norway specifically referred to paragraph 15 of the Commission's report in support of their draft resolution calling for an expansion of UN population activities. Catholic countries were dismayed, and at the 12th session of the Commission in 1963, Mr de Wilmars, who was once again in the chair, sought to restore the situation. He said that paragraph 15 had been adopted 'too hastily'. The Commission, he claimed, had not intended to endorse the provision of assistance for operational activities connected with family planning and population programmes.[2]

At the 31st session of ECOSOC in April 1961, Eugene Black, President of the World Bank, devoted almost half his statement to the population problem. 'Unless population growth can be restrained', he said, 'immediate hopes of economic progress in the crowded lands of Asia and the Middle East would have to be abandoned'.[3] The delegates of Spain, Argentina, Italy and the USSR strongly criticized Mr Black's remarks, maintaining that the question did not come within the terms of reference of the World Bank.[4]

In August 1961 the Permanent Representatives of Sweden and Norway formally requested that the item 'Population growth and economic development' be placed on the agenda of the 16th session of the General Assembly. In the note setting out the reasons for the move they drew attention to the 1960–61 censuses, which showed a much higher rate of population increase than had been previously estimated, and to the effects of rapid population growth on the prospects for economic development. They quoted the speech of the President of the World Bank and emphasized the benefits of planned parenthood for the health of mothers and children.[5]

When the Assembly met at the end of 1961 the item was assigned to the agenda of the Second Committee. Sweden and Norway had meanwhile obtained the support of Ghana, Greece, Pakistan and Tunisia. On 1 December the six countries intro-duced a draft resolution calling, inter alia, for an intensification

[1] UN Doc. E/CN.9/SR.148, p. 3.
[2] UN Doc. E/CN.9/SR.178, p. 8.
[3] OR of ECOSOC, 31st session, 1961, pp. 14–15.
[4] Ibid., pp. 17–19.
[5] UN Doc. A/4849.

of studies and research on the inter-relationship between population growth and economic and social development, and inviting member states to seek technical assistance from the UN to deal with their population problems.[1] However, it was by then evident that the committee would not be able to complete all the items on its agenda. The sponsors of the draft resolution therefore proposed that the item be carried over until the next session and that in view of its importance it should be given priority.[2]

In the discussion on the assignment of agenda items several governments had stated their opposition to the discussion of 'birth control' by the UN. Irked at having been denied the opportunity to condemn the subject, the representatives of Argentina and Lebanon took their revenge on the resolution for postponement. They called for a roll call vote on whether the item was 'important' and whether it 'should be given priority' because, they said, the inclusion of these words in the text of the resolution prejudged the issue. By 27 votes to 15 the committee rejected the word 'important' and, by 25 votes to 17, the phrase 'should be given priority' was also deleted. Britain and the United States abstained on the question of the importance of the item but voted against it being accorded priority. The Communist delegates, on the other hand, abstained in the voting on the priority of the question but voted for the deletion of the word 'important'.[3]

At the 15th World Health Assembly in May 1962 the question of population was not raised. However, in July, the final declaration of the Cairo conference of developing countries included the following statement: 'Countries that suffer from the pressure of population on resources available should accelerate their rate of economic development and in the meantime take all appropriate legitimate measures to deal with their population problems.'[4]

THE 1962 GENERAL ASSEMBLY

Several of the governments which signed the Cairo declaration became sponsors of the draft resolution on population growth and economic development when it was presented to the General Assembly of the United Nations, with minor modifications, in October 1962.[5] Introducing the resolution in the Second

[1] UN Doc. A/C.2/L.601.
[2] U.N. Doc. A/C.2/L.601/Rev. 1.
[3] OR of the General Assembly, 16th session, 1961. Summary Records of the Second Committee, pp. 430–2.
[4] Conference on the Problems of Economic Development, Cairo, 9–18 July 1961, para. 13 of Final Declaration.
[5] UN Doc. A/C.2/L.657 and Add. 1. Sponsors were now as follows: Ceylon, Denmark, Ghana, Greece, Nepal, Norway, Pakistan, Sweden, Tunisia, Turkey and the UAR. To this list was added the names of Uganda and Thailand.

Committee, Mrs Lindstrom denied allegations that the sponsors intended to make technical and economic assistance dependent on acceptance of birth control by the recipient countries. She pointed out that the resolution clearly stated that economic development and population policy were not to be considered as alternatives. At the same time, she said, 'there was no denying the connection between poverty, nutrition, health and literacy on the one hand and rapid population growth on the other'. She emphasized that family planning was 'first and foremost a question of human rights', but, she added, in this case there was 'no contradiction between the interests of the nation and those of the family'.[1]

Opposition to the resolution was led once again by Argentina, whose representative, Mr Bernado, said that the draft 'proclaimed as recognized facts three dogmatic assertions which were equally false ... namely that population growth was an obstacle to economic development, that birth control was an efficient and adequate means with which to overcome the consequences of population growth, and that the UN should furnish technical assistance in order to enable governments to introduce or disseminate birth control techniques'. The UN, he said, had no authority to take a decision with regard to birth control. 'That question', he continued, 'had a religious aspect; the adoption of the principle of birth control would place those countries whose conception of natural law excluded that principle in a very difficult moral position, as it would compel them to choose between the UN and their own moral obligations.'[2]

Similar arguments came from the representatives of Ireland, Italy, Lebanon, Liberia, the Philippines and Spain. Mr Hakim of Lebanon said that he firmly believed that 'each dollar spent on technical improvement in developing countries would contribute more to economic development than a dollar spent on propaganda for population control'.[3] The Spanish representative Mr Temboury, said that 'if birth control were to be admitted it would only be a matter of time before such monstrous practices as abortion, "mercy killing" and the destruction of the old were accepted'.[4] Mr Zadotti, for Italy, said that his government could not possibly support the draft resolution, since the Italian penal code severely punished anyone encouraging contraceptive practices or engaging in propaganda for birth control.[5] Several speakers hinted that they might feel obliged to reconsider their

[1] OR of the General Assembly, 17th session, 1962. Summary Records of the Second Committee, pp. 441–2.

[2] Ibid., pp. 443–4.   [3] Ibid., p. 449.
[4] Ibid., p. 459.   [5] Ibid., p. 452.

contributions to UN technical assistance funds if the draft resolution were adopted.

Support for the resolution came notably from India, Tunisia, Syria, Pakistan and Greece. Richard Gardner for the United States said his government believed that 'obstacles should not be placed in the way of other governments which sought solutions to their population problems'. The United States government, he said, was willing to help these countries 'in their search for information and assistance on ways and means of dealing with this problem.'[1]

The sponsors of the draft resolution were greatly encouraged. Mr Gardner's speech, which was cleared by President Kennedy, seemed to indicate a change in American policy with regard to international assistance in the population field.

Midway through the debate in the Second Committee, which lasted through six sessions, Mr Viaud of France, supported by Lebanon, Liberia, Spain and Gabon, introduced a series of amendments. The two most important involved the deletion of operative paragraph 6, relating to the provision of technical assistance, and the addition of a proposal for an inquiry among governments on 'the problems confronting them as a result of the reciprocal action of economic development and population changes.'[2]

The sponsors of the resolution argued that sufficient evidence was already available regarding the adverse effects of rapid population growth on the prospects for economic development. Finally, however, they accepted the amendment calling for an inquiry, as well as a preambular paragraph recognizing the need for further studies of the relationship between population trends and economic and social conditions, in the hope that this would facilitate agreement on the technical assistance clause. The opposition, however, remained adamant and pressed for a vote on the proposal to remove paragraph 6. The amendment was narrowly defeated with 30 votes for deletion, 32 against and 35 abstentions. At the request of the Netherlands, a separate vote was taken on the words 'that the UN should give technical assistance as requested by governments for national projects and programmes dealing with problems of population'. The phrase was upheld by 32 votes to 27, with 35 abstentions. Fourteen countries, the most determined opponents of UN involvement voted against the resolution as a whole.[3]

[1] OR of the General Asssembly, 17th session, 1962. Summary Records of the Second Committee, p. 458.
[2] UN Doc. A/C.2/L.709 and Rev. 1 and Rev. 2.
[3] Summary Records of the Second Committee, op. cit., pp. 496–8. The countries which voted against the draft resolution as a whole were Argentina, Austria, Belgium, Colombia, France, Ireland, Italy, Lebanon, Liberia, Luxembourg, Peru, Portugal, Spain and Uruguay.

The United States and the UK abstained in the voting on the provision of technical assistance. The American abstention was a result of domestic Catholic pressure, though Mr Gardner skilfully explained it on the grounds that paragraph 6 'neither extended nor restricted the authority already held by the UN'.[1] The British representative, Mr Unwin, stated that his delegation had not taken part in the debate because it had no well-defined views on the subject.[2]

The question was reopened in the Plenary Session of the General Assembly under the guise of 'explanations of vote'. The representatives of Argentina, Lebanon, and France reiterated the criticisms they had made in Committee. Mr Bernado of Argentina quoted at length from the records of the Population Commission which, he claimed, had been misrepresented by the sponsors of the resolution.[3] Mr Viaud of France argued that the Assembly could take no decision until they had results of the inquiry which his delegation had proposed. Consequently the reference to technical assistance should be deleted.[4] In an impassioned speech against the resolution, Dr Belaunde of Peru dwelt on the mysteries of human existence. 'Do we know', he asked, 'what moral consequences may flow from population control measures . . .? Do we know what effect a widespread tendency to interfere with the normal genetic processes . . . would have on the very spirit of future generations?' He recalled the fate of the Roman Empire, and ended with an appeal to all countries 'which wish to retain their national personality' not to vote for 'a provision which compromises the honour and responsible character of the UN General Assembly'.[5]

In his speech Dr Belaunde had said that under the rules of procedure the question should be treated as 'important', therefore requiring a two-thirds majority. The representatives of Argentina and Lebanon supported this proposal although, as Mr Malm of Sweden pointed out, only the year before their representatives had insisted that the question was *not* important. Mr Malhotra of Nepal observed that it was most unusual for economic questions to be declared important under rule 87. Nevertheless, on the insistence of Mr Bernado, the question was put to the vote and as a result declared 'important' by 42 votes to 26.[6] The British and American delegations, who had abstained in 1960 on the question of the importance of the topic, voted for the motion.

[1] Ibid., p. 499. For Mr Gardner's own account of the debate see R. N. Gardner: *In Pursuit of World Order*, New York, 1964, chapter 8.
[2] Summary Records of the Second Committee, op. cit., p. 499.
[3] OR of the General Assembly, 17th session, op. cit., Plenary meetings, pp. 1172–4.
[4] Ibid., p. 1174.   [5] Ibid., pp. 1174–5.   [6] Ibid., pp. 1175–8.

At the request of Mr Viaud a separate vote was taken on the last part of paragraph 6 which referred to the provision of technical assistance. There was little chance that the clause would secure the necessary two-thirds majority. The voting was in fact 34 for and 34 against with 32 abstentions. The extra votes against the technical assistance clause came from Congo (Leopoldville), Paraguay and the Dominican Republic, which had not voted in the Second Committee, and from Chad, the Central African Republic, China, Ecuador and El Salvador which had previously abstained. Several other countries which had voted for the retention of the technical assistance clause in Committee abstained in Plenary. The resolution, less the contentious part of paragraph 6, was adopted by 69 votes to nil with 27 abstentions.[1]

The American representative once again explained the reasons for his abstention on the technical assistance clause. While reaffirming his belief that the UN already had the necessary authority, he said that in its technical assistance activities the UN 'should emphasize those three areas on which there appears to be broad agreement among members'. The three areas according to Mr Gardner were providing information, training personnel for demographic studies and promoting discussion of population problems.[2]

Britain, which had abstained on the question of UN technical assistance in the Second Committee somewhat surprisingly voted in favour of the retention of paragraph 6 in Plenary. Significantly the Communist bloc took little part in the proceedings and abstained in all the votes.

THE 1960 POPULATION CENSUS

Many of the speakers who supported the draft resolution referred to the results of the 1960–61 population censuses.[3] They pointed out that the censuses confirmed the projections of the United Nations and showed beyond any doubt that world population was increasing at an unprecedented rate. The census results were particularly dramatic in the less developed countries. The figures exceeded by far all previous estimates, in one case, Ghana, by as much as 26%. In India the enumeration indicated a population some 30 million higher than the estimates published

---

[1] OR of the General Assembly, 17th session, op. cit., Plenary meetings, p. 1178. For the text of the final resolution, see OR of the General Assembly, 17th session, 1962, supplement 17, p. 25, Resolution 1838(XVII).

[2] Idem., Plenary meetings, p. 1178.

[3] Between 1958 and 1963 comprehensive national censuses were carried out in 157 countries and territories covering about 70 per cent of world population. The majority of these censuses were held in 1960 and 1961 as part of the UN World Population Census Programme.

in 1953 and between 10 and 12 million higher than the figures prepared only two years earlier for the Third Five Year Plan.[1] The UN projections, which had been greeted with scepticism in many quarters, were also found to be too low. In Asia and Africa census results were, on average, 5% above the UN 'median' figure: in Latin America the difference was around 4%.[2]

The results, which came as a surprise and a shock in most of the countries concerned, necessitated a substantial revision of estimates of the rate at which population was increasing. In many underdeveloped countries the 1950–51 censuses had been the first ever undertaken. Since many of the countries had no adequate system for the registration of births and deaths before that time, it was not until the results of the 1960–61 censuses became available that rates of growth could be calculated with any degree of accuracy. Even after allowances had been made for earlier under-reporting, it was clear that the population of most underdeveloped countries was growing very much faster than had been predicted either in national estimates or in UN projections. In India, for example, the average annual rate of population growth was 1·4% according to official estimates and 1·7% according to the latest UN projections. After the census the figure for the period 1951–61 had to be revised to 2·0% and the current growth rate was estimated at 2·3%.[3] Elsewhere the same pattern was repeated. The UN Demographic Yearbook for 1961 revised its rates upwards for all less developed regions. Its figure for the world as a whole rose from 1·7% to 1·8%.[4]

The impact of the census results was greatest in Latin America. Since 1920 the population of the region had been increasing more rapidly than that of all other regions of the world. Between 1950 and 1960 the population was found to have increased by almost 30%, an indication that the rate of growth had risen still higher. In many countries the annual rate of growth was found to be in excess of 3%; this implied a doubling of the population in less than 25 years. In Costa Rica, where the rate was an astonishing 3·9%, the doubling period was under 20 years.[5]

[1] See H. Gille: 'What the Asian Censuses Reveal', *Far Eastern Economic Review*, 29 June 1961, p. 636.

[2] See A. Sauvy, 'Rhythme de croissance des populations du Tiers Monde d'après les recensements de 1960–61', United Nations Conference on the Application of Science and Technology for the Benefit of the Less Developed Areas, Geneva, 1963. UN Doc. E/Conf. 39/8/30, pp. 3–4.

[3] H. Gille, op. cit., pp. 637 ff.

[4] UN Demographic Yearbook, 1960, p. 118, and UN Demographic Yearbook, 1961, p. 124. See also *World Population Prospects as assessed in 1963*, Population Studies no. 41 (ST/SOA/Series A/41).

[5] A Sauvy, op. cit. See also UN Doc. E/CN.12/604, 'Preliminary Survey of the Demographic Situation in Latin America'.

The crucial distinction between population size and population growth was beginning to be understood. A UN seminar on the use of census data in Latin America pointed out in 1959: 'Of course for each new mouth there is also a pair of hands. But the mouth has to be fed now; the hands become useful only some years later.'[1] Although most of the countries in the region considered that they were under-populated in relation to their area and resources, all faced considerable difficulties as a result of rapid population growth. Since 1955 per capita income had been stagnant or had declined in nearly all countries of the region.[2] 'It seems evident', continued the report of the seminar, 'that in spite of the advantages that might accrue to them from a larger population, their economic progress would be more satisfactory if they could arrive at those larger numbers at a more leisurely pace.'[3]

In 1961 a report on population trends in relation to economic and social policy, written with the assistance of the regional Demographic Training and Research Centre, contained a veiled hint that measures to slow the rate of population growth might be desirable.[4] The Economic Commission for Latin America was, however, unwilling to become involved in a public debate on the question and limited itself to a recommendation that studies of the question be intensified.[5] Nevertheless within many countries of the region the census results sparked off a fierce debate over the population question while, at the same time, the high incidence of abortion and infant mortality led many doctors to give discreet endorsement to contraception.

The proposals for action prepared in connection with the launching of the United Nations Development Decade in 1961 contained several allusions to the relevance of population growth rates to the achievement of the goals of the Development Decade. A short section entitled 'Demographic Studies' stated that if governments decided that it would be in the national interest to seek to influence population trends 'it becomes important also to study the means of making such policies effective'.[6]

[1] Seminar on the Evaluation and Utilization of Population Census Data in Latin America, Santiago, Chile, November–December 1959 (ST/SOA/SER.C/46), p. 37.
[2] UN Doc. E/CN.12/659/Add.1, 'Economic Development of Latin America in the Post War period'.
[3] Seminar on the Evaluation and Utilization of Population Census Data, op. cit.
[4] UN Doc. E/CN.12/583, 'Population trends in Latin America in relation to economic and social policy', p. 21.
[5] Economic Commission for Latin America, 9th session, May 1961. OR of ECOSOC, 32nd session, supplement no. 4, p. 34.
[6] UN Development Decade: Proposals for Action (Sales number 62 II.B.2), p. 115.

The launching of the Development Decade coincided, paradoxically, with the widening of the gap between rich and poor countries. In the sixties food production in less developed regions failed to expand as rapidly as in the previous decade. In some countries supplies were maintained only by massive imports of food from North America.[1] External assistance, which contributed approximately ten per cent of all investment in less developed countries also increased more slowly after 1961. Despite an increase in private overseas investment, the net transfer of resources from rich to poor countries virtually dried up. The 'one per cent' target endorsed by the General Assembly at its sixteenth session was met only by France, while in other rich countries the percentage of national income allocated to aid programmes declined. Meanwhile the terms of trade continued to move against primary products and the share of developing countries in world trade decreased still further.[2]

The proposals for action pointed out that even if countries were successful in achieving an annual rate of economic growth of 5%, per capita incomes would rise very little in countries where population was increasing at 2·5 or 3% per annum. The problem was not, however, merely that there would be more people among whom additional benefits had to be shared. The UN report *The Determinants and Consequences of Population Trends* and the work of Coale and Hoover and other economists suggested that high fertility actually impeded economic development through its effect on the age structure and the dependency ratio. Some commentators went still further and argued that without a prior reduction in the rate of population growth economic development would prove impossible. The combination of high fertility and poverty tended to impede those social changes associated with economic growth which had led to the transition from high to low birth rates in the now-developed countries. The less developed countries were thus caught in a 'trap'.[3] The replies to the questionnaire sent out by the Secretariat in pursuance of Resolution 1838(XVIII) indicated that an increasing number of governments in less developed regions were coming to share this view.[4]

Certainly there was growing interest in measures and policies to moderate fertility as part of overall plans for economic and

---

[1] See Chapter 11, pp. 127–8.

[2] *Partners in Development*, Report of the Commission on International Development, New York, 1969, chapter 2, p. 45 ff.

[3] See for example, R. R. Nelson: 'A Theory of the Low-level Equilibrium Trap', *American Economic Review*, December 1956, pp. 894–908.

[4] UN Doc. E/3985/Rev/1, 'Inquiry among Governments on Problems Resulting from the Reciprocal Action of Economic Development and Population Changes', Report of the Secretary-General.

social development. In November 1961 Korea joined the list of countries with national population policies. Several governments, including those of Turkey, Tunisia, Thailand, Kenya and Colombia, began discussions on national population policies with the help of the Population Council. In other countries—for example Ceylon, Malaysia, Taiwan and Singapore—existing voluntary programmes were taken over by the government and expanded on a national scale. Many other governments were beginning to adopt a more favourable attitude towards family planning and either offered services through government health centres or gave financial support to voluntary planned parenthood organizations.[1]

The UN has claimed some credit for these changes in attitude towards the need for population policies.[2] Certainly the discussion of the implications of demographic trends in the General Assembly accorded a seal of respectability to the question. Moreover, the debates in the UN obliged governments to assess their own situations in order to participate in the discussions at the international level. Before seeing what effect these changes had on the activities of the UN and WHO, the role of FAO, and in particular of its Director-General, B. R. Sen, deserves further consideration, since, in retrospect, it seems that it was fear of a breakdown in food supplies which played a major part in the outcome of the debate on the population question.

[1] See chapter 2, 'Developments in Family Planning 1960–66' in the 1967 *Report on the World Social Situation*, UN, Dept. of Economic and Social Affairs, 1967; and D. Kirk and D. Nortman: 'Population Policies in Developing Countries' *Economic Development and Cultural Change*, January 1967, pp. 129–142.

[2] See UN Doc. E/CN.9/239, p. 102 and 1967 *Report on the World Social Situation*, chapter 2, op. cit.

I I

B. R. Sen and the World Food Crisis

BETWEEN 1950 and 1958 food production in the less developed regions had increased at about 3·5% per annum. After 1958 food supplies increased less rapidly and per capita food production began to decline. The deterioration was due partly to a slowing down in the rate of growth of production but mainly to the acceleration of population growth.[1] The situation was particularly disturbing in Latin America, because of the very rapid growth of population, and in the Far East. Although population growth was less rapid in the latter region, the high density and the large, absolute increases in population size constituted an ever present threat of a breakdown in food supplies.

Under B. R. Sen, who became Director-General in 1956, FAO began to place less emphasis on the theoretical possibilities of increasing world food production and directed attention instead towards the inadequacies of existing food supplies and patterns of consumption.

It was partly to dramatize the problem that in 1959 Sen launched the Freedom from Hunger Campaign.[2] According to the estimates prepared in connection with the Campaign, more than half the world's population suffered from hunger or malnutrition or both. Despite the efforts made since the Second World War, the amount of food available per person was only fractionally above the already inadequate pre-war levels. Moreover most of the increase in total food production had taken place in the more developed regions. As a result, the gap between the rich countries and the poor countries had widened. In many parts of the world, food production was not keeping pace with population growth, and consumption levels had only been maintained by massive imports of food supplies.[3] Before the Second World War the less developed countries of Asia, Africa and Latin America had been net exporters of cereals to the

---

[1] P. V. Sukhatme, 'The World's Food Supplies', *Journal of the Royal Statistical Society*, Series A (General), vol. 129, part 2, 1966, pp. 234-9.

[2] FAO, Report of the 10th session of the Conference, 1959, Resolution 13/59. The aims and methods of the campaign are described briefly in *Freedom from Hunger: Outline of a Campaign*, Rome, 1960.

[3] *Third World Food Survey 1963*, Freedom from Hunger Campaign Basic Study, no. 11, FAO, Rome, 1963, especially chapter 2; and P. V. Sukhatme, 'The World's Hunger and Future Needs in Food Supplies', *Journal of the Royal Statistical Society*, Series A (General), vol. 124, part 4, 1961, pp. 474-94.

industrialized parts of the world. By 1950 they had become net importers. Their dependence on imported cereals increased from 4 million tons in 1950 to 25 million tons in 1965.

In 1963, on the basis of the 'medium' variant of the UN population projections, FAO calculated that world food supplies would need to be increased by over 35% 'merely to sustain the world's population at its present unsatisfactory level of diet'. To achieve 'a reasonable improvement in the level of nutrition' it was estimated that a 50% increase in total food supplies would be required for the world as a whole and an 80% increase in the less developed regions. Looking further ahead, total food supplies would need to be doubled by 1980 and trebled by 2000 in order to provide a reasonably adequate level of nutrition.[1] On the basis of past performance the prospects for achieving such increases were far from reassuring. Sen himself warned that famines would occur in the Far East in the early 1980s unless drastic measures were taken to increase food production.

Sen, a former member of the Indian Civil Service, had been profoundly marked by the famine which occurred in 1943 in his own province of Bengal and in which it was estimated between 1½ and 3 million people died. He realized that population control could not solve the immediate problem of hunger and malnutrition. At the same time he believed that efforts to raise food production had to be accompanied by measures to slow down the rate of population growth. Like McDougall, Sen recognized that population policies were not the responsibility of FAO. But whereas his predecessors had been unwilling to do more than draw attention to the failure of food production to keep pace with population growth, Sen sought ways of promoting discussion of the implications of this situation.

In 1959 he asked Arnold Toynbee, the British historian, to give the first McDougall Memorial lecture at the opening session of the ninth FAO Conference. In his lecture, entitled 'Population and Food Supply', Toynbee raised the moral question: 'What is the true end of Man? Is it,' he asked, 'to populate the Earth with the maximum number of human beings that can be kept alive? Or is it to enable human beings to lead the best kind of life that the spiritual limitations of human nature allow?' The answer he gave was that 'living human beings, whatever their number, shall develop the highest capacities of their nature . . . and what we should aim at is the optimum size of population for this purpose in the economic and social circumstances of each succeeding generation'.[2]

[1] *Third World Food Survey*, op. cit., pp. 8–10, Conclusions.
[2] Arnold Toynbee: *Population and Food Supply*, McDougall Memorial Lecture, 1959, FAO, Rome, 1959, pp. 17–18.

At the Second World Population Conference in Belgrade in 1965 Sen recalled that Professor Toynbee's address had made a considerable impact, but the reactions of delegates to the Conference at the time were that public opinion was not yet ready to face the question and discuss its implications. The second McDougall lecture, in 1961, was given by John D. Rockefeller III, who devoted his lecture to the theme of 'people, food and the well-being of mankind'. He lamented the fact that the controversial nature of birth control made governments reluctant even to investigate their demographic situation. Population growth, he said, 'is second only to the control of atomic weapons as the paramount problem of our day'.[1]

Two years later, in 1963, the World Food Congress met in Washington against a background of increasing concern at the failure to achieve substantial improvements in the world's food situation. Arnold Toynbee, who was invited to address the Congress, once again warned that 'in the long run the Campaign cannot be won unless the planet's hundreds of millions of wives and husbands voluntarily decide to regulate the number of human births'.[2]

In his summing up B. R. Sen made a direct reference to birth control. 'It is obvious', he said, 'that the increase in numbers cannot continue at the present rate, let alone at an accelerated pace, if the food supply invariably lags behind. In the final analysis it will be up to the individual to decide, bearing in mind his responsibility to his family and to his society, how he should conduct himself. Even so, the time may come when not only the nation to which the individual belongs, but also the world as a whole, may have to take a more direct and even a more dynamic role in assisting family planning measures through social education and hygiene'.[3]

The Congress did not endorse Toynbee's plea for population stabilization. The final declaration did, however, include a reference to the alarming implications of the 'explosive growth of population'.[4]

Encouraged by the impact of the campaign to dramatize the seriousness of the world food situation and by the growing evidence that attitudes towards the population question were now less rigid, Sen decided to throw the weight of his position behind

[1] J. D. Rockefeller III: *People, Food and the Well-Being of Mankind*, McDougall Memorial Lecture, 1961, FAO, Rome, 1961, pp. 17–18.
[2] Report of the World Food Congress, Washington, 1963, FAO, Rome, 1963, p. 21.
[3] Quoted in *Around the World News of Population and Birth Control*, no. 117, September 1963. This part of Sen's speech was not included in the official report of the conference.
[4] Report of World Food Congress, op. cit., p. 307: Final Declaration.

the need for population control. The occasion he chose for his entry into the debate was characteristically bold; the International Eucharistic Congress, one of the most important gatherings of Roman Catholic laymen and hierarchy and attended by Pope Paul VI. Invited to address the Congress, held in Bombay in November 1964, Sen, after painting a grim and moving picture of world hunger asked, 'Can we any more turn our faces away from the concept of family planning when the alternative is starvation and death? This is a question on which we await guidance from the great moral and spiritual leaders of the world.'[1] Six months later, addressing the UN Population Commission, he stated: 'the situation certainly calls for the adoption of population stabilization as an urgent social priority'.[2]

Now with remarkable boldness and considerable adroitness, he entered into a dialogue with the Vatican. Pope Paul VI, in addressing the General Assembly at the end of 1965, urged 'the need to multiply bread so that it suffices for the tables of mankind rather than to rely on measures which diminish the number of guests at the banquet of life'.[3] Dr Sen, in a speech to the 50th anniversary meeting of the American family planning association Planned Parenthood—World Population in October 1966, picked up this phrase. He admitted that some scientists believed that the production of land and ocean could be greatly increased, a view from which he did not dissent, but all these possibilities were still in the realm of research, and moreover the adoption of methods to increase food production were conditioned by social and economic factors. Meanwhile, India and Pakistan had been forced to adopt family limitation programmes. Was the world to ignore their appeal for aid for these programmes? And, returning text for text, he quoted Pope John's Encyclical 'Pacem in Terris' which had proclaimed 'man's right to life, to bodily integrity and to the means which are necessary and suitable for the development of life'. The implication of this pronouncement, Dr Sen suggested, surely is clear; that a continuation of present trends in population growth may well lead to a situation where the right to life of those not yet living will no

---

[1] 'Freedom from Hunger—Challenge of the Century'. Text of an address delivered by Dr B. R. Sen at the Plenary Session of the 38th International Eucharistic Congress, Bombay, 26 November 1964, reproduced in *Food, Population and Development*, FAO, Rome, 1965, p. 8.

[2] Text of the address given by Dr B. R. Sen to the 13th Session of the Population Commission, 24 March 1965. See *Food, Population and Development*, op. cit., p. 30. See also E/CN.9/SR.181, pp. 7–11.

[3] OR of the General Assembly, 20th Session, 1965. 1347th Plenary Meeting, p. 4.

longer be a right parallel to, but will be in conflict with, the right to a worthy standard of living.[1]

In March 1967 Pope Paul VI issued an encyclical on the 'Development of Peoples' which contained a somewhat ambiguous statement on 'Demography'. It admitted, however, that 'It is certain that public authorities can intervene within the limits of their competence by favouring the availability of appropriate information and by adopting suitable measures, provided these be in conformity with the moral law'.[2] Dr Sen immediately called a press conference to express 'the deep gratitude' of FAO for the encyclical. He described the passage quoted as being 'of tremendous significance in the context of the question of population stabilization'. The population explosion, Dr Sen pointed out, involved large areas of the world which were not Catholic. The encyclical therefore opened up more possibilities for family planning than anything the Catholic Church had said before. For whilst the moral law of the Catholic Church was the moral law interpreted by the Pope, the moral law of other religions raised no objections to family planning.[3]

Several questioners asked whether FAO had been involved in the preparation of the encyclical. Dr Sen replied that there had been no consultations but that he understood that documents produced by FAO had been extensively used in the discussions of the Oecumenical Council.[4] However, in the opinion of several observers one of the more important contributions made by B. R. Sen was that he had managed to take a bold line without seriously antagonizing the Catholic Church on a question which only a few years earlier was so controversial that it could not be mentioned in Rome.

The pessimistic picture of the extent of hunger in the world drawn by FAO, and in particular Sen's warnings of imminent disaster, incurred considerable criticism. A leading critic was Colin Clark, the Australian economist and a Roman Catholic. Clark, who had attended the International Eucharistic Congress in Bombay, consistently challenged the accuracy of the FAO's estimates of the number of hungry and undernourished people of the world. Other criticism was directed as much against the style in which the campaign was carried out as the substance of the calculations. As John D. Rockefeller III had observed in his McDougall Memorial lecture, 'It is easier to say that the

[1] Text of the address given by Dr. B. R. Sen at the 50th Anniversary Banquet of Planned Parenthood—World Population, New York, 18 October 1966, FAO/MI/51682.
[2] Encyclical letter of Pope Paul VI, *Populorum Progressio* . . ., 1967, para. 37.
[3] Press conference of Dr B. R. Sen, Rome, 30 March 1967, FAO/MI/58455, p. 3 and p. 11 ff.
[4] Ibid., pp. 4 ff.

world's larder is half full than to say that it is half empty'.[1] To some observers the so called 'Green Revolution', which hit the headlines in 1968, the same year that Sen failed to secure re-election as Director-General, seemed to confirm that the critics were right and that Sen had been wrong. However, it was significant that his successor, A. H. Boerma, was quick to point out the need for caution. 'It is true' he said 'that we may be on the verge of a breakthrough in agriculture' but, he continued, 'both the developed and the developing countries must realize that what has been achieved so far is not a revolution but a challenge and an opportunity to bring it about. We are in a critical stage of transition, and the dangers confronting us are as great as the opportunities.'[2] Three months earlier in an interview he had said: 'I share my predecessor's views on the urgency of measures that will lead to a slowing down in the rate of population increase.'[3]

It seems probable that B. R. Sen's intervention was instrumental in finally committing the United States government to the need for population control. In the course of the Senate hearings on the world population problem in 1965 and 1966 the problem of hunger was seen as one of the three most serious consequences of over-rapid population growth.[4] President Johnson, in his message to Congress on the Foreign Aid Program in February 1966 said 'We cannot meet the world food needs of the future, however willing we are to share our abundance.'[5] Sen's warnings, coupled with the realization that American grain stocks were insufficient to avert a major disaster such as nearly occurred in India in 1965–66, would appear to have carried more weight than arguments based on considerations of health, human rights or economic development.

[1] *People, Food and the Well-Being of Mankind*, op. cit.
[2] Statement by A. H. Boerma on the world situation, Rome, 20 June 1968, FAO/MI/75832, p. 1.
[3] *Ceres*, March–April 1968.
[4] 'Population Crisis', Hearings Before the Senate Sub-Committee on Foreign Aid Expenditures (Gruening Committee)—United States Senate, 89th Congress, 1965.
[5] Presidential Message on the US Foreign Aid Program, 1 February 1966. Quoted in *Department of State Bulletin*, 28 February 1966.

Part V

THE BREAKTHROUGH
(1965–1967)

'Once as President of the United States I thought and said that birth control was not the business of the Federal Government. The facts changed my mind . . . I have come to believe that the population explosion is the world's most critical problem.'

Ex-President Eisenhower (1968)

12

The Breakthrough in the United Nations

RICHARD GARDNER's observation at the 17th session of the General Assembly that the UN already had the necessary authority under its general technical assistance resolutions to provide assistance to governments in the formulation and execution of population policies would appear to have been legally sound. However, it was doubtful from the debate in the Assembly and from the reports of the Population Commission whether the majority of member states were yet ready to support active UN involvement in questions of population policy and family planning. Indeed, some member states which were opposed to birth control for religious reasons claimed that the vote on operative paragraph 6 of Resolution 1838(XVIII) actually precluded the UN from providing technical assistance in this field. Most, however, were simply unwilling to commit themselves, either through lack of conviction or, more often, because of the controversy aroused by the question. Pressure on the General Assembly, as the supreme legislative organ of the UN, for a clear decision came from several of its subsidiary bodies.

ECAFE AND THE ASIAN POPULATION CONFERENCE

As early as 1954, ECAFE had given high priority to a study of the relationship between population growth and economic development.[1] Following the Bandung seminar in 1955, and the endorsement by ECAFE of its conclusions,[2] the study was put on a 'continuing high priority basis'.[3] There was pressure from India, Ceylon and Indonesia for a more active role. In 1959 it was decided to hold a regional population conference. In the following year, the Commission decided that the conference 'should not limit itself to theoretical discussions but should seek practical solutions to population problems'.[4]

[1] Report of the 10th session of ECAFE, 1954, OR of ECOSOC, 17th session, 1954, supplement no, 3, p. 32.
[2] See chapter 7.
[3] Report of the 13th session of ECAFE, Resolution 20(XIII), OR of ECOSOC, 24th session, 1957, supplement no. 2, p. 41.
[4] Report of the 15th session of ECAFE, Resolution 28 (XV), OR of ECOSOC, 28th session, 1959, supplement no. 2, pp. 27–8 and p. 38.

This decision caused some embarrassment in the Population Commission. At the 11th session in 1961, Mr Castellano of Italy asked what was meant by the words 'should seek practical solutions to population problems'. John Durand adroitly evaded the question, saying that ECAFE alone could provide a satisfactory answer.[1]

The conference had been originally planned for 1961 or 1962 but was postponed until late 1963 to allow time for more detailed preparations. This gave the Population Commission a second chance to comment on the arrangements, which were finalized in February 1963. The preparatory committee had decided that the conference should be attended by representatives of governments and interested Specialized Agencies as well as by individual experts. The provisional agenda included discussion of 'government measures to affect population trends'. It also envisaged that the final report would include recommendations to governments.[2]

At the 12th session of the Population Commission, several members objected to the involvement of the UN in a conference which would be able to adopt recommendations on questions of demographic policy. Mr Mertens de Wilmars said that this would be contrary to the general philosophy which had guided the work of the Population Commission in the past and which was reflected in Resolution 1838(XVIII) of the General Assembly. Mr Castellano suggested dividing the conference into two parts, one of which would be devoted to discussions and studies in which the UN might participate, and a second devoted to practical solutions at which the UN would not be represented.[3] There was, however, little the Commission could do. As John Durand pointed out, the conference had been convened by ECAFE which assumed full responsibility for it. Ainsley Coale, the US member on the Commission, and Mr Bhadamarkar of India reminded members that it was not for the Population Commission to give instructions to ECAFE concerning the procedures to be followed.[4]

The Asian Population Conference met in New Delhi in December 1963. It lasted ten days and was attended by over two hundred participants from fourteen Asian countries and five members of ECAFE from outside the region.[5] There was

[1] UN Doc. E/CN.9/SR.154, pp. 10–11.
[2] Report of the Preparatory Committee of the Asian Population Conference, February 1963, in UN Doc. E/CN.9/175.
[3] UN Doc. E/CN.9/SR.169, pp. 6–9.
[4] Ibid., p. 7. See also Report of the 12th session of the Commission, paras. 91–2, OR of ECOSOC, 35th session, 1963, supplement no. 2.
[5] Report of the Asian Population Conference, New Delhi, India, December, 1963, UN, New York, 1964, Annex II, pp. 56–62.

widespread agreement that rapid population growth was an obstacle to the achievement of a satisfactory rate of economic growth and that lower fertility would ease pressure on health services, education, housing and other social welfare facilities.

The conference unanimously adopted a resolution and a series of recommendations. The first part of the resolution invited governments in the region 'to take account of the urgency of adopting a positive population policy related to their individual needs and to the general needs of the region'. The second part of the resolution and several recommendations dealt with international co-operation. The Executive Secretary was requested to expand regional population activities, particularly training and research, and to promote the exchange of experience and information on population policies among member states in the region. The UN and the Specialized Agencies were urged to 'expand the scope of the technical assistance which they are prepared to give at the request of governments in the development of statistics, research, experimentation and action programmes relating to population'.[1]

A surprising feature of the Conference was the sympathetic attitude taken by the traditional opponents of birth control. A Roman Catholic participant said he believed that the Church would not object to 'a family centred programme for responsible parenthood in which Catholic couples as well as others would be encouraged to limit the number of their children'.[2] The Soviet Union was represented not by a demographer but by the First Secretary of the Soviet Embassy in India. During the discussion on the economic and social implications of prospective population trends, he said that the Soviet Union did not object to birth control providing the measures used did not disregard human dignity or involve compulsion. He pointed out that in the USSR voluntary parenthood was an established principle. However, he stressed that in the long run 'rapid socio-economic development was the most important means of successfully settling population problems'.[3] The conference readily agreed that, by itself, population control was not a solution to development problems. Nevertheless it was accepted that, in some circumstances, a reduction in the rate of population growth would assist in raising living standards.

In March 1964 the report of the Asian Population Conference was discussed by ECAFE which endorsed the recommendations and unanimously adopted a resolution repeating the main provisions of the resolutions passed by the conference. Operative

[1] Ibid., pp. 49–51. [2] Ibid., p. 34. [3] Ibid., p. 20.

paragraph 5 of this resolution invited the UN and the Specialized Agencies to expand the scope of their technical assistance activities.[1]

Also in March, the newly formed Advisory Committee on the Application of Science and Technology to Development, at its first session, had included the provision of adequate food supplies and a better understanding of population trends among the 'especially important problems of research or application'.[2]

THE ENQUIRY ON POPULATION AND ECONOMIC DEVELOPMENT

ECAFE's report, together with Resolution 54(XX), was submitted to ECOSOC in July 1964. The agenda for the session also included consideration of the replies to the 'Enquiry among governments on the problems resulting from the reciprocal action of economic development and population change' which had been called for in Resolution 1838(XVIII).[3]

Replies had been received from fifty-three governments and the Vatican. Twenty-eight were from the governments of less developed countries. Despite the lack of uniformity in the depth and scope of the answers it was clear that many governments viewed the current rate of population growth with concern, and considered it to be a serious handicap to their economic and social development. Lebanon, which had been one of the most outspoken critics of the joint resolution in 1962, admitted: 'While population pressure in Lebanon may not hamper economic development, it is at least retarding it.'[4] While several governments replied that a larger population would be an economic advantage, very few said that currently high rates of population growth were beneficial. On the other hand, only six African and six Latin American countries answered the enquiry. Significantly, many of the governments which had opposed the original draft resolution in 1962 failed to reply, including Argentina, Brazil, Peru and nearly all the French-speaking African countries.

Despite objections from some members of the Population

[1] Resolution 54(XX) adopted at the 311th meeting of ECAFE, 17 March 1964. See Report of ECAFE for 1963–4, OR of ECOSOC, 37th session, 1964, supplement no. 2, pp. 113 and 128–9.

[2] Report on the first session of ACAST, February–March 1964, OR of ECOSOC, 37th session, 1964, supplement no. 14, p. 24. See also Second Report, 1965, OR of ECOSOC, 39th session, 1965, supplement no. 14, paras 20–68 and 75–84.

[3] UN Doc. E/3895/Rev. 1, 'Inquiry Governments on Problems Resulting from the Reciprocal Action of Economic Development and Population Changes.' Report of the Secretary-General. [4] Ibid., p. 20.

Commission who had claimed that this would give the enquiry 'a specific bias',[1] the questionnaire also enquired about government policies aimed at affecting population trends. The replies from India, Iran, Jamaica, Korea, Pakistan, Tunisia, Turkey and UAR referred to the efforts being made or contemplated to moderate fertility.[2]

The two reports were referred to the Council's Economic Committee. A strong lead was given by the Japanese representative, Mr Kakitsubo, who argued that population policies were an essential component of national development plans. He called on the UN to expand its technical assistance activities as requested in the ECAFE resolution.[3] Three Asian countries, Japan, India and Iran, supported by Mexico and Yugoslavia, introduced a draft resolution noting the 'serious concern' expressed by many governments of less developed countries in their replies to the enquiry, and calling on the General Assembly, the regional economic commissions and the Population Commission to examine the replies and to 'make recommendations with a view to intensifying the work of the UN in assisting . . . governments . . . to deal with the population problems confronting them'. Operative paragraph 4 called on ECOSOC to 'endorse' the resolution of ECAFE. The resolution also suggested that other regional commissions should hold similar conferences.[4]

The representative of Ecuador, one of the countries which had not replied to the enquiry, alleged that the questionnaire had been 'slanted'.[5] Mr Viaud of France maintained that further studies were necessary before any action could be contemplated at the international level. In what was seen as yet another delaying tactic, he proposed that the replies of governments should be circulated in full to the General Assembly. The issue he said was 'too controversial and sensitive' for the UN to run the risk of becoming involved, and he advised countries which needed technical assistance to seek it through bilateral agencies.[6] Italy, Luxembourg and Austria also spoke against the draft resolution and in particular its operative paragraph 4 endorsing ECAFE Resolution 54(XX).

Fearing that the resolution might be rejected, the sponsors finally agreed to replace 'endorses' with the words 'draws the attention of the General Assembly to . . .'. With this change, the resolution was approved without objections at the very last

---

[1] UN Doc. E/CN.9/SR.163, pp. 6 ff.
[2] UN Doc. E/3895/Rev. 1, op. cit., chapter VI.
[3] UN Doc. E/AC.6/SR.355, p. 10.
[4] UN Doc. E/AC.6/L.309 and Rev. 1.
[5] UN Doc. E/AC.6/SR.356, p. 12.
[6] Ibid., pp. 14–15.

meeting of the committee.[1] The Council, also at its last meeting, unanimously adopted the resolution.[2]

In the course of the discussion in the Economic Committee the UK representative (whose name appropriately enough was Mr Pill), indicated that the British government was now willing to furnish technical assistance in the population field. He hoped that developing countries would make their needs known at the forthcoming session of the General Assembly.[3]

The dispute over the financing of peace-keeping operations completely disrupted the work of the 19th session of the General Assembly. Resolution 1048 of ECOSOC and the findings of the Secretary-General's enquiry could therefore not be discussed until the 20th session in 1965.

THE APPROVAL OF ACTION PROGRAMMES

Several events occurred in the months preceding the 20th session of the General Assembly which led many observers to refer to 1965 as the turning point in the history of the involvement of the United Nations in population action programmes. An important development was the evolution in the position of the United States government. At the 37th session of ECOSOC in July 1964, the US representative intimated that a change was under way. Explaining his vote on Resolution 1048(XXXVII) he said that while the US government was 'opposed to the UN undertaking any activity involving the supply of specific birth control devices, since such devices were repugnant to many people' it approved assistance 'connected with the study of problems and the dissemination of knowledge about birth control'.[4] In his State of the Union Address to Congress in January 1965 President Johnson said: 'I will seek new ways to use our knowledge to help deal with the explosion in world population and the growing scarcity in world resources.' Shortly afterwards American missions abroad were instructed that the government was now prepared to respond to requests for assistance with family planning projects. The provision of contraceptive supplies was excluded because, it was claimed, 'experience has made it clear that the cost of these . . . items is not a stumbling block in most countries'.[5]

[1] UN Doc. E/AC.6/SR.358, p. 9.
[2] Resolution 1048(XXXVII), OR of ECOSOC, 37th session, 1964, supplement no. 1, p. 13.
[3] UN Doc. E/AC.6/SR.355, p. 13.
[4] OR of ECOSOC, 37th session, p. 253.
[5] US Agency for International Development, Statement on Population Program, February 1965.

THE BREAKTHROUGH IN THE UN 141

In the same month, the UN Technical Assistance Board approved a request from the Indian government for an expert mission to review the Indian family planning programme and to make recommendations for its intensification. A five-man mission, led by Sir Colville Deverell, Secretary-General of the IPPF, spent two months in India from mid-February till mid-April 1965. The mission was the first of its kind to be provided by the United Nations.[1]

In March, the Commission on the Status of Women adopted a resolution introduced by UAR, Finland, Austria and USA affirming that 'married couples should have access to all relevant educational information concerning family planning'. The resolution requested the Secretary-General to investigate the relationship between family planning and the advancement of women and commended the resolutions adopted by ECAFE and ECOSOC.[2] In the Social Commission, too, which met in May 1965, there was agreement that national family planning programmes were essential in strengthening family life and improving the status of women.[3]

The Population Commission also met in March 1965 for its 13th session. It had a full agenda. In addition to the results of the Secretary-General's enquiry and ECOSOC Resolution 1048 (XXXVII), the Commission had before it the report of an ad-Hoc Committee of Experts on a Long-range Programme of Work in the Field of Population which it had requested at its 11th session. The Committee, which had met in September 1964, recommended an expansion and redirection of UN activities in the field of population. It identified five areas in which research and technical work should be intensified: fertility, mortality, internal migration and urbanization, demographic aspects of economic development, and demographic aspects of social development. Among these, top priority was given to fertility. The committee also recommended that the UN should provide assistance on all aspects of population problems, 'including inter alia the formulation and execution of family welfare planning programmes . . .'[4]

The Commission began by discussing the Secretary-General's report on his enquiry and ECOSOC Resolution 1048. Almost

[1] The report was issued in February 1966. See Report on the Family Planning Programme in India, UN Doc. TAO/IND/48.
[2] Report on the 18th session of the Commission on the Status of Women, March 1965, OR of ECOSOC, 39th session, 1965, supplement no. 7, pp. 43–4.
[3] Report on the 16th session of the Social Commission, May 1965, OR of ECOSOC, 39th session, supplement no. 12, p. 35.
[4] UN Doc. E/CN.9/182. 'Report of the Ad-Hoc Committee of Experts on the Long-Range Programme of Work in the Field of Population'.

immediately Mr Schmid of Austria, a new member of the Commission, challenged the right of the UN to provide technical assistance for family planning programmes. Mr Sauvy of France and Mr Podyachick of the Soviet Union questioned the legality of the mission sent to India in the light of the decision of the General Assembly in 1962 to delete the technical assistance clause from Resolution 1838(XVII).[1] The Secretariat, however, stood firm. As a mark of the importance which it attached to this question, the Under Secretary for Economic and Social Affairs, Philippe de Seynes, came in person to the opening session. In his opening statement he said that 'there were indisputable signs of a willingness to re-examine views relating to even the most delicate and controversial aspects of the problem'. He argued that the population problem 'could no longer be dealt with as if it was subject ... to self-regulating mechanisms and could solve itself, without direct intervention, as a result of economic and social measures'.[2] Julia Henderson, head of the Bureau of Social Affairs, strongly defended the decision to respond to the request of the Indian government. It had been taken, she said, with the greatest of care in the light of the recent resolutions adopted by ECAFE and ECOSOC. She emphasized the right and duty of the UN under Resolution 222(IX) of ECOSOC and Resolution 418(V) of the General Assembly to respond to requests from governments in all economic and social fields. It was for governments to decide what sort of assistance they required. Finally, she reminded members that the Population Commission itself had stated at its 11th session that the UN should give technical assistance, as requested by governments, for national projects of research, experimentation and action in the field of population.[3]

The question came up again when the Commission discussed the future programme of work. The Secretariat's proposals were based on the recommendation of the Ad-Hoc Committee of Experts, and included plans for an intensification of research on human fertility and ways of controlling it. The Secretariat also proposed that the UN should be prepared to respond to requests for technical assistance for family planning programmes.[4]

A proposal by the USSR, supported by Ukraine and Austria, to delete the section relating to research into fertility control was defeated by eleven votes to three.[5] The chapter on future tech-

[1] UN Doc. E/CN.9/SR.181, p. 14 and SR.182, p. 12.
[2] UN Doc. E/CN.9/SR.179, pp. 5–6.
[3] UN Doc. E/CN.9/SR.182, p. 10.
[4] UN Doc. E/CN.9/196. 'Long-Range Programme of Work in the Field of Population'. Note by the Secretary-General.
[5] UN Doc. E/CN.9/SR.190, p. 7.

nical assistance activities fared less well. After a heated debate a French proposal that the recommendation be made conditional on a favourable vote in the General Assembly was adopted by nine votes to six with two abstentions. However, other amendments which would have expressly prohibited assistance for family planning programmes were outvoted.[1]

The Commission's final report recognized that the scope of the work which the UN had carried out until then was no longer sufficient to meet the needs of member states. It called for an expansion of activities, particularly at the regional level, and recommended that greater weight be given to population work within the Secretariat.[2]

During the adoption of the report at the final meeting, the USA and Panama introduced a draft resolution for submission to ECOSOC summarizing the main recommendations of the Commission and calling on the General Assembly to provide the necessary resources to enable the organization to carry out the expanded programme of work.[3] Austria and the USSR opposed the move, claiming that the draft resolution had not been submitted in due time. Mr Schmid of Austria said he would need to obtain instructions from his government, while Mr Podyachick insisted that there could be no question of diverting funds away from existing technical assistance programmes. In view of the difficulties, the sponsors agreed to modify the controversial sections of their resolution, which was added to the report.[4]

When the Social Committee of ECOSOC considered the Commission's report and the draft resolution in July 1965, India and Iraq put forward an amendment explicitly authorizing the UN to provide 'advisory services and training in action programmes in the field of population . . .'[5] Introducing the amendment, the Indian representative said: 'Those who felt their moral conscience would be violated should not allow their feelings to hinder those who had no such problems'. He insisted that there was nothing in the UN Charter to prohibit the organization from assisting family planning.[6] There was opposition from Argentina, whose representative described family planning as 'an infringement of human rights' and claimed that the sole effect of the resolution would be to permit state interference in family life.[7] Mr Astafyev for the Soviet Union remarked

[1] UN. Doc. E/CN.9/SR.191. See also Report of the 13th session of the Population Commission, Annex I, para. 26 and footnote g, OR of ECOSOC, 39th session, supplement no. 9, p. 49.
[2] Report of the 13th session of the Population Commission, op. cit., para. 106.
[3] UN Doc. E/CN.9/L.80.   [4] UN Doc. E/CN.9/SR.198.
[5] Un Doc. E/AC.7/L.480.
[6] UN Doc. E/AC.7/SR.529, p. 10.   [7] Ibid., p. 11.

that the Commission had been unanimous in its belief that
population control was not substitute for economic development.
In that case, he wondered why the Committee was not more
concerned with increasing the resources available for economic
development rather than transferring already scarce funds to
family planning.[1]

In addition to the expected support from countries of Asia, the
Middle East and Scandinavia, there was backing from UK and
USA, while a number of developing countries, such as Ghana
and Mexico, which considered that they themselves had no
population problems, supported the right of other governments
which had such problems to receive assistance from the UN. The
French representative got little encouragement for his proposal
that the decision should be delayed until after the World
Population Conference in September 1965. The amendment was
easily adopted by 15 votes to 2, with seven abstentions.[2] When the
draft resolution was considered by ECOSOC as a whole the
chairman, either intentionally or by oversight, did not put the
resolution to the vote but merely asked whether anyone wished
to speak. Since none of the delegates took the floor, the resolution
was recorded as having been adopted unanimously.[3]

In July 1964 the IPPF had finally gained consultative status
at ECOSOC. Sir Colville Deverill, Secretary-General of IPPF,
attending the Council meeting for the first time as an official
observer, commented: 'The passing of this resolution by so
important a body as ECOSOC suggests that it is no longer
likely that the blocs traditionally opposed to the active involvement of the UN in this field will in future feel disposed to pursue
their opposition to the length of voting against any proposals
advanced by the developing countries which are assured of
strong additional support.'[4] The adoption by the World Health
Assembly of a resolution authorizing advisory services on the
medical aspects of fertility control in May 1965,[5] seemed to confirm that the way was now open for a rapid expansion in international action. The second World Population Conference, held in
Belgrade in September 1965, provided further evidence of the
shift in opinion regarding the seriousness of the demographic
situation and the need to moderate fertility.[6]

[1] UN Doc. E/AC.7/SR.530, p. 4.   [2] Ibid., p. 16.
[3] OR of ECOSOC, 39th session, 1966, Summary records of the 1394th
meeting. For the text of the resolution see Resolution 1084(XXIX), OR of
ECOSOC 39th session, op. cit., supplement no. 1, p. 18.
[4] Quoted in *IPPF News*, no. 139, September 1965.
[5] Resolution 18.49 of the World Health Assembly, see Chapter 13, pp. 152–3.
[6] See *World Population—Challenge to Development*, Summary of the highlights of the World Population Conference, Belgrade, August–September,
1965 (UN Sales no. 66 XIII.4). See also 'Le deuxième Congrès Mondial de
la Population', *Population*, Novembre–Decembre, 1965.

THE BELGRADE WORLD POPULATION CONFERENCE

There were almost twice as many participants at the Belgrade Conference as there had been at Rome in 1954 and a greater proportion of them were from less developed countries.[1] Like the Rome Conference, but unlike the Asian Population Conference, there was no question of the conference adopting resolutions or recommendations. The ECOSOC resolution authorizing the holding of a second World Population Conference stated that it would be 'devoted to the exchange of ideas and experience on population matters among experts in the relevant fields.'[2] The Preparatory Committee defined the purpose of the conference as being to improve understanding of population problems, to stimulate interest in research and to explore ways of improving basic data.[3] However, in his opening statement to the participants, Philippe de Seynes asked 'What is it then that makes us feel, in opening this Conference—ostensibly a technical Conference—that we are taking part in an exceptional occurrence, with a political dimension . . .?' Referring to the changes in attitude which were taking place 'within the very groups which in the past showed themselves to be most concerned about possible conflicts with transcendental principles', he said that the world community expected more from the Conference than a better understanding of demographic phenomena.[4] Julia Henderson, opening the session on fertility, said that although 'prescribing solutions for population problems is not part of the terms of reference of this assembly of experts' it was hoped that the discussions would shed 'light on the paths of policy and action'.[5]

More meetings were devoted to fertility than any other topic and one whole session was devoted to 'studies relevant to family planning'. The latter proved surprisingly non-controversial. It was readily agreed that couples should have access to information to enable them to achieve the number of children they wanted, and that countries should have access to external assistance, especially advice and research.[6] In other sessions, the confrontations between demographers from Communist countries and Western countries were also less acute than in previous years. The Soviet demographer A. Boyarsky disagreed with the UN population projections which, for the first time, were

[1] *World Population Conference, 1965*, vol. I: Summary Report, p. 2.
[2] Resolution 820c(XXI) of ECOSOC, OR of ECOSOC, 31st session, 1961, supplement no. 1, p. 4.
[3] Report of the first session of the Preparatory Committee, July 1962, UN Doc. E/Conf.41/PC.1, p. 3 and p. 8.
[4] *World Population Conference, 1965*, vol. 1, op. cit., pp. 27–9.
[5] Ibid., p. 35.   [6] Ibid., pp. 110–11.

calculated to the end of the century. Instead of the 6 billion projected by the UN medium variant, he estimated that world population would be between 4·2 and 5 billion in the year 2000. Consequently, he urged, there was no cause for alarm.[1] The session on population and natural resources split along classical lines into 'technocrats' and 'neo-Malthusians'. However, as the rapporteur pointed out, 'symptoms of a new synthesis ... had been felt throughout the discussions'.[2] Marxist demographers were more willing to acknowledge the need for family planning programmes in some less developed countries, while the western proponents of birth control showed a greater awareness of the limitations of family planning and the importance of economic and social changes in bringing about changes in population trends.

Hopes that the General Assembly would give its blessing to the new interpretation of UN responsibilities were not immediately fulfilled. A draft resolution sponsored by Denmark, Ghana, India, Iraq, Iran, Kenya, Libya, Nepal, Norway, Nigeria, Pakistan, Sweden, Syria, UAR and Yugoslavia[3] met with determined opposition from Catholic countries when it was introduced in the Second Committee. They quoted Pope Paul's statement to the opening session of the Assembly that 'their task was to ensure that there was enough bread on the table of mankind and not to favour an artificial limitation of births ... in order to lessen the number of guests at the banquet of life'.[4] The representative of Ireland, which was not a member of ECOSOC, introduced a series of amendments intended to dilute the force of the draft resolution, including one which would prohibit the UN from undertaking 'operational activities in the field of family planning'.[5] A similar amendment had been successfully added to the resolution adopted by the World Health Assembly in May 1965.[6]

Despite energetic manoeuvring by the Indian delegation, no agreement was reached on the scope of technical assistance activities. Catholic countries were under strict instructions. As on previous occasions at which the Assembly had discussed population questions, the item had been placed at the end of the

[1] A. Y. Boyarsky: 'A Contribution to the Problem of World Population in the Year 2000', World Population Conference, 1965, vol. II, pp. 5–11, and vol. I, pp. 203–4.
[2] World Population Conference, 1965, vol. 1, op. cit., p. 271.
[3] UN Doc. A/C.2/L.835 and Corr. 1 and Add 1.
[4] OR of the General Assembly, 20th session, 1965. 1347th Plenary meeting, p. 4.
[5] UN Doc. A/C.2/L.842.
[6] See chapter 13.

agenda. Arguing that there was insufficient time to arrive at a satisfactory conclusion, Mr Velladao of Brazil proposed that further discussions be postponed until the next session of the Assembly. Despite protests from the sponsors of the draft resolution, the chairman, Mr Forthomme of Belgium, refused to consider a rearrangement of the work programme. The Brazilian motion was put to the vote and narrowly carried by 34 votes to 28, with 17 abstentions.[1]

This, however, would seem to have been the last stand of the opposition. When the Assembly met in 1966, the number of governments with official policies aimed at moderating the rate of population growth had grown to fourteen, while at least ten other countries were actively supporting family planning activities.[2] In May, the World Health Assembly had confirmed the right of WHO to give advisory services on the medical aspects of family planning, and the General Conference of UNESCO had adopted a resolution authorizing studies of the effect of population growth on education.[3]

On 9 December, three days before the Assembly's Economic Committee was due to discuss the question, the Secretary-General circulated a statement on population problems signed by twelve heads of state. The Declaration, issued on Human Rights Day, drew attention to the effects of rapid population growth on hopes for a better life and called on heads of state everywhere to recognize family planning as a vital interest of both the nation and the family. In a long statement to the Committee, Philippe de Seynes maintained that the Assembly had not yet tackled the problem 'with all the vigour that such an important subject deserves'. He called on members to give the necessary 'political impetus' which would enable the UN 'to go full speed ahead'.[4]

The sponsors of the draft resolution whose numbers had now increased to twenty-five, including the United States, UK and several Latin American countries, had made several changes to the text presented the previous year designed to meet the objections of Roman Catholic countries. After consultations a paragraph had been added to the preamble recognizing 'the sovereignty of nations in formulating and promoting their own population policies' and the principle that 'the size of the family should be the free choice of each individual family'. The operative paragraph, calling on interested member states, the UN and

[1] OR of the General Assembly, 20th session, 1965, Summary Records of the Second Committee, pp. 393–4.
[2] *1967 Report on the World Social Situation*, chapter 2, op. cit.
[3] See chapters 13 and 14.
[4] UN Doc. A/C.2/L.941.

the Specialized Agencies to provide technical assistance, drew attention to regional and national differences in the character of population problems.[1] As a further compromise the sponsors dropped a clause calling on member states of the UN to provide assistance with population action programmes.

These changes and what the Italian representative called 'the spirit of compromise and understanding'[2] shown by the sponsors brought about unanimous approval of the draft resolution in the Second Committee.[3] At its 1497th Plenary meeting, the Assembly also unanimously adopted the resolution.[4]

The unanimous adoption of Resolution 2211 (XXI) by the General Assembly was the cue for which those members of the Secretariat who favoured active involvement by the UN were waiting. In February 1966 the Population Branch had been upgraded to the level of Division. John Durand, who had been in charge of the Population Branch since 1955, resigned. The new director of the Population Division was Milos Macura of Yugoslavia, the first non-American to be in charge of population activities in the Secretariat. Macura had been chairman of the Ad-Hoc Committee of Experts on the Long Range Programme of Work which had drawn up the guidelines for an expanded, action-oriented role for the United Nations in the population field. In addition to being a leading professional demographer, he had also had field experience as an expert in development planning in India and Africa. Under his leadership the Population Division placed an increasing emphasis on activities at the regional level and on technical assistance. The number of staff was increased and a new unit created to deal with operational activities.[5]

At the same time, however, it was clear that existing resources were insufficient to carry out the whole of the expanded programme of activities called for in Resolution 1084 (XXXIX) of ECOSOC. Although the Assembly had endorsed the need for such an expansion, it was not at all certain that those countries which still had reservations on this question would be willing to vote the necessary extra resources, particularly since the greatest expansion was likely to be precisely in the field of technical assistance. At the 39th session of ECOSOC several delegates had suggested that it would be preferable to finance an expanded programme of activities in the population field from extra-

[1] UN Doc. A/C.2/L.936.
[2] OR of the General Assembly, 21st session, 1966, Summary Records of the Second Committee, p. 443.
[3] Ibid., p. 446. See also A/6604, Report of the Second Committee.
[4] Resolution 2211(XXI), OR of the General Assembly, 31st session, 1966, supplement, no. 16, p. 43.
[5] UN Doc. ST/SGB/128/Amend. 9, February 1966.

budgetary sources.[1] Moreover it seemed at that stage unlikely
that UNDP support would be forthcoming, since many governments would oppose any diversion of funds from economic
development into family planning. Consequently, in July 1967,
U Thant announced the creation of a special Trust Fund for
Population Activities to supplement regular budget appropria-
tions. It was estimated that an additional 5·5 million dollars
would be required over a five-year period, the major portion of
which would be allocated to the regions, principally to build up
staff resources.[2]

[1] OR of ECOSOC, 39th session, 1965. Summary records of the 1394th
meeting. See also the final paragraph of the ECOSOC Resolution 1048
(XXXVII), op. cit.
[2] Aide-Memoire on Additional Financing of the Expanded United Nations
Population Programme, July 1967. See also OR of ECOSOC, 43rd session,
July 1967, p. 3.

13

The Turning Point in WHO

O NE of the factors which complicated the debates on the population question in the UN was the lack of agreement on the fundamental question of whether rapid population growth helped or hindered economic development. Simple correlations of the two variables were, not unsurprisingly, inconclusive, while the models developed by population economists, showing that a reduction in fertility would shorten the period required to achieve a given rise in per capita income, were not properly understood by many of the delegates to ECOSOC and the General Assembly.

There was no such uncertainty regarding the effects of large families and frequent pregnancies on the health of mothers and children. Indeed, the problem had been recognized by an expert committee of the League of Nations Health Organization as early as 1931.[1] In 1951 a WHO expert committee on maternal care once again drew attention to the problem.[2] Moreover, the fact that small, planned families were healthier than large, unplanned ones, had induced several governments to accept responsibility for providing family planning advice and services. In less developed countries the problem was seen from a national, as well as an individual perspective. High fertility and the resulting high dependency ratios placed a considerable strain on already inadequate health services.

Roman Catholic countries had succeeded for many years in blocking consideration by WHO of the health aspects of population by hinting, when necessary, that they might leave the organization. After 1961, however, they found it increasingly difficult to impose their will in this field. The increase in membership, and the concern with which a growing number of governments viewed their demographic situation encouraged those who felt that WHO should be involved in family planning to discount the risks of splitting the organization.

In the general debates in the World Health Assembly in 1963[3] and 1964,[4] several delegates, including those of Jamaica, Thailand, Indonesia and Korea, urged that WHO recognize the health problems associated with rapid rates of population

[1] See Chapter 3, p. 25. [2] See Chapter 6, pp. 61–2.
[3] OR of WHO, no. 128, pp. 40 ff.
[4] OR of WHO, no. 136, pp. 51 ff.

growth. At the 17th Health Assembly in 1964, the Indian Minister of Health, Dr Sushila Nayar, said that it was no longer a matter of debate whether or not population control or population problems should figure in the activities of health agencies. She welcomed the interest taken by WHO in research into the physiology of human reproduction but hoped that before long population control would figure on the agenda of the Assembly.[1] The Brazilian delegate on the other hand declared his government's 'complete disagreement with all shades of neo-Malthusianism', and stated that 'any measures which contribute to increasing the rate of population growth are beneficial to us'.[2]

The Western Pacific region of WHO, containing three countries—Japan, Korea and Taiwan—with successful family planning programmes, was the most advanced of the WHO regional committees with regard to the involvement of the organization in family planning and population questions. In September 1964 Korea, Taiwan and the USA tabled a loosely worded resolution calling for studies of 'human population in a demographic sense' and requesting governments to exchange information on population programmes.[3] The Regional Director, Dr Fang, suggested that this would duplicate work already being carried out by the United Nations. He was supported by the Deputy Director-General of WHO, Dr Dorolle. Mr Lee, the United States sponsor, emphasized that the proposal was concerned exclusively with the health aspects of the problem which, he said, did not come within the terms of reference of the UN. The resolution was rephrased to make this clear and adopted with only one dissenting vote, that of France whose delegate explained that French territories in the Pacific had no population problems.[4]

Early in the following year, the question came up at the 35th session of the WHO Executive Board. The resolution adopted by ECOSOC in July 1964 was addressed to the Specialized Agencies as well as to the UN.[5] Dr Mutendam, Netherlands member of the Board, argued that the time had now come for WHO to decide what were its responsibilities in the field of population. He submitted a draft resolution requesting a report on the possible fields of action by WHO.[6] Support for this proposal came from several members of the Board, including Dr Evang of Norway and those from Turkey, Sierra Leone and the United Kingdom.

[1] Ibid., p. 120.   [2] Ibid., pp. 136–7.
[3] WHO Doc. WPR/RC.15/Min.3/Rev. 1, p. 128.
[4] WHO Doc. WPR/RC.15/Min.5/Rev. 1, p. 194. For the text of the resolution WPR/RC.15/R5, 'Health Aspects of Population Dynamics'.
[5] Resolution 1048(XXXVII), see Chapter 12, pp. 139–40.
[6] WHO Doc. EB.35/Min.13/Rev. 1, p. 441.

The Director-General, Dr Candau, sounded a note of caution. He described the research which WHO was already carrying out, with American funds, into the biology of human reproduction and indicated that it was intended to expand the scope of the research in order to include medical and social aspects of fertility and the relationships between population trends and health services. On the question of family planning, he said the organization was in a very different position. The Secretariat, he argued, could not be expected to take any initiative on this matter without prior approval from the World Health Assembly. He said that WHO would not participate in the meetings devoted to family planning at the forthcoming World Population Conference because it had neither the necessary authority nor experience. The same reasoning would, he concluded apply to requests for technical assistance. [1]

After some difficulties over the precise wording, a resolution was adopted which requested the Director-General to report to the 18th World Health Assembly on 'activities in health aspects of world population which might be developed by WHO'. [2]

The report, presented to the Assembly in May 1965, was mainly concerned with the research already carried out by WHO. There was, however, a short section, in the chapter on future action, referring to 'advisory services' which stated: 'WHO should be prepared to give advice on request . . . on the medical aspects and treatment of sterility and the medical aspects of family planning. It should also be in a position to advise on the place such subjects should have in the health services of the community.' [3]

Two resolutions were introduced in the Committee on Programme and Budget when it discussed the Director-General's report. The first, presented by Dr Engel of Sweden on behalf of twelve countries from Asia, the Middle East and Protestant Europe, requested the Director-General to 'develop further the programme proposed in the fields of reference services, studies and advisory services'. [4] The second, sponsored by six Latin American countries, approved the proposals for research and reference services but called for further study of the extent and variety of advisory services which WHO might provide. [5] The delegates of Ireland and Italy asked for clarification of the sort of advisory services which the Director-General envisaged that

[1] WHO Doc. EB.35/Min.13/Rev. 1, pp. 452–5.
[2] WHO Doc. EB.35/R.31. See also OR of WHO, no. 140, p. 21.
[3] OR of WHO, no. 143, Annex 18, p. 158.
[4] Ceylon, Denmark, Finland, Iceland, India, Norway, Pakistan, Korea, Sweden, Tunisia, UAR, UK. OR of WHO, no. 144, pp. 359–60.
[5] Brazil, Chile, Panama, Paraguay, Peru, Venezuela. ibid., p. 360.

WHO would provide. Dr Canaperia of Italy agreed that WHO should be able to give technical advice on the medical aspects of the methods which a government might wish to adopt. However, his government could not approve WHO involvement in decisions about population policy or 'operational-type activities in the matter of birth control'.[1]

A notable change could be seen in the position of the USA, whose representative could now quote President Johnson's pledge 'to seek new ways to use our knowledge to deal with the population explosion'. Even more striking was the admission by the observer from the Holy See that there might be circumstances in which it was a patriotic duty to limit the size of families.[2]

At Dr Canaperia's suggestion, a working group was set up to see if the two resolutions could be combined. Protracted discussions, lasting eight hours, were necessary before the working group could reach agreement. The compromise resolution which was eventually adopted made it clear that while WHO might provide advisory services on the medical aspects of fertility control, these services were to be limited to technical advice, and should not involve operational activities. The resolution emphasized that it was 'a matter for national administrations to decide whether and to what extent they should support the provision of information and services' and confirmed that it was 'not the responsibility of WHO to endorse or promote any particular population policy'.[3]

Although the chairman of the working group, Dr Watt of the USA, said that the resolution represented a 'consensus' on the question, it soon became apparent that there were conflicting interpretations of what in fact WHO was authorized to do. Some representatives believed that the reference to operational activities meant merely that WHO would not assume responsibility for the actual running of family planning clinics. It seems, however, that those who had insisted on this reservation intended a more restricted interpretation. They were also unhappy at the cordial reception given by the Secretariat to the organizers of an international conference on population and family planning programmes held in Geneva in mid-1965. The Secretariat's understanding of its mandate was outlined in the report on activities presented to the 19th Health Assembly in 1966. The report stressed the importance of training professional and nonprofessional staff, and said that WHO's main role should be to 'advise governments, on request, in the development of programmes on a demonstration basis where there is an organized

[1] Ibid., p. 369.
[2] Ibid., pp. 363–4.
[3] Resolution WHA 18.49, OR of WHO, no. 143, p. 35.

health service, without impairing its normal preventive and curative activities'.[1]

In order to clarify the situation, seventeen countries, including the USA, put forward a draft resolution at the 19th World Health Assembly in 1966 specifying that advisory services should include 'expert advice on programme planning and execution, training of personnel and programme evaluation'.[2] This was seen by other delegations as an attempt to extend the mandate given to WHO at the 18th Assembly. Dr Sow of Mali, who had been a member of the working party on that occasion, said that the draft resolution would allow WHO to assist member states in setting up family planning programmes. He argued that this contradicted the provision in the resolution adopted at the 18th Assembly that responsibility for deciding whether to disseminate information or provide services rested with national administrations.[3] Several other delegates from French-speaking African countries also spoke strongly against any extension of the existing mandate and particularly the suggestion that family planning should be considered as a normal part of maternal and child health services. Professor Vannugli of Italy said that, in his view, the programme outlined in the Director-General's report also went beyond the terms of resolution 18.49.[4] The Pakistan representative, however, asked pointedly, 'would malaria or smallpox have been eradicated . . . if WHO had merely given advice?'[5]

The Director-General, Dr Candau, made what was perhaps a decisive intervention in the debate. He said that countries were diverting funds from public health in order to establish family planning programmes. In some countries, T.B. and malaria eradication programmes had suffered accordingly. Promoters were going round the world trying to convince people that family planning should be given high priority, regardless of the size of the population. He attacked the notion that a few dollars spent on birth control gave better returns than hundreds of dollars invested in economic development, and said that if it was decided that what was necessary was not really just family planning but a reduction in the population, it was very difficult for an international organization to be party to such a decision.[6]

Almost immediately Dr Dolo, head of the Mali delegation, proposed the closure of the debate. As a result of a procedural misunderstanding, an Indian proposal to set up a working group to seek a compromise was not considered. As the Argentinian delegate pointed out, however, this made little difference, since

[1] OR of WHO, no. 151, Annex 13, pp. 63–4.
[2] OR of WHO, no. 152, pp. 367–8.
[3] Ibid., pp. 368–9.　　　　　　　　　　[4] Ibid., p. 368.
[5] Ibid., p. 372.　　　　　　　　　　　　[6] Ibid., pp. 383–4.

the area of disagreement between the two sides was so great. The chairman, Dr Nabulsi of Jordan, ruled that the committee would vote first on a counter-resolution confirming existing policy, introduced earlier by Brazil, Argentina, Austria, France, Belgium and Mexico.[1] At the request of the American delegate, the vote was taken by roll call. The resolution endorsing existing policy was easily approved by 64 votes to 19, with 13 abstentions.[2] The seventeen-power resolution was not put to the vote.

Somewhat surprisingly, several French-speaking African countries objected to a reference in the six power resolution to the need for training, and successfully pressed for its deletion.[3] The resolution as adopted did, however, state clearly that WHO could give advice 'in the development of activities in family planning, as part of an organized health service'.[4] Previous resolutions had used various circumlocutions for family planning.

When the twentieth World Health Assembly met in May 1967, the UN General Assembly had meanwhile adopted Resolution 2211 (XXI) authorizing a wide range of activities in the field of population, including the provision of technical assistance for action programmes. The emphasis placed by advocates of family planning on respect for individual and sovereign rights helped to some extent to allay the fears and misunderstandings surrounding the question. The discussion on the topic in the Committee on Programme and Budget of the World Health Assembly was visibly less tense than in the previous years.

The debate was once again marked by a vivid description from the new Indian Minister of Health and Family Planning of his country's problems. He appealed to WHO for assistance in men, money and materials.[5] Doubtless by preconcerted arrangement, delegate after delegate, including several from Latin America, got up to stress that current abortion practices were much more undesirable than contraceptives. In Colombia, abortion was stated to be the main cause of death among women of child-bearing age.[6] A unanimous resolution, introduced by Trinidad and Tobago, India and the UK, once again endorsed existing policy. It also recognized the urgent need for suitably qualified personnel and confirmed that WHO could assist 'in securing the training of university teachers and of professional staff'.[7]

*   *   *

[1] Ibid., pp. 374-5.   [2] Ibid., pp. 388-9.
[3] Ibid., pp. 381-2 and p. 388.
[4] Resolution WHA 19.43. OR of WHO, no. 151, p. 20.
[5] OR of WHO, no. 161, pp. 351-3.   [6] Ibid., p. 364.
[7] Ibid., p. 370. Resolution WHA 20.41, OR of WHO, no. 160, p. 25.

One of the factors which seems to have prompted Dr Candau to intervene in the debate in 1966 was a suggestion by the US delegate that, if requested, WHO should help to develop family planning services even where the programme was not an integral part of the maternal and child health services.[1] It was significant that the resolution presented by Brazil and other countries in 1966 repeated a remark made by Dr Candau to the effect that family planning activities should not impair the normal preventive and curative functions of health services.[2] It was generally considered within WHO, as a result of the experience with the campaign for malaria eradication, that countries needed first to concentrate on building up an infra-structure of basic health services before attempting to organize specialized services to meet specific needs.

At the 20th Health Assembly, Dr Kim of Korea pointed out that many developing countries did not have adequate maternal and child health services. Although agreeing with the principle of integration he suggested that, where necessary and acceptable, family planning services could be provided immediately and integrated within the MCH services at a later stage.[3] The Pakistan delegate, Brigadier Haque, suggested that the long term strategy implied by the approach favoured in the Secretariat did not correspond to the urgency with which many developing countries viewed the problem.[4] Most delegations, however, agreed with the strategy put forward by Dr Candau. The resolution adopted in 1967 emphasized: 'the development of basic health services is of fundamental importance in any health programme aimed at health problems associated with population'.[5] The following year the resolution adopted by the World Health Assembly recognized the difficulties involved in this approach, and requested that special attention be given to the problems connected with the integration of family planning in maternal and child health services.[6] After the meeting of the WHO/UNICEF Joint Committee on Health Policy in February 1967, UNICEF also endorsed the principle that assistance should only be given to family planning within the context of an organized health service and as part of maternal and child care.[7]

At the 19th World Health Assembly in 1966 the suggestion that family planning should be a normal part of maternal health

[1] OR of WHO, no. 152, op. cit., p. 384.
[2] Resolution WHA 19.43, op. cit.
[3] OR of WHO, no. 161, op. cit., p. 354.   [4] Ibid., pp. 361–2.
[5] Resolution WHA 20.41, op. cit.
[6] Resolution WHA 21.43. OR of WHO, no. 168, p. 21.
[7] Report of the Executive Board of UNICEF, June 1967, paras. 44–50, OR of ECOSOC, 43rd session, 1967, supplement no. 8, pp. 14–16.

services everywhere had been strenuously resisted. The resolution adopted two years later at the 21st World Health Assembly confirmed the dramatic change in attitudes that had taken place with respect to birth control. Resolution WHA 21.43, adopted unanimously, recognized that family planning was viewed by many governments as an important component in the promotion of family health and expressed the view that 'every family should have the opportunity of obtaining information and advice on problems connected with family planning'.[1]

[1] Resolution WHA 21.43, op. cit.

14

The Effects on Other UN Agencies

AFTER the breakthrough in the United Nations and in WHO, several of the Specialized Agencies, as well as UNICEF and the World Bank, embarked upon or intensified their activities in the field of population, including operational activities connected with family planning programmes. The involvement of the other members of the UN system, and the efforts directed towards coordinating activities in a multi-agency and multi-disciplinary strategy, were not achieved without controversy or considerable difficulty. Whereas there was fairly widespread agreement on the forms of assistance which the UN and WHO might provide, it was not immediately clear what role the other agencies could play. Demographic factors, particularly the very rapid increase in population in the less developed regions, had a direct effect on the work of the agencies and on their prospects for achieving the aims which they had set themselves in their respective fields. The impact of population growth on food supplies has already been noted.[1] Although the agencies used the population projections prepared by the UN, there was little co-operation between them and the UN Department of Economic and Social Affairs in demographic research into the relationships between population trends and economic and social conditions. The only Specialized Agency to have undertaken its own research in the demographic field was UNESCO. However, after the departure of Julian Huxley, this programme had been allowed to run down. In 1957, UNESCO had one professional demographer, whose work was primarily concerned with migration.

The resolutions adopted by ECOSOC in 1964 and 1965[2] called specifically on the Specialized Agencies to expand their activities in the field of population. In WHO it was the Secretariat itself which drew attention to the ECOSOC resolution. In the other agencies the initiative was taken by member states. But whereas in the earlier debates in the UN and WHO, most pressure had come from the less developed countries themselves, the leading protagonists of greater involvement were now the

[1] See Chapters 6, pp. 56–7, and 11.
[2] Resolutions 1048(XXXVII) and 1084(XXIX) of ECOSOC, op. cit., see Chapter 12, pp. 139–44.

Western capitalist countries, and in particular Sweden and the United States.

UNICEF

During the 1960s individual members of the UNICEF Executive Board, in particular Mr Thedin of Sweden, had frequently urged that an important contribution which the organization could make would be in assisting to ensure that families were so spaced as to give all children a better chance of survival and well-being. Since UNICEF functions were to provide equipment, supplies and training facilities, several governments had in fact made enquiries about the possibility of UNICEF assistance being made available to family planning programmes. A more urgent note was sounded at the Executive Board meeting in Bangkok in January 1964. Several members suggested that countries in the region should adopt population policies along the lines indicated in the recommendations of the Asian Population Conference which had just ended.[1] In a parting speech Mr Keeny, who had just retired as UNICEF Regional Director for Asia to take up a job with the Population Council, said he believed that family planning should be an integral part of every mother and child care programme.[2]

It was not, however, until June 1965 that the Executive Director, on the proposal of the USA, was asked to prepare a report on possible UNICEF action in the field of family planning. He was authorized to submit to the Board one or two requests from governments for such assistance, which would be considered in the event of a favourable decision on UNICEF involvement.[3]

Henry Labouisse, an American, had only recently become Executive Director on the death of UNICEF's first Executive Director, Maurice Pate. In May 1966 he presented a report arguing the case for UNICEF assistance for family planning on economic, social and medical grounds. The most cogent arguments were that in many less developed countries the rate of population growth was seriously outstripping the ability of the government to provide services for children, and that all too often, the early arrival of a younger brother or sister had a disastrous effect on the state of health and nutrition of older

[1] Report of the Executive Board, para. 23(b), OR of ECOSOC, 37th Session, 1964, supplement 3A, p. 9.
[2] UN Doc. E/ICEF/SR.301, p. 4.
[3] UN Doc. E/ICEF/SR.324, pp. 6 ff. See also Report of the Executive Board, June 1965, paras. 107–119, OR of ECOSOC, 39th session, 1965, supplement no. 15, pp. 32–5.

children and their mother.[1] He also presented requests for assistance, mainly vehicles and audio-visual equipment, from India and Pakistan.[2] He proposed that UNICEF should be prepared to offer assistance with training, public health education, supplies and equipment for family planning centres, transport and support for maternal and child health centres which included family planning activities. Where family planning services were provided through maternal and child health centres, he said that there should be no difficulty about UNICEF assistance. But he also invited the Board to extend assistance to services which were provided outside the framework of maternal and child health organizations of member states. He felt that UNICEF should not provide contraceptive supplies or equipment for their manufacture because, he said, 'inter alia, other sources of supply seem to be adequate for the moment'.[3]

The debate in the UNICEF Executive Board in June 1966 was almost as impassioned as that in the World Health Assembly in 1952. The opposition was led by Switzerland, whose representative said he was disturbed at UNICEF's 'unseemly haste' and warned that UNICEF must not get ahead of WHO. He insisted on the need to safeguard the rights of the individual and the integrity of the human person, and referred to the existence of 'sterilization camps' in India, an allegation refuted by the Indian representative.[4] The Belgian member felt that the proposals could endanger the organization's very existence. He warned that if they became UNICEF policy as a result of a majority vote, 'a number of members would doubtless consider themselves released from their obligations'.[5] This line of argument was stated even more bluntly by the chairman of the Irish National Committee for UNICEF, Mr Donohue. He said he would be 'reluctant to hand the private contributions raised in his country over to UNICEF, if they were to be used to prevent children being born'.[6] Senegal suggested that the spread of contraceptive methods would increase prostitution. The USSR considered that UNICEF participation in family planning activities would be 'contrary to the spirit and letter of its mandate'.

The most eloquent support came from India and Pakistan. In response to arguments that there was insufficient knowledge of the medical aspects of family planning, the latter said that Pakistan 'could not afford to wait'. Among the principal contributors, the

[1] UN Doc. E/ICEF/L.1259, 'Family Planning: Report of the Executive Director on the possible role of UNICEF'.
[2] UN Doc. E/ICEF/P/L.754 and E/ICEF/P/L.755.
[3] UN Doc. E/ICEF/L.1259, op. cit., pp. 46–7 and p. 51.
[4] UN Doc. E/ICEF/SR.357, pp. 5–8.
[5] Ibid., p. 9.   [6] UN Doc. E/ICEF/SR.349, p. 7.

USA, UK and Sweden were firmly behind the proposals. Some-what surprisingly, the French member of the Board also approv-ed UNICEF involvement, providing certain conditions, similar to those agreed in WHO, were accepted. There was general Asian support. Of the African members who spoke, Nigeria was in favour, Morocco indecisive, whilst Ethiopia and Senegal were opposed. The Latin American countries were all opposed, Brazil arguing that there were many other projects which deserved priority.

Finally, as in the debate in WHO in 1965, a working party was set up, consisting of Ethiopia, France, Peru, Sweden, Switzerland, Tunisia, USSR and USA, to see if a compromise could be found. The resolution which was eventually adopted was a disappointment to those members who wished to see UNICEF active in this field. The Executive Director's report was not endorsed, and the whole matter was referred to the UNICEF–WHO Joint Committee on Health Policy. The requests from India and Pakistan were withdrawn, since they would not have met the conditions on which the working party had insisted. It was agreed that discussions would be held with the governments concerned to see if revised requests could be drawn up.[1]

The Joint Committee on Health Policy met in February 1967. The principle that UNICEF assistance should only be given as part of a country's health service and not as a separate category of assistance was endorsed by the WHO representatives, who argued that family planning was most effective where it was introduced as an integral part of maternal and child care. The Committee therefore recommended that UNICEF assistance should be given to requesting governments for the development of maternal and child health services, including family planning, and drew attention to the need for trained personnel. The deci-sion to exclude contraceptive supplies was upheld.[2]

The recommendations were approved by the UNICEF Execu-tive Board when it met in June 1967.[3] Sweden, Pakistan and India were not fully satisfied with the arrangements, but said that they would accept the decision as a compromise.[4] The requests for assistance from India and Pakistan, substantially revised, had meanwhile been approved by a mail poll of members.

[1] UN Doc. E/ICEF/SR.351. See also Report of the Executive Board, May 1966, paras. 166–91, OR of ECOSOC, 41st session, 1966, supplement no. 13, pp. 54–61.
[2] UN Doc. E/ICEF/556, section 10, pp. 13–15. Report of the 15th session of the JCHP.
[3] Report of the Executive Board, June 1967, para. 56, OR of ECOSOC, 43rd session, 1967, supplement no. 8, p. 17.
[4] UN Doc. E/ICEF/SR.361.

The forms of assistance offered by UNICEF, especially vehicles and clinical equipment, were a valuable addition to the external assistance available for family planning. In many less developed countries, the foreign exchange costs of such items constituted a serious bottleneck in the expansion of programmes. Between 1967–70, UNICEF provided help to India, Korea, Malaysia, Pakistan, Singapore, Thailand and UAR. By August 1969, more than 3·3 million US dollars had been allocated for the development of family planning programmes within maternal and child health services.[1] Such was the demand that in 1970 it had proved impossible to meet requests from four countries because of lack of funds. The Executive Director made an appeal for special contributions and entered into discussions with the United Nations Fund for Population Activities.[2]

UNESCO

As seen earlier, Julian Huxley, the first Director-General of UNESCO, had sought, unsuccessfully, to draw the attention of member states to the disastrous effects that overpopulation would have on the quality of human civilization.[3] When, in 1966, the population problem was raised in UNESCO for a second time, the approach was markedly different. The Swedish representative at the General Conference in 1966 proposed that an advisory committee be set up to advise on sociological factors relating to population, as part of the long range programme of work called for in Resolution 1084(XXXIX) of ECOSOC.[4] Although there was some criticism from Ireland, Italy and Argentina, the conference unanimously adopted a resolution approving the inclusion of a small sum in the regular budget to finance research into the relationship between the development of education and the evolution of population, and requesting the Director-General to report to the Executive Board on the question of UNESCO's responsibilities in the field of population. He was invited to convene a meeting of experts to advise on the subject and in particular on the possibility that UNESCO might act as a clearing house for information on family planning.[5] The Director-General was also authorized 'to help member states, on

---

[1] UN Doc. E/CN.9/234/Add.4. 'Activities and Programmes of UNICEF in the Field of Population', pp. 2–3.
[2] UN Doc. E/ICEF/602. General progress report of the Executive Director, March 1970.
[3] See Chapter 6, pp. 53–4.
[4] 14th General Conference of UNESCO, 1966. Programme Committee, 20th meeting.
[5] Resolution 3.252. 14th General Conference, op. cit.

request, to conduct scientific studies on the effectiveness of various means of education and information used (in) family planning'.[1]

The report of the experts was presented to the Executive Board at its 77th session in October 1967. Its main emphasis was on research, including the use of mass media, to promote family planning and ways of educating populations, particularly women, about the implications of rapid population growth. The report proposed that no decision be taken on the clearing house until more was known about the needs for such a centre and the plans of other organizations interested in this field.[2] In the Executive Board Mr Hela of Finland, who said he was speaking on behalf of all the Scandinavian countries, criticized the report for its conservatism. 'Scientific studies', he said, 'would not solve the population problem.' The representatives of India, Nigeria and the USA also felt that the programme should be more action-oriented.[3] The Board approved the general lines of policy laid down in the report, but noted the comments made in the discussion.[4]

During the discussion the Secretariat had pointed out in defence of its proposals that no requests for assistance with action programmes had been received. Shortly after the session three countries, UAR, Pakistan and Tunisia, submitted projects, and six others, including India, indicated interest in obtaining assistance.

When the General Conference met in November 1968, the Swedish delegation introduced a long draft resolution setting out a comprehensive programme of research and operational activities which covered almost every aspect of the UNESCO programme. It suggested that the purpose of UNESCO's involvement in this field should be 'to promote a better understanding of the serious responsibilities which population growth imposes on individuals, nations and the whole international community . . .'[5] Although several delegations continued to have reservations about the direction in which UNESCO seemed to be moving, the Swedish proposal was finally adopted without opposition and with only minor modifications.[6] The Swedish government had also indicated its willingness to provide 'seed money' to allow a rapid expansion of operational activities.

[1] 14th General Conference, op. cit., Approved Programme and Budget, para. 1233-7.
[2] UNESCO Doc. 77/EX/13. Report by the Director-General on UNESCO'S responsibilities in the field of population.
[3] UNESCO, Minutes of the Executive Board, 77th session, 1967, pp. 202 ff.
[4] Resolution 4.4.1 of the Executive Board, 77th session.
[5] UNESCO Doc. 15.C/DR.52.
[6] 15th General Conference of UNESCO, 1968. Report of the Programme Committee, part II, section 1.24.

Belgium, France and several other delegations expressed their concern at this move, claiming that it would duplicate the Trust Fund created by the Secretary-General of the United Nations. However, it was pointed out that the Director-General could not very well refuse money offered by member states, and the matter was not pursued.

An unusual incident occurred during the final discussion of the draft resolution in plenary session. The Director-General objected to an operational paragraph requesting him to appoint a programme specialist whose job would be to stimulate and advise on projects and to coordinate the activities of the various technical departments of the Secretariat. Mr Maheu pointed out that it was not the responsibility of the Conference to tell him what sort of staff to appoint. He asked if they also intended to specify the colour of the specialist's eyes and the length of his hair![1] The offending paragraph was removed and the resolution was adopted by 56 votes to none with 13 abstentions.[2]

In several countries, where the initial response to the provision of family planning services had been encouraging, programmes were now running into difficulties in persuading young couples with small families to practice contraception. It was found that acceptors tended on the whole to be older couples who had already reached the family size they wanted. Moreover, many of them were merely switching from a relatively inefficient method of fertility control, such as coitus interruptus, to the more effective methods provided by the family planning clinics. At the same time it was clear that in most of the less developed countries the mere provision of family planning services was unlikely to lead to any significant reduction in the birth rate because desired family size was between four to six children. For governments concerned with the economic consequences of rapid population growth, the problem was essentially one of how to bring about suitable changes in traditional pro-natalist beliefs and customs. Fertility surveys showed a definite link between the level of education and family size. It was therefore felt that UNESCO, as the agency in the UN system with responsibility for education and mass communication, was potentially in a position to make a key contribution to the further development of family planning programmes.

[1] Idem, 40th Plenary meeting, p. 30.
[2] Resolution 1.241, 15th General Conference of UNESCO, Resolutions, pp. 23-5.

THE INTERNATIONAL LABOUR ORGANIZATION

Since 1950 the reports of the Director-General had contained occasional allusions to the problems posed by rapid population growth. There was, however, no further mention of the need for a 'positive population policy'.[1] In 1964 the International Labour Conference adopted a recommendation on employment policy which contained a discreet reference to population growth. Countries in which population was increasing rapidly were urged to 'study the economic, social and demographic factors affecting population with a view to adopting economic and social policies which made for a better balance between the growth of employment opportunities and the growth of the labour force'.[2]

The question of the involvement of the ILO in family planning in order to support population control policies was first raised openly in 1966. As in several other agencies, the initiative was taken by the Swedish delegation. Mr Bengtsson, Swedish government representative, introduced a resolution which re-affirmed concern with the effects of rapid population growth on employment opportunities and referred also to its adverse effects on living standards. Although population growth clearly affected the work of the ILO, it was not immediately clear what role the organization could play in measures to slow it down. The Swedish resolution ingeniously listed the various activities carried out by the ILO through which family planning education and services might be channelled. He proposed, for example, that family planning education be included in the curricula of vocational training programmes which were supported by the ILO, and that employers be encouraged to offer services to their workers. The resolution also called for a comprehensive study of the problem of population growth, living standards and employment, in cooperation with UN, to serve as a basis for future action in this field.[3]

The resolution was opposed by many delegations, particularly those of France and the French-speaking countries of Africa. They argued that it was not for the ILO to become involved in the provision of family planning services or the promotion of contraception among workers. As in the UN General Assembly, where the Catholic countries had succeeded in preventing a vote

[1] See Chapter 6, pp. 57–8.
[2] Recommendation 122 concerning employment policy, para. 28. International Labour Conference, 48th Session, 1964. Record of Proceedings, p. 918.
[3] Resolution concerning activities of the ILO in the field of population. ILC 50th session, 1966. Record of Proceedings, Appendix IV, Resolutions, pp. 508–9.

on the resolution submitted by ECOSOC, their efforts behind the scenes at the International Labour Conference proved successful. The Committee on resolutions declared that it was unable to find time to give proper consideration to the Swedish resolution.[1]

The debate, however, continued at the regional level. At the Conference of American States Members of the ILO, held in Ottawa in September 1966, Willard Wirtz, US Secretary of Labour, argued that efforts to promote the development of human resources would be wasted if they failed to take into account the resources required to educate and equip the rapidly growing population.[2] The government representative of Argentina, Mr Tamborena, argued that while he recognized the gravity of the problem in some regions he could not accept any solution which would limit what he called 'the sacred right to life'.[3] In reply, Wilfred Jenks, the ILO's Principal Deputy Director-General, suggested that it was precisely respect for the sacred character of human life which imposed an obligation to ensure that population growth did not outstrip the resources required to provide everyone with a full and useful life.[4]

In November, the ILO's Asian Advisory Committee recommended that, in view of the effects of rapid population growth on family income and welfare and on the employment situation, 'countries should consider the adoption of a population policy suited to national considerations.'[5] The Governing Body adopted the Committee's report despite an observation by the government delegate of the USSR, Mrs Mironova, that other international organizations were more competent to deal with population questions and that 'no useful purpose would be served by discussing them in the Governing Body'.[6]

When the International Labour Conference met in June 1967, Mr Bengtsson, supported by the government representatives of India and Kenya, introduced a new resolution under the heading 'the influence of rapid population growth on opportunities for training and employment and on the welfare of workers'. Referring to recommendations of the Asian Advisory Committee and to the General Assembly resolution, the new draft emphasized that 'governments as well as trade unions and employers'

[1] ILC, 50th session, 1966. Record of Proceedings, op. cit., p. 528.
[2] Octava Conferencia de los Estados de América Miembros de la Organización Internacional de Trabajo, Ottawa, Septiembre de 1966. Actas, p. 38.
[3] Ibid., p. 84.
[4] Ibid., p. 203.
[5] Report of the 13th session of the Asian Advisory Committee, Singapore, November–December 1966, para. 4. See Minutes of the Governing Body, 168th session, February–March 1967, p. 69.
[6] Minutes of the GB, 168th session, op. cit., p. 20.

organizations have an important role to play in creating awareness of the implications of rapid population growth in developing countries'. The operative paragraphs were deliberately restrained. The Governing Body was invited to request the Director-General to arrange for a study of the problem in co-operation with other agencies and, in the light of the study, to submit proposals for action.[1]

There was widespread support in the resolutions committee for the new text which, the committee pointed out, was 'moderate, precise and devoid of rhetoric'.[2] Carefully shepherded by Wilfred Jenks, the resolution was unanimously adopted by the International Labour Conference.[3]

At the next session of the ILO's Governing Body, the sponsors of the resolution emphasized the urgency of the problem which, according to Mr Mbathi of Kenya, was not fully conveyed in the proposals put forward by the Office.[4] The Director-General explained that the ILO's activities had to be coordinated with those of the other UN agencies, particularly the United Nations itself which had primary responsibilities in this field. Nevertheless, he welcomed the comments as proof of a desire to see the organization fully involved in family planning. It was agreed that the Office should 'pursue as a matter of urgency' the preparatory work on the study. The Director-General was asked to report to the May 1968 session of the Governing Body on the progress made on the study and the results of inter-agency consultations.[5] The progress report was not ready for the May session and further discussion was postponed until November.

Meanwhile vigorous support for an active role had come from the Asian members of the ILO. The Sixth Asian Regional Conference, meeting in Tokyo in September 1968, declared its conviction that 'there can be no lasting solution of employment problems in most Asian countries unless the current high rate of population growth is reduced'. The resolution was introduced by Nawal Tata, employers' representative from India. The Tata industrial group, one of the largest in India, had for several years provided family planning services to its employees. The resolution urged Asian countries '(a) to adopt population policies suited

[1] Resolution concerning the influence of rapid population growth on opportunities for training and employment and on welfare of workers. ILC, 51st session, 1967. Record of Proceedings, Appendix IV, Resolutions, pp. 550–1.
[2] Record of Proceedings, pp. 564–5.
[3] Ibid., p. 500. For the final text, see Resolutions adopted by the ILC at its 51st session, Geneva, 1967, resolution IV, pp. 5–7.
[4] Minutes of the GB, 170th session, November–December 1967, p. 20. See also Appendix III: Action to be taken on resolutions adopted by the ILC, pp. 64–5. [5] Ibid.

to national conditions ... (b) to consider ... the provision of adequate information, practical education, health and advisory services ... to workers and their families and (c) to enlist the full cooperation of employers and workers and their organizations in planning and carrying out these activities'. The resolution further requested the Governing Body to authorize the provision of technical assistance to deal with population problems as a complement to the Asian Manpower Plan.[1] Fifty-four delegates voted in favour, none against, while fifteen, including the USSR, Vietnam and Iran, abstained.

When the Governing Body met in November, it had before it a preliminary draft of the study on the influence of rapid population growth on opportunities for training and employment and on the welfare of workers, as well as proposals for future action by the ILO in the population field.[2] The first part of the paper submitted by the Office dealt with ILO activities to further economic and social development in order to meet the 'population challenge'.[3] The second part was concerned with the possible contribution of the organization to the problem of slowing the rate of population growth. It pointed out that, although population control did not fall directly within the ILO's mandate, continuing high fertility was frustrating the attainment of ILO objectives in the economic and social field. Because of its experience and its contacts with workers and employers, the ILO could make a 'distinctive' contribution to lowering birth rates by supporting the other international agencies which had primary responsibility in this field.[4]

The lines of action put forward in the paper reflected the proposals contained in the original Swedish resolution. These included information and educational activities among employers and trade unions and the inclusion of family planning in the health services provided at the plant-level or as a part of social security. The latter represented a change in thinking on the part of the Office: until the resolution of the Asian Regional Conference, it had been felt that the provision of family planning advice and services was the exclusive responsibility of WHO. The paper also emphasized the need for research, particularly in respect of the effect of social security measures on family building patterns.[5]

---

[1] Resolution concerning the Asian Manpower Plan and population policy. Sixth Asian Regional Conference, Tokyo, 1968. Proceedings, pp. 227–8. See also 6th Report of Selection Committee, Discussion of a draft resolution, p. 205, and Record of Twelfth sitting of conference, pp. 166–82.

[2] Minutes of the GB, 173rd session, Appendix IV, 'ILO Action on Population Questions', pp. 63–82.

[3] Ibid., paras. 17–23, pp. 65–6.   [4] Ibid., para. 26, p. 66.

[5] Ibid., paras. 31–44, pp. 67–9.

The proposals were welcomed by the Governing Body. Mr Aström of Sweden expressed his government's satisfaction at the action taken on its resolution. Mr Parodi of France, made one of the most positive statements by a French representative on the need to control population growth.[1] Mr Lawyer, government delegate of the USA, also supported the proposals for action and hinted at American support for an increase in the funds allocated for population activities in the regular budget. However, he criticized the study on the influence of population growth on employment and welfare, because, he said, it placed insufficient emphasis on the benefits to workers of family limitation and because it failed to express a clear-cut opinion on the effects of rapid population growth on the economic and social development of less developed countries.[2]

In view of Mr Lawyer's comments, the Office decided to retain the study for substantial revision before publishing it. The proposals for action were endorsed[3] and work began on the preparation of specific projects. It was not, however, until after the decision in June 1969 to extend the Trust Fund to the Specialized Agencies that operational activities began.

THE FOOD AND AGRICULTURE ORGANIZATION

In UNESCO and ILO the immediate response to the changes in national and international attitudes on the population question was to give greater recognition to the effects of rapid population growth on the work of these agencies. Thus, in UNESCO, the resolution adopted in 1966 called for a programme of studies on the relationship between population changes and educational development, while, in 1967, the International Labour Conference authorized a study of the effects of rapid population growth on opportunities for training and employment and on the welfare of workers. FAO, on the other hand, had itself been instrumental in bringing the population problem to the attention of the world community.[4] For B. R. Sen, population control was an integral part of development strategy and a necessary complement to efforts to increase food production. His aim, however, was to get others to act since, as he had said with reference to Arnold Toynbee's lecture, 'We in FAO, must concentrate on the responsibilities set out in our charter.'[5] His successor, A. H. Boerma shared this view. 'I do not believe', he said, 'it is our task

[1] ILO, Minutes of the GB, op. cit., Fourth sitting, p. 21.
[2] Ibid., p. 19.   [3] Ibid., p. 22.
[4] See Chapter 11.
[5] FAO Doc., C/59/PV.3, p. 17.

to pioneer the introduction of family planning techniques as such.'[1]

However, FAO, like ILO, carried out programmes through which information about population problems and family planning could be transmitted. Moreover, most national family planning programmes were making slow progress among FAO's constituents—the rural population—who generally had little inducement to practice family planning. In 1967 the FAO Conference approved a new educational programme, 'Planning for Better Family Living', which would operate through home economics centres and include information on the relationship between rapid population growth and hunger, malnutrition, ill-health and low standards of living.[2]

THE WORLD BANK

The World Bank is one of the most important sources of finance for development projects. Like any bank it is interested in the performance of its borrowers, although its ability to effect changes in the policies of countries to which it lends money is limited by the need to respect the susceptibilities of national sovereignty.

The Coale and Hoover study on India, published in 1958,[3] had received financial and technical support from the World Bank. Its conclusions, notably that a reduction in fertility would facilitate a more rapid increase in per capita income, made a considerable impact on thinking on this question within the Bank. However, the hostility which greeted Eugene Black's remarks to ECOSOC in 1961 on the need for fertility control[4] reinforced the feeling that extreme care should be exercised in this area. Nevertheless, some World Bank country reports drew attention to the demographic situation and its implications. In Thailand, for example, official discussion of the need for measures to slow down the rate of population growth were prompted by the report of a World Bank mission.[5]

In June 1967 it was decided that all country reports should contain information on the country's demographic situation and, where relevant, information on government population policies. The President of the World Bank, George Woods, in a statement in January 1968, welcomed the changes in attitude on the population question which had taken place in recent years and said

[1] Interview in *Ceres*, March–April 1968, op. cit.
[2] Report of the 14th session of the FAO Conference, 1967.
[3] A. J. Coale and E. M. Hoover, *Population Growth and Economic Development in Low-Income Countries*, op. cit.   [4] See Chapter 10, p. 117.
[5] Population Council, *Country Profiles*, 'Thailand', May 1969, p. 3.

that the Bank favoured policies to reduce the birth rate in countries where excessive population growth inhibited economic development. He warned that population control should not be viewed as 'a bargain basement substitute for development aid' but said that the Bank was giving increasing attention to its borrowers' policies on population as an indication of their commitment to economic growth.[1] This statement was reflected in new instructions issued for World Bank missions in April 1968.

A development of far-reaching significance occurred in September 1968. In his first address to the Bank's governors, the new President, Robert S. McNamara, announced active involvement by the Bank in population control measures. He proposed three courses of action: 'first, to let the developing countries know the extent to which rapid population growth slows down their potential development, . . . second, to seek opportunities to finance family planning programmes and third, to join with others in programmes of research to determine the most effective means of family planning'.[2]

Mr McNamara followed up his statement to the Board of Governors in a speech on the population question at the Roman Catholic University of Notre-Dame in May 1969. Referring to the question as 'the most delicate and difficult issue of our era' he said: 'To put it simply, the greatest single obstacle to the economic and social advancement of the majority of the peoples in the underdeveloped world is rampant population growth.'[3]

The speech was greeted with enthusiasm in the United States and in other donor countries where public opinion regarding population growth had swung rapidly from indifference to alarm. In the underdeveloped countries themselves the response was mixed. In a number of countries, particularly in Latin America and Africa, there was suspicion of the motives behind the speech. It was alleged that the 'population explosion' was an 'imperialist smokescreen' designed to divert attention away from the real causes of poverty. The drop in foreign aid added to these suspicions.[4]

If, as Mr McNamara claimed, rampant population growth was the single most important obstacle to economic development, the logical conclusion might be to make World Bank loans and other forms of external assistance conditional on the adoption of effective policies designed to moderate fertility. The

[1] Statement on population problems and family planning, 25 January 1968. A modified version appears in *Victor Fund Report*, no. 8, Spring 1968, pp. 16–17.

[2] Address to the Board of Governors, Washington, 30 September 1968.

[3] Address to the University of Notre-Dame, 14 May 1969.

[4] See, for example, J. Mayone Stycos: 'Politics and Population Control in Latin America', *World Politics*, October 1967, pp. 66–82.

dangers of even appearing to impose such a condition were obvious. In his speech at the University of Notre-Dame, Mc-Namara had said that it was 'essential to recognize the right of a given country to handle its population problem in its own way'. The developed countries, he continued, 'can—and should—inform. They should not—and cannot—pressure'.[1]

The scope for direct action by the World Bank appeared in fact somewhat limited. In most countries the need was for technical advice rather than financial assistance. Nor was it certain that governments would seek loans on standard World Bank terms for family planning activities in light of the growing amount of finance available on more favourable terms from bilateral sources and other international agencies. The indications were that the World Bank was prepared to relax its normal conditions in this field. Negotiations were held with the Indian government and, in July 1970, the World Bank announced its first loan, to Jamaica, to finance the expansion of the main Kingston maternity hospital, where one quarter of all the island's births took place, and for the construction and equipment of ten rural maternity centres.

[1] Address to the University of Notre-Dame, op. cit.

Part VI

THE DEVELOPMENT OF AN ACTION PROGRAMME (1967–1970)

'The achievement of the objectives of social progress and development . . . requires the formulation and establishment, as needed, of programmes in the field of population, within the framework of national demographic policies and as a part of the welfare medical services, including education, training of personnel and the provision to families of the knowledge and means necessary to determine freely and responsibly the number and spacing of their children.'

Declaration on Social Progress and Development; United Nations General Assembly Resolution 2542(XXIV), 1969

15

Towards a World Population Policy?

IN July 1967 U Thant, in referring to the population question in his statement to ECOSOC, stated that 'on the strength of a historic General Assembly resolution the UN can now embark upon a bolder and more effective programme of action'.[1] Resolution 2211(XXI) had not only confirmed that the UN had the right to provide assistance for national family planning programmes, but also endorsed recommendations made by its subsidiary bodies that the future programme should give more attention to fertility and ways of controlling it.

Controversy on the population question was, however, far from over. Apart from the practical difficulties of translating new mandates into a coherent work programme, of obtaining the necessary resources and of ensuring coordination between the agencies involved, there were still important areas of disagreement. These included, notably, the central but unresolved question of the relationship between population growth and economic development and the extent to which governments, and therefore, by implication, the international community, could legitimately intervene in individual decisions about family size.

Many of the governments which had voted for the General Assembly resolution in 1966 had done so with reservations. It was to be expected that they would show little enthusiasm for substantial increases in the resources allocated to population activities, especially if these were to be used to support family planning. The establishment of the Secretary-General's Trust Fund in July 1967 to finance the expanded programme of work removed this difficulty, at least to some extent. However several developments which occurred after 1967 served to increase their hesitations with regard to the direction in which the UN seemed to be moving.

The most important was that in several of the developed countries of the West, in particular the USA, it began to be argued with much greater conviction that rapid population growth not only made economic development more difficult but could in many cases frustrate it completely. Although the representatives of the countries involved did not draw the conclusion, publicly at least, that economic assistance should be made conditional on the adoption of effective measures to slow down the

[1] UN Doc., SG/SM/51, 11 July 1967, p. 3.

rate of population growth, some of them pointed out that they could not be indifferent to the attitude of a potential aid recipient towards this question. This position had been World Bank policy for several years.[1] In 1969 it was supported by the Pearson Commission, the 'grand assize' set up by Robert McNamara[2] and by a panel of experts, under the chairmanship of John D. Rockefeller III, established by the United Nations Association of the USA.[3]

Meanwhile there was a reawakening of interest in developed countries in the global and ecological aspects of the population question to which Julian Huxley and others had drawn attention in the early fifties. It was calculated that if all the world were to enjoy the same standard of living as the presently developed countries even a rate of population growth of only 1 or 1·5 per cent would place intolerable strains on the earth's finite resources and delicate ecological balance.[4] Population control aiming at a 'zero growth' rate, was urged as an essential part of the preservation of the environment and, by implication, of human existence itself.[5] From the less developed countries the reply came that whilst the rich countries might be alarmed at what they called the 'effluent society', for the poor countries this represented a paradise in comparison to their present poverty. Not surprisingly they were suspicious of the motives behind the call for 'population' control. The Victor-Bostrom Fund Report for Spring 1970 was devoted to the topic 'Population: A Challenge to the Environment': juxtaposed on the cover were two scenes, one of a quiet New England countryside and the other of a vast crowd of impoverished Asians.[6] Several observers warned that the Western obsession with population control served only to arouse controversy, thereby hindering the development of family planning programmes.[7]

A second factor which influenced the evolution of attitudes within the UN was the debate among demographers, economists

[1] See Chapter 14, p. 171.
[2] *Partners in Development: Report of the Commission on International Development*, op. cit., chapter 10.
[3] *World Population—A Challenge to the United Nations and its System of Agencies: Report of a National Policy Panel* established by the United Nations Associations of the USA, New York, 1969.
[4] See, for example, 'Population and Resources: the Coming Collision', *Population Bulletin* (Population Reference Bureau), June 1970; and Preston Cloud: 'Resources, Population and Quality of Life', Address to the Annual Meeting of the American Association for the Advancement of Science, Boston, 29 December 1969.
[5] See, for example, Paul Ehrlich, *The Population Bomb*, New York, 1968.
[6] *Victor-Bostrom Fund Report*, no. 13, Spring 1970. The editorial began 'Whatever your cause, it's a lost cause unless we control population'.
[7] See, for example, G. Myrdal, *Asian Drama*, op. cit., vol. II, pp. 1494–5.

and family planning professionals over the kind of measures required to make family planning programmes effective. The debate was mainly occasioned by an article by a leading American demographer, and former member of the Population Commission, Kingsley Davis, in which he argued that it was illusory to expect family planning to solve the population problem. 'There is no reason,' he said, 'to expect that the millions of decisions about family size made by couples in their own interest will automatically control population for the benefit of society'. Family planning strategy was based on the assumption that couples had more children than they wanted, and that the provision of services would therefore bring about a reduction in fertility. Davis argued that even if the programmes were successful in reducing the gap between wanted and unwanted children, the desired family size in most of the less developed countries implied a rate of population growth in excess of that considered necessary from the point of view of economic development. He said that if what was needed was population control, governments would have to intervene more actively, for example, through encouraging later marriages and by providing incentives for smaller families.[1]

In 1960 the American economist Stephen Enke had proposed the introduction of a system of cash incentives to couples who accepted contraception or who abstained from childbearing for a given period.[2] Other critics of contemporary family planning programmes now went still further and suggested the addition of fertility control agents to water supplies or to staple foods.[3]

Bernard Berelson, President of the Population Council, replied to the various proposals for making programmes more effective in a speech at an international conference of family planners in Pakistan in January 1969.[4] It was, he said, ironic that no sooner had family planning been accepted as a human right by the major organs of the UN system than others were seeking to take away this right. He argued that none of the proposals which had so far been advanced satisfied basic criteria of technological readiness, political viability, administrative feasibility, economic

[1] Kingsley Davis: 'Population Control: Will Current Programs Succeed', presented at the annual meeting of the National Research Council, 14 March 1967, and reprinted in *Science*, vol. 158, 10 November 1967, pp. 730–9.

[2] Stephen Enke, 'The Economics of Government Payments to Limit Population', *Economic Development and Cultural Change*, July 1960, pp. 339–48.

[3] See, for example, M. Ketchel, 'Fertility Control Agents as a Possible Solution to the World Population Problem', *Perspectives in Biology and Medicine*, vol. 11, 1968, pp. 678–703.

[4] B. Berelson, 'Beyond Family Planning', paper presented at the International Family Planning Conference, Dacca, Pakistan, January 1969, reprinted in *Studies in Family Planning*, no. 38, February 1969.

capability, ethical acceptability and presumed effectiveness. He urged instead that current family planning programmes should be implemented more energetically. Both sides in the debate agreed, however, that governments could not be passive or indifferent with regard to population growth and that they should accept responsibility not only for encouraging the practice of contraception but also for encouraging couples to want fewer children.

FAMILY PLANNING AS A BASIC HUMAN RIGHT or FAMILY PLANNING AND HUMAN RIGHTS

As Berelson had pointed out, family planning had been proclaimed as a basic human right. There was in the words of the Secretary-General in his statement to ECOSOC in July 1967 a willingness to look at the population question 'not simply in its strict economic aspects, more or less linked to the Malthusian dilemma, but rather in the broad perspective of human progress in modern societies . . .'[1] The principle that every couple had the right to decide on the number and spacing of their children had been included in resolutions adopted by the World Health Assembly and the UN General Assembly. It was also stressed in the Declaration on Population, issued in December 1966 and subsequently signed by thirty heads of state.[2] The continued interest in family planning shown by the Commission on the Status of Women also helped to emphasize the aspect of human rights.[3]

The International Conference on Human Rights sponsored by the United Nations in Teheran in May 1968 marked a further step in this direction. Forty-nine countries, including the Holy See, voted in favour of a resolution introduced by UAR on behalf also of Chile, Finland, India, Morocco, Pakistan, Sweden, Tunisia, Turkey, UK and Yugoslavia. The resolution affirmed that couples had a basic human right, not only to decide freely and responsibly on the number and spacing of their children, but also to have adequate education and information on how to do so. Even more strikingly it included the observation that 'the present rate of population growth in some areas of the world hampers the struggle against hunger and poverty and in parti-

[1] UN Doc. SG/SM/51, op. cit.
[2] Declaration on Population by World Leaders, December 1967. See *Population Newsletter*, no. 1, April 1968, NY, UN Population Division, pp. 43–5.
[3] In June 1968 ECOSOC approved a proposal by the Commission on the Status of Women for the appointment of a special rapporteur to continue the study of family planning and the status of women. See Resolution 1326(XLIV) of ECOSOC, 44th session, 1968, supplement no. 1. See also UN Doc. E/CN.6/497, 'Family Planning and the Status of Women' Interim report of the Secretary-General, 1968.

cular reduces the possibilities of rapidly achieving adequate standards of living . . . thereby impairing the full realization of human rights'.[1]

The inclusion of this principle in these key resolutions was seized on by the family planning movement and its supporters among member governments. They had argued for many years not only that all children should be wanted children, but also, by implication, that governments had an obligation to accept responsibility for the provision of family planning advice and services in order to enable couples to plan the size of their families. Some who voted for the resolutions, however, seem to have intended the insistence on the right of couples to decide on the number and spacing of their children as a disavowal of government measures, such as mass education campaigns or bonuses and incentives, designed to influence decisions about family size. Thus in July 1968, the French representative on ECOSOC drew a distinction between family planning and birth control. He said: 'That process whereby the population un-balance resulting from the fall in the death rate was to be corrected by deliberately reducing the birth rate was called "family planning" although, in fact, it implied birth control measures resulting not from the free decisions of individuals or families, but from the application of a veritable national policy.' He asked, 'How could a state population policy be justified . . . if birth control rested upon a basic human right?'[2]

The division became very apparent later in 1968 when the General Assembly discussed the draft Declaration on Social Progress and Development. After heated discussion it was agreed to include a clause in the section on 'Principles' reaffirm-ing the exclusive right of parents to decide on the number and spacing of their children.[3] Part III of the draft Declaration covered 'Means and Methods'. When this was discussed by the Third Committee in 1969 there was strong opposition to the suggestion that couples should have not only the knowledge but also the means to enable them to decide on the number and spacing of their children. The representative of Argentina said 'the establishment of norms . . . in a declaration by the UN amounted to an inadmissible interference in something which was exclusively a matter for individual conscience'.[4] Brazil complained that birth control was presented as some kind of 'magical solution'.[5] However, the Finnish representative argued

[1] Resolution XVIII of the International Conference on Human Rights, Teheran, April–May 1968 (UN Doc. A/CONF.32/41), chapter III.

[2] UN Doc. E/AC.6/SR. 453.

[3] UN Doc. A/C.3/SR.1599–1601. See also A/7374, Report of the Third Committee.   [4] UN Doc. A/C.3/SR.1682, p. 2.   [5] Ibid., p. 3.

convincingly that couples had to have both the knowledge and the means to plan their families, otherwise the right to do so would remain an empty word. A leading role in obtaining agreement was taken by the representative of Sierra Leone, who pointed out to his African colleagues that the text did not state that government policies should necessarily have as their objective a reduction in the rate of population growth. The Irish representative nevertheless insisted on a separate vote on the words 'and means', which were upheld by 64 votes to 16 with 17 abstentions.[1] Finally, only six countries, Argentina, Brazil, Cuba, Gabon, Nicaragua and Portugal, opposed as a whole the paragraph which called for the 'formulation and establishment, as needed, of programmes in the field of population, within the framework of national demographic policies and as part of the welfare medical services, including education, the training of personnel and the provision to families of the knowledge and means necessary to enable them to exercise their right to determine freely and responsibly, the number and spacing of their children'.[2]

The difference of emphasis with respect to the role of the UN system was underlined in the discussions in ECOSOC and in the Populations Commission in 1967.

On the one hand, in June 1967, several delegates in the newly reorganized Committee on Programme and Co-ordination of ECOSOC, including those of Britain, USA, India and Ghana, pressed strongly for firm evidence that the UN Secretariat was responding to its new mandate.[3] In its report the Committee recognized the importance of research and projections, but suggested that these should be restricted to studies which could serve as practical tools for policy making.[4] On the other hand when the Population Commission met in October 1967 to consider the two and five year programmes of work, several members warned against the danger of an imbalance developing in the UN's population programme. They argued that the main role of the Commission, and therefore of the Population Division, was to provide information and analysis on which governments could base their policies. A vote was necessary on the question of giving high priority to the study of fertility and to technical assistance for family planning.[5]

[1] UN Doc. A/C.3/SR.1684, pp. 2–6.

[2] UN Doc. A/PV.1829. For the text of the Declaration see Resolution 2542(XXIV), articles 4 and 22, OR of the General Assembly, 24th session, 1969, supplement no. 30, pp. 49–52.   [3] UN Doc. E/AC.51/SR.42–44.

[4] UN Doc. E/4383, Report of the Committee on Programme and Co-ordination on the first part of its first session, May 1967, para. 65.

[5] UN Doc. E/CN.9/SR.218, p. 5 and Report of the 14th session of the Population Commission, OR of ECOSOC, 44th session, 1968, supplement no. 9, paras. 23–4.

The Commission's report was a disappointment to some delegations. When the Commission's recommendations were discussed in the Economic Committee of ECOSOC in July 1968, the US representative strongly criticized what he called the conservatism of the Population Commission. 'His country' he said, 'had hoped that when the Commission marked its twentieth anniversary . . . it would reorient its work in the light of the increased attention being given by the UN system to the developing countries' needs in the population field. Unfortunately, the Commission had continued to spend virtually all of its time on problems which were primarily of interest to a small number of specialists in demography and statistics, and had given limited attention to the practical problems of population growth and economic development and to technical assistance problems.'[1]

Other countries, including India, Turkey, Japan, Sweden and Iran, also considered that the work programme should place greater emphasis on technical assistance activities, particularly family planning. The representatives of less developed countries were, however, noticeably less insistent on this approach than the United States, while the Swedish representative pointed out that 'family planning was basically a social and medical question rather than an economic one'.[2] Some delegations interpreted the American intervention as an attempt to subordinate the whole of the UN's activities in the field of population to population control. The delegate from Upper Volta hoped it was not the policy of the UN 'to wage war against fertility in all States'. He said that 'what was wanted in Africa was to increase people's skills, not to limit their numbers'.[3] The representative of Venezuela said that 'it was essential to recognize . . . that there was no simple solution to the problem and that it would be a mistake to try and solve it solely by means of birth control measures'.[4] Argentina, France and the Soviet Union also emphasized the complexity of the population problem and the dangers of attempting to apply a universal solution.

Finally, the Committee passed by 14 votes to 4 a resolution containing a clause requesting UNDP to give 'due consideration to . . . projects designed to assist developing countries in dealing with population problems'.[5] When the draft resolution was put to the vote in plenary session, France joined the countries opposed to UNDP involvement. Mr Viaud said that 'the resources of UNDP were too limited for part of them to be devoted to a small group of countries whose problems, though acute, were not

[1] UN Doc. E/AC.6/SR.454, pp. 5–6.   [2] Ibid., p. 3.
[3] UN Doc. E/AC.6/SR.456, p. 3.
[4] UN Doc. E/AC.6/SR.453, p. 18.
[5] UN Doc. E/AC.6/SR.463, p. 10.

universal.'[1] The clause was once again upheld, but by only 12 votes to 7.[2]

The greater opposition which the action clause encountered in the plenary was due to the publication of the Papal encyclical 'Humanae Vitae' in the course of the session. To the surprise and indeed consternation of many Catholics, the encyclical rejected the advice of the majority of the Church's Commission on birth control. Of particular significance in the United Nation's debates was a section addressed to the 'Rulers of Nations'.[3] A passage in an earlier encyclical by Pope Paul VI, 'Populorum Progressio', given in March 1967, had been seized on by many as an indication that the Church would not stand in the way of those whose religious beliefs did not condemn birth control.[4] 'Humanae Vitae', however, made it clear that the teaching of the Vatican was intended to apply to Catholics and non-Catholics alike.

Further proof that controversy was still alive came at the end of 1970 when the General Assembly debated a resolution coming up from ECOSOC which proposed that 1974 be designated 'World Population Year'. The representative of Senegal suggested that the function of the UN was to foster and protect human lives and not to prevent them from blooming even if they disturbed the peace of mind which the affluent societies sought to conserve.[5] The ECOSOC report was attacked because it was considered to imply that the world's population needed to be reduced. Among African representatives who claimed that their countries were under-populated were those of Senegal, the Central African Republic, Upper Volta, Gabon and Libya: Latin American representatives who took the same line were those of Brazil, Bolivia, Argentina, Chile and Peru. Syria also claimed to be under-populated. The representative of Chile alleged that population growth problems were artificially emphasized by developed countries as an excuse for them to escape from their obligations to the international community. The USSR joined in the attack on the ECOSOC report, which was described as more a form of advertisement than a scientific attempt to solve important population questions. Although the ECOSOC proposal for the designation of 1974 as 'World Population Year' was eventually passed by 53 votes to 9, it was in a modified form and there were 33 abstentions.[6]

[1] OR of ECOSOC, 45th session, 1968, p. 159.
[2] Ibid. For the text of the resolution see Resolution 1347(XLV), OR of ECOSOC, 34th session, 1968, supplement no. 1, p. 2.
[3] Encylical letter of Pope Paul VI, 'Humanae Vitae . . .', 1968, para 23.
[4] See Chapter 11, p.131.   [5] UN Doc. A/C.2/SR.1324, p. 23.
[6] UN Doc. A/C.2/SR.1352-3. For the text of the resolution see Resolution 2683(XXV), OR of the General Assembly, 25th session, 1970, supplement no. 28, pp. 55-6.

The opposition seems, in part, to have been provoked by the insistence of the President of the World Bank on the need of population control. In the debate in the General Assembly in 1970 several delegates referred specifically to recent speeches by Mr McNamara in which they claimed he had failed to recognize that some countries needed larger populations. In his first address to the Board of Governors in September 1968 he had indeed said, 'More than anything else it is the population explosion, which by holding back the advancement of the poor, is blowing apart the rich and the poor and widening the already dangerous gap between them.' Emphasizing that what he called 'the drag of excessive population growth' operated quite independently of population size or density, he asserted: 'It is a false claim that some countries need more population to fill their land or accelerate their economic growth'.[1] In his addresses to the Board of Governors in 1969 and in 1970 he devoted a major part of his report to the urgent need to bring about a decline in fertility.[2]

The resolutions adopted by the United Nations had repeatedly affirmed the right of governments to formulate their own population policies. Moreover, these resolutions had almost invariably included a reference to the need to take into account regional and national differences when proposing action programmes. However, the implication of the position adopted by Mr McNamara and others appeared to be that the economic development of all poor countries was threatened by rapid population growth. Opposition to this point of view was clearly reflected in the place assigned to population in the Declaration on the Second United Nations Development Decade.

POPULATION AND THE SECOND DEVELOPMENT DECADE

The Economic and Social Council had appointed a group of experts under Professor Tinbergen of Rotterdam to advise on plans for the Decade. The group, whose formal title was the Committee on Development of Planning, suggested an overall target for the Decade of a 6 to 7% annual increase in GNP and a 3·5 to 4·5% annual increase in per capita income. These targets were, however, based on an average rate of population growth of 2·5% per annum, which was lower than the figure of around 2·8% then forecast by the United Nations Population Division. To achieve a more rapid rate of growth in per capita income, it

[1] Address to the Board of Governors, September 1968, op. cit.
[2] Address to the Board of Governors, September 1969, and idem, September 1970.

was argued, would require a further reduction in the rate of population growth. The Committee suggested that 'the world community should formulate its position with regard to population growth' and that the Declaration on the Second Development Decade should call on countries which suffered from a problem of population growth 'to introduce effective population policies including the possession, by the end of the Decade, of a family planning service which is truly available to at least half the population'.[1]

At the fifteenth session of the Population Commission in November 1969, General Draper, the new American member, introduced a draft resolution calling on the Preparatory Committee to include in the Declaration a text recognizing that 'throughout most of the world efforts to promote economic and social development ... will be in large measure offset and frustrated if present rates of population growth continue.'[2]

This resolution received a mixed reception. Alfred Sauvy of France, supported by Mr Podyachick of the USSR and Mr Madeira of Brazil, argued that it was a gross oversimplification to say that rapid population growth was the major impediment to economic development and that, as a result, all developing countries should seek to moderate fertility. Although Sweden and the UAR welcomed the American draft, other members who normally supported population programmes, including UK, Jamaica, Ghana, Indonesia and India, expressed reservations. In the draft resolution which was finally adopted the American proposal was considerably modified; the key sentence recommended for consideration by the Preparatory Committee stated that 'in some parts of the world (economic and social development) could be frustrated by the continuance of present high rates of population growth'.[3] The resolution was supported by all representatives except those of Brazil, Venezuela and the Communist countries.[4]

Meanwhile the Preparatory Committee established by the General Assembly had begun consideration of policy measures in key areas, including population. The draft paragraphs prepared by the Secretariat were as forthright as the original draft

[1] UN Doc. E/4682. Report of the 4th and 5th sessions of the Committee on Development Planning, para. 19.

[2] UN Doc. E/CN.9/L.84.

[3] UN Doc. E/CN.9/L.84/Rev.2.

[4] Report of the 15th session of the Population Commission, OR of ECOSOC, 48th session, 1970, supplement no. 3, paras. 88–90 and Draft Resolutions, p. 50. The resolution was adopted by ECOSOC with only minor changes. See E/AC.6/SR.507 and Resolution 1483(XLVIII), OR of ECOSOC, 48th session, op. cit., supplement no. 1, p. 2.

resolution tabled in the Population Commission by General Draper: it was suggested that in order to minimize the adverse effects of rapid population growth on living standards each government should formulate a population policy; governments should encourage responsible attitudes towards family size and should make family planning advice and services widely available; and finally, developed countries should increase the amount of their assistance to population activities.[1]

The text which was adopted by the Preparatory Committee, however, stated merely that 'those developing countries which consider that their rate of population growth hampers their development will adopt measures which they deem necessary in accordance with their concept of development'. While international organizations and those developed countries which considered this to be important would continue to assist less developed countries in research and family planning, it was emphasized that such assistance was not a substitute for other forms of development assistance.[2]

The representatives of Norway, Pakistan and the United States expressed their disappointment with the paragraph, which they said did not adequately reflect the urgency of the problem. The US representative, Mr Reinstein, said that his delegation was also disappointed at the manner in which the Committee had considered the question. No consideration had been given to the text proposed by the Population Commission and endorsed by ECOSOC. The representatives of Latin American countries, on the other hand, expressed satisfaction that governments which did not consider population growth to be a crucial issue were left free to adopt whatever measures they considered appropriate.[3]

When the General Assembly met at the end of 1970 to adopt the strategy for the Second United Nations Development Decade, it approved without discussion the paragraphs relating to population policy proposed by the Preparatory Committee. In the section dealing with objectives the Declaration noted that the targets for the decade were based on an annual rate of population growth of 2·5% which was lower than that estimated by the UN. 'In this context,' it said, 'each developing country should formulate its own demographic objectives within the framework of its development plan.'[4]

[1] UN Doc. A/AC.141/L.20. 'International Development Strategy for the 1970s. Draft Paragraphs Relating to Human Development'. Note by the Secretariat, pp. 2–3.

[2] UN Doc. A/7982, Report of the Preparatory Committee for the Second United Nations Development Decade on its 6th session, para. 62.

[3] UN Doc. A/AC.141/SR. 58.

[4] Resolution 2626(XXV) paras. 15 and 65, OR of the General Assembly, 25th session, 1970, supplement no. 28, pp. 39–48.

The Committee on Development Planning had suggested that the world community should formulate its position with regard to population. As we have seen, however, in the preparation of the development strategy for the 1970s, as in earlier debates, the member states of the UN had deliberately avoided taking up a position either on the desirability of family planning or on the need to control population growth in the interests of economic and social development.

The right of couples to obtain advice and information on family planning had been affirmed in resolutions adopted between 1967 and 1970. However, the responsibility of governments to provide the necessary advice and services was not made explicit. The Committee on Development Planning had recommended that the development of family planning programmes should be one of the objectives of the Decade. The Executive Heads of the UN agencies in a collective statement to ECOSOC in July 1969 had also urged that all governments, regardless of their demographic objectives, should take steps to provide each family in the community with access to family planning services.[1] WHO as the agency within the UN system with the primary responsibility for family planning was placed in a delicate position. From a health point of view the need for planned parenthood was overwhelming. However, under the terms of the mandate established by resolutions of the World Health Assembly it was to be the responsibility of the government requesting assistance, without advice from WHO, to determine its attitude towards family planning.[2]

A somewhat similar contradiction existed with regard to population policies. Once it was recommended that governments should have population policies, it became difficult for the UN, as part of its economic planning advisory services, to avoid responsibility for advising, on request, as to what the size or rate of increase should be. The Population Commission had argued in 1961: 'it is in the interests of the UN that decisions on national policies should be taken in the light of knowledge of the relevant facts and that the programmes should be adequate to ensure satisfactory economic and social progress'.[3] To many the facts seemed fairly clear: rapid population growth was not only a hindrance to the economic and social development of less developed countries but also, if the present rates of increase

[1] UN Doc. E/4718. Statement on the Second United Nations Development Decade, June 1969, para. 19.

[2] UN Doc. E/ICEF/556. Note by the WHO Secretariat to the WHO/UNICEF Joint Health Policy Committee, February 1967, p. 3.

[3] Report on the 11th session of the Population Commission 1961, para. 15, op. cit.

were to continue, a threat to the well being, and possibly even the survival, of both rich and poor countries. What was needed therefore, they considered, was a world policy for restricting population growth.

However, although in the UN and in the World Bank there were signs of a willingness to advance beyond neutrality on this issue, on the evidence available at the end of 1970 it seemed that it could be many years before national states were ready to accept more than a very gentle guidance from the UN.

16

The Search for a Combined Strategy

WHEN in July 1967 the Secretary-General of the United Nations established a Trust Fund for Population Activities, to which governments, non-governmental organizations and private sources were invited to contribute, family planning was not emphasized. The purpose of the Fund was to finance the five year programme of work of the United Nations itself; the main elements in this were the training of demographers, the provision of research and information services of current importance for policy formulation by governments and the extension of advisory and technical assistance services. The sum of $5·5 million was stated to be required for the programme over the period 1967–1971.

This modest initiative was seen, however, in various influential quarters as an opportunity to involve the whole United Nations system of agencies in a much more ambitious role of assistance to governments in the population field, and in particular in family planning.

Much of the pressure came from the United States. In November 1967 the US Congress had approved a bill introduced by Senator Fulbright, providing for greatly increased American assistance for family planning and population programmes. The large amount of money available was, paradoxically, something of an embarrassment in view of the cut back in the overall aid budget. The American government therefore was anxious to channel as much of these funds as possible through the UN system and through non-governmental bodies, provided that there was a guarantee that the money would be used for operational activities. Shortly after the Fund was established, the United States Government made an earmarked grant to it to enable the United Nations Population Division to appoint Population Programme Officers in the field who would help governments to prepare requests for assistance. Professor Richard Gardner, a former American representative in the General Assembly, in a book published early in 1968, suggested that a World Population Programme be established with an annual budget of $50 million, to be administered by UNDP and operated through the UN and the Specialized Agencies, with the aim of making contraceptive facilities available to all fertile couples in

188

developing countries.[1] About the same time, General Draper, Chairman of the Population Crisis Committee, submitted proposals to the Secretary-General for the massive involvement of the UN agencies in family planning programmes: when the Republicans came into office in 1969 he became the US representative on the UN Population Commission. Whilst the Democrats were still in office the US representative in ECOSOC was Arthur Goldschmidt, a former senior official of UNTAA who had long felt that the UN should be more active in the population field. The statements of Robert McNamara, who was not only President of the World Bank but also an influential figure in the Democratic establishment, have been mentioned in the last chapter. Henry Labouisse, the American Executive Director of UNICEF also played a leading part in interagency discussions on population, and eventually in May 1970 was to persuade the UNICEF Executive Board to remove restrictions on the supply of contraceptives.[2]

In 1968 the Secretary-General appointed a consultant, Richard Symonds, to advise on the use of the Trust Fund and on the role of the UN in population action programmes. Symonds' report, submitted in 1968 and published in an abbreviated form in 1969, recommended that the Fund be expanded to support programmes of the Specialized Agencies and UNICEF, as well as of the UN itself, at an annual level of $5 million in the first year, $10 million in the second and $20 million in the third. The Fund should be used to finance not only technical assistance but research, transport and equipment: it should also be more flexible than other UN technical assistance programmes in financing local costs and using local institutions to carry out research. Whilst not rejecting the ultimate establishment of a UN population agency, the report proposed as an immediate measure the appointment of a UN Commissioner for Population Programmes, with a staff drawn from all the UN agencies concerned, who would co-ordinate the programme and whose status would enable him to attend the ACC meetings of the Executive Heads of Agencies.[3]

At about the same time the United Nations Association of the USA appointed a panel which produced a report in 1969 entitled *World Population—A Challenge to the United Nations and its*

[1] R. N. Gardner, 'Toward a World Population Program' in R. N. Gardner and M. Millikan (eds.) *The Global Partnership: International Agencies and Development,* New York, 1968, pp. 357–61.

[2] Report of the Executive Board.

[3] Report on the United Nations Trust Fund for Population Activities and the Role of the United Nations in Population Action Programmes, UN Doc. ST/SOA/Ser.R/10, pp. 28–9.

System of Agencies. The composition of the panel was impressive and the weight of its report correspondingly important. John D. Rockefeller III was chairman and George Woods, former President of the World Bank, vice-chairman. Among the members were David Bell of the Ford Foundation, the demographers Ansley Coale and Frank Notestein, the future Secretary of State William D. Rogers, David Hannah, Director of USAID, Professor Richard Gardner and William Thorp, former chairman of the Development Assistance Committee of OECD. The rapporteur was a young Englishman, Stanley Johnson, who was a former official of the World Bank. The UNA report called for an expansion of the UN Population Trust Fund to $100 million a year in order to support activities of the Specialized Agencies as well as of UN, and recommended that a Population Commissioner be appointed within UNDP.[1]

As noted in both reports, the distinctive role of several of the UN agencies was beginning to emerge as a result of new mandates. The role of the UN itself was seen as (*a*) to assist governments in determining the size of their populations and to assess population trends; (*b*) to assist governments to understand the consequences of population trends in relation to economic and social development; (*c*) to assist governments to formulate population policies, taking into account all factors which affect fertility; (*d*) to assist governments which adopt population policies in carrying out and evaluating measures to which affect fertility. The main role of WHO was seen as helping governments to establish family planning services within health services, the training of medical and paramedical personnel and research on human reproduction. That of UNESCO would be in mass communication, training of demographers at university level, education on population questions in schools and through adult education programmes. UNICEF would support WHO programmes, and perhaps those of other agencies, with supplies and equipment. ILO and FAO would have a less important role, the former through workers' education and health services in industry, the latter through its home economics programmes. The World Bank would provide loans to finance the establishment of family planning clinics and the local manufacture of contraceptives.

The American approach was centralist. By making a substantial contribution to a central fund, which would then allocate resources to the various UN Agencies with relevant mandates, it was believed that a positively co-ordinated direction could be assured in the population field at a time when the UN system

[1] *World Population—Challenge to Development,* op. cit.

was under considerable criticism for the general lack of co-ordination in its approach to economic and social development. In contrast, the Swedish Government adopted quite different tactics by offering special contributions, earmarked for family planning activities, directly to individual agencies, such as UNESCO and UNICEF, in order to persuade them to broaden the interpretation of their mandates.

These pressures on the whole fell on willing shoulders in the secretariats of the UN agencies, though WHO for some time remained in a special position. Thus the Secretary-General of the United Nations, U Thant, told ECOSOC in 1968: 'From all the quarters directly interested in this problem there is a call for UN leadership. Now that certain inhibitions have finally been lost, it is for us to establish the need and the programming machinery to help governments in preparing projects, including pilot projects in family planning . . . The financial requirements involved are not so considerable that they should be invoked against more widespread and effective efforts.'[1]

Within the UNDP Governing Council, though there was strong support for involvement in family planning, there was also considerable opposition which took the form of argument that funds contributed for economic development should not be diverted to this field. Paul Hoffman, the Administrator of UNDP, made no secret of his view that the UN agencies needed to play a much more important part in population action programmes. In May 1967 Resident Representatives had been instructed to assist governments to formulate requests in this field. Hoffman therefore indicated his interest in obtaining additional contributions, in the form of funds-in-trust, to finance family planning activities.

Although the Commission on International Development, of which Lester B. Pearson was chairman, also endorsed the proposal that a UN Population Commissioner be appointed,[2] a somewhat different arrangement was made in the middle of 1969, when action was taken which did much to implement the recommendations of the Symonds and UNA reports. Responsibility for the operation of the Trust Fund, now called UN Fund for Population Activities (UNFPA) was transferred by the Secretary-General to UNDP, within which Paul Hoffman appointed Rafael Salas, a former Filipino cabinet minister and senior official, as Director of the Fund. Under the new arrangements the Director of the Fund was to use the technical resources of the United Nations Population Division in developing its programme. The Specialized Agencies and UNICEF were

---

[1] UN Doc. SG/SM/65, 8 July 1968.
[2] *Partners in Development*, op. cit., p. 197.

informed that their programmes were now eligible for financing by the Fund. Further, its scope had been extended to cover types of aid other than the conventional forms of technical assistance, so that it could be used to provide equipment and supplies and to support local costs.[1]

Announcing these decisions to the 15th session of the Population Commission in November 1969, Salas concluded 'The Secretary-General and Mr Hoffman intend the Fund to be "action orientated", that is, to be devoted to the most effective ways available towards the solution of population problems by those countries having such problems and requesting the assistance of the Fund . . . Since population problems relate to the whole fabric of a society, projects and programmes will, in many cases, not break down neatly along the lines of academic disciplines or organizational jurisdictions. An imaginative approach and the closest possible co-operation and co-ordination on population projects and programmes will be required among the various elements of the UN system.'[2]

Here indeed was a problem. At the end of 1969 there appeared Sir Robert Jackson's *Study of the Capacity of the UN Development System*,[3] the most vivid, and indeed brilliant, critical account of the UN agencies' approach to development ever to appear as an official UN document. Jackson's criticism of 'a system without a brain' and of consequent competition for business between the UN agencies in their technical assistance programmes described a general situation in which hitherto population had been an exception. For, whereas in various fields such as agricultural education, water use and the establishment of small industries, the UN agencies had been in competition to assert mandates which often overlapped, in the field of population the position had been quite different. For years WHO had been reluctant to give advice on the health aspects, whilst UNESCO had avoided involvement in the educational aspects of family planning. On the other hand, the United Nations, a number of whose officials believed that family planning and population policies were essential to development, had been more prepared to stretch its mandate to fill the vacuum. Thus in the Indian family planning evaluation mission of 1965 the United Nations appointed physicians as members of the team, because WHO was unable to collaborate.

[1] UN Doc. DP/CM/189. Circular Letter on the UN Fund for Population Activities, October 1969.

[2] Population Commission, 15th session, Conference Room Paper no. 9: Statement by Mr R. Salas, Director of the UN Fund for Population Activities, 10 November 1969.

[3] *Study of the Capacity of the United Nations Development System.* UN Doc. DP/5 1969.

However, between 1967 and 1969, as has been seen, the mandates of all agencies concerned UN, WHO, UNESCO, ILO, FAO, UNICEF, as well as the World Bank and UNDP were extended to authorize them to collaborate in action programmes in family planning, even though there was still the distinction that WHO and UNICEF could only give assistance to family planning programmes which were within the health services.

Moreover, the inhibitions of the Executive Heads of the UN Agencies regarding their involvement in population action programmes seemed completely to have disappeared. In July 1969, in a joint statement on the Second Development Decade, they affirmed that rapid population growth would be a major limiting factor on development in the 1970s, particularly in the fields of education, housing and employment. They suggested that all countries, regardless of their population situation, needed to introduce family planning as part of their health services.[1]

The creation of a substantial Population Fund within UNDP also considerably altered the picture. It had been an argument in the legislatures of the UN agencies, and even in the secretariats, that development funds should not be diverted to population programmes. Now additional resources, specifically earmarked for population activities were available. All who wrote on the subject—Gardner, Symonds, the UNA report and Pearson, emphasized the distinctive role of the UN agencies in a situation in which bilateral agencies had to tread delicately to avoid accusations of 'genocide'. In some countries, ministers who wanted to adopt population policies, but who had to guard their flanks against Church, Army, Marxist or nationalist criticism, were eager for a UN initiative.

Yet even for the United Nations agencies an individual approach was needed in this delicate field, related to the special situation of each country. It might be through the Ministry of Economic Affairs, whose development and employment targets were not met because of population increase; or through the Ministry of Education, unable to fulfil a commitment to provide free universal primary education; or through a Ministry of Health, preoccupied both with providing health and family planning services; or through a Ministry of Food and Agriculture harassed by the spectre of famine. To develop and carry through the right approach might require the skills of demography, economics, sociology, public health, education, mass communications and public administration. Whereas in bilateral aid programmes representatives of these disciplines could quite easily be brought together or consulted, in the UN system the responsi-

[1] ACC Statement on the Second Development Decade, op. cit.

bilities were scattered between different agencies whose head-quarters were located in different places.

As mandates were extended and funds for action programmes became available, the question of how to co-ordinate and make maximum use of the resources of each of these agencies assumed importance. From 1968 the Population Sub-committee of ACC had enabled the agencies to exchange information on their evolving mandates and activities. At the fifteenth session of the Population Commission in November 1969 Mrs Lindstrom of Sweden doubted whether the existing machinery 'would be strong and effective enough to create the necessary leadership for an integrated approach'. She suggested that the Fund needed a director with the status of a high commissioner and with sufficient authority to enable him to negotiate with heads of state and members of the ACC on an equal footing.[1] As has been seen the United States also urged the Fund to assume a much more active role in coordinating and promoting operational activities by the UN organizations concerned. Other donors to UNFPA also looked to the Fund to act as the 'brain' of the system in the field of population.

When the administration of the Fund was transferred to UNDP in June 1969, responsibility for the technical appraisal of projects was at first retained by the UN Population Division. At the end of 1969 UNFPA took over the function and began to build up its own expertise and staff. The Fund showed itself to be more flexible than the normal technical assistance programmes of the United Nations system, for example, in the negotiation of comprehensive family planning projects in Pakistan and Mauritius in which a number of UN agencies would be involved, in the provision of grants for the construction of facilities, and in making use of agencies outside the UN family. It had also made rapid financial progress. In 1969 it financed programmes costing $5 million. In 1970 over $10 million were contributed by twenty-four governments and the target for 1971 was $24 million.

Not surprisingly, the growing autonomy and resources of the Fund were viewed with mixed feelings in the Secretariats of the UN agencies. In addition, several members of the Population Commission in 1969 saw the expansion of the Fund, and in particular the decision to create an Advisory Board, as a threat to the Commission's own responsibilities for population policies and programmes. Alfred Sauvy made a strong intervention in which he complained that the Fund was run by a small group of donors and that no means existed whereby the majority of member states could exercise control over its activities. He was supported by Brazil and the Soviet Union. Mr Podyachick also

[1] Population Commission, 15th session, Conference Room Paper no. 11.

opposed the idea of an UN Commissioner for population programmes.[1]

The Commission's final report reaffirmed the responsibility of the Population Commission for the population activities of the UN and stressed the need to preserve a balance between family planning and other activities and to safeguard the international character of the Fund.[2]

As Sauvy had pointed out, the Fund was not responsible to any inter-governmental body. The Administrator of UNDP in deciding on the policy and programmes of the Fund drew on the advice of three bodies: an Advisory Board composed of twenty eminent persons, including B. R. Sen and John D. Rockefeller III, chosen by the Secretary-General; an Inter-Agency Consultative Committee; and a Programme Consultative Committee consisting of government donor agencies and non-governmental organizations engaged in population activities.[3]

The establishment of a World Population Agency, as foreseen by Lord Brain in his presidential address to the British Association in 1964[4] at first sight might appear the best way to cut through the jungle of co-ordination and to enable the resources of all relevant disciplines to be concentrated in population action programmes: certainly independent Specialized Agencies have been set up in fields of less importance. The membership of such an agency would, however, be much less than universal at present. In July 1968, after the publication of the Papal encyclical 'Humanae Vitae', the paragraph in an ECOSOC resolution which asked UNDP to give assistance in population programmes was approved only by 12 votes to 7, with 4 abstentions while, as late as 1970, there were 33 abstentions and 9 negative votes on a resolution designating 1974 as 'World Population Year'.[5] Acquiescence in the present rather untidy and ambiguous arrangements might be considerably easier for a number of governments than would be the positive action of joining a new agency, at least until the Vatican alters its attitude. Moreover, experience in other fields indicated that when a new agency is created the problems of co-ordination are not necessarily settled, since it may encounter considerable resistance in persuading existing agencies to surrender part of their responsibilities to it.

Meanwhile effective co-ordination might be fostered in two

[1] Report of the 15th session of the Population Commission, op. cit., para. 60.
[2] Ibid., para 61.
[3] UN Doc. DP/L.168/Add.1 Activities of UNDP in 1970—Trust Fund Administration. See also *Population Newsletter*, no. 8, March 1970, NY, UN Population Division, pp. 9–13.
[4] See Lord Brain: *Science and Man*, New York, 1968, p. 33.
[5] See Chapter 15, p.182.

ways. Firstly the Director of the Fund for Population Activities might build up a combined planning staff of experts in the main relevant fields, such as demography, health and administrative aspects of family planning, education and communications, who could be on secondment from the UN and Specialized Agencies. Secondly the inter-disciplinary attack might be carried on at a more profound level through the proposed World Population Institute. It was encouraging that in 1970 a joint mission of UN, WHO and UNESCO representatives, led by David Morse, the former Director-General of ILO, proposed the early establishment of such an institute jointly by the United Nations, WHO and UNESCO. Out of the teaching and research programmes of this institute, if established, it could be hoped that a deeper recognition of the respective contributions of the various disciplines, as well as new habits of co-operation in action, might permeate the agencies themselves.[1]

If eventually a new UN agency is created, its mandate may perhaps encompass the problems of the environment as well as of population. Indeed it is likely to seem remarkable to future generations that whilst much attention was given in the 19th and early 20th centuries to the relationship between animals and their environment (the science of game cropping being a recent example) so little was given to that between man and his environment. An agency which was concerned both with population and environment problems, which are confronted both by rich and poor countries, could have a broader and more successful appeal than one which was only concerned with population, and which could be seen by the people of poor countries as an arena in which the patronizing representatives of rich countries urged them to have smaller families and to accept population control programmes, in order to avoid the much heavier burden of having to finance economic and social development.

[1] Report on the Feasibility of Establishing a World Population Institute, UN Doc. ST/SOA/Ser.R/12, 1971.

17
Conclusions

DURING the period covered by this study, 1945–70, the world's population increased by 40 per cent and in 1970 it was expected to double by the end of the century.

Within the period international interest in the population question shifted to focus on quite different aspects. The consequences of malaria eradication and improved public health at first concentrated attention on the dramatic rate of population increase. 'Will there be room for us all on the planet in a few hundred years'? was the kind of question popularly asked. Then the problem was seen as one of food. *Nous allons à la Famine* was the title of a book by a famous French agronomist which had the misfortune to appear just as the 'green revolution', with its sensational rise in wheat and rice yields, caused a relaxation of concern as to the world's capacity to feed itself. The emphasis now changed to the limits set by population growth on the rate of economic and social development in the poor countries, in terms of the percentage of inhabitants for whom schools, health services and jobs could be provided; whilst in the rich countries there was a wave of alarm about pollution and the damage to the environment caused by an increase in population and in consumption.

There were still countries which wanted larger populations, France, Australia, Brazil and some of the sub-Saharan African countries being among them. Far more countries were concerned to limit the rate of population increase. Perhaps the most important change within the period was recognition that population growth was a variable which was susceptible to influence. It was increasingly agreed that every country should have a population policy, and that there were measures quite apart from provision of family planning facilities, such as education of girls, regulation of age of marriage, taxation and housing policies, which could be used to influence the rate of growth. Whilst there was still no global population policy, at least in Asia and in some western countries there appeared to be consciousness of a need for one.

Another major change was an almost universal recognition, despite the theological morass from which the Roman Catholic Church was struggling to extricate itself, that every family had the right to the knowledge and means of controlling reproduction.

It would be somewhat ingenuous to ask 'could the United Nations have done more' to bring such changes about more rapidly, or even to promote a world population policy: for the United Nations and its associated agencies are collectivities of sovereign states, and a lesson of our study seems to be that reluctant members, even when in a minority, can halt the pace of change. In favourable circumstances the Executive Heads could exercise leadership. The contrast is interesting between the attitudes of Chisholm and Candau in WHO: between that of Sen and his predecessors in FAO; between that of Huxley and his successors in UNESCO, and indeed in the United Nations itself between that of Hammarskjöld and of U Thant. It is natural that some of the Executive Heads were influenced by their own national and cultural background and experience. Some observers considered that Chisholm, although, as a psychiatrist, in favour of making birth control facilities widely available, was too pessimistic about making progress in WHO when opposed by the Roman Catholic Church because of his experience in Canada, where the Church's opposition had been particularly formidable. Sen and U Thant as Asians could probably take a more positive attitude than European or American Executive Heads at a time when Asian governments were the first to adopt population policies. There was a considerable difference between their positions however. Sen did not have to carry his Conference and Council with him: his was a propaganda campaign for which budgetary support was not required. U Thant and some of his senior colleagues in UN on the other hand were exercising leadership in relation to ECOSOC and the General Assembly and were interpreting resolutions as broadly as possible in order to enable action programmes to be carried out.

Some of those involved in the UN technical assistance programmes in the fifties and sixties felt considerable frustration at the inability of the UN system to assist governments who wished to control the rate of population increase. Hugh Keenleyside, the Canadian Director-General of the UN Technical Assistance Administration wrote in 1965, after his retirement: 'Perhaps by the end of the sixties it will have become clear that neither an increased capacity to produce nor any conceivable increase in production itself, will solve humanity's problems as long as unrestricted procreation continues to add to the sum of human needs and to impede most efforts to meet them.'[1] Not all his former colleagues, however, would have agreed with the antithesis which he presented that 'education in birth control is today vastly more important than training in the maintenance

[1] H. L. Keenleyside: *International Aid: A Summary*, New York, 1966, p. 187.

of health'.[1] Indeed the experience of family planning projects in the sixties suggested that, in some communities, it is only when the infant mortality rate falls that people become motivated to have fewer babies.

Keenleyside's compatriot and colleague in UNTAA, George Cadbury, unofficially assisted early family planning projects in Ceylon and Jamaica and after leaving the UN became Vice-Chairman of the IPPF Governing Body. In August 1969 David Owen, who had been Executive Chairman of the UN Technical Assistance Board and Associate Administrator of its successor, UNDP, for nearly twenty years, resigned to become Secretary General of the IPPF. After his death in June 1970 he was succeeded by another senior UN official, Julia Henderson, former Head of the Bureau of Social Affairs and later Assistant Commissioner and Director of Technical Co-operation Operations. In Asia Sam Keeny retired from the position of Director of the Regional Office of UNICEF, to become a field representative of the Population Council.

It is difficult to think of any successful major economic or social initiative to which the American government, which has contributed between 25 and 50% of the budgets of the UN agencies and their extra-budgetary funds, has been unsympathetic. Professor Richard Gardner, who was closely involved, suggests that the American conversion in the mid-sixties was the largest single factor in bringing about UN involvement in family planning programmes. On the other hand, to one of the authors of this book it seems possible that the change from a very cautious approach in the early sixties to determined advocacy of population control after 1967 hindered the development of family planning programmes in some of the less developed countries. Statements like that of President Johnson's in 1965 to the effect that five dollars invested in population control was worth as much as a hundred dollars invested in economic development[2] aroused considerable hostility and suspicion of Western motives. In either case, American enthusiasm for population control has ensured that in recent years there has been no shortage of funds for population work.

The change in the official American position seems in part to have been due to the fact that a Catholic President — Kennedy — had less to fear from the opposition of the Bishops than a Protestant. It took place in a climate of growing permissiveness in sexual behaviour. But it also developed at a time when many Catholics believed that the Pope would sanction the use of the

[1] Ibid., p. 279.
[2] Address at the 20th Anniversary of the United Nations, San Francisco, 25 June 1965.

contraceptive pill after the long deliberations of the Church's Commission. By the time the encyclical 'Humanae Vitae' was published in 1968, the solidity of the Church's position had been undermined. The teaching of St Augustine and St Thomas Aquinas, which had been unquestioned for centuries, had become the subject of liberal interpretation and commentary. All over the world Catholics were practising prohibited methods of contraception and, at a time when the whole authority of the Pope was being challenged within the Church, little effort seems to have been made to impose the doctrine of the encyclical rigidly. To protagonists of birth control there was an encouraging precedent in the fact that the Church, which had once regarded usury as illegal, had eventually established the Banco di Sants Spirito.

The combination of the lobby of the family planners, who saw birth control as a basic human right, with that which believed that population increase had to be controlled in order to prevent an intolerable strain on the world's resources and on the environment was formidable. Perhaps in WHO in 1952 the Catholics won a Pyrrhic victory which provided the stimulus which the opposition required at the international level, just as the Catholic inspired police raids and confiscation of medical records of Margaret Sanger's clinic in New York twenty years earlier had a decisive effect in rallying hitherto uncommitted and influential opinion to the defence of the family planning movement.

In America, the protagonists of UN involvement in population control were now no longer 'jailbirds' (as Margaret Sanger's children had heard her described by their schoolfellows) but pillars of the 'establishment'. Three only need be mentioned. General William H. Draper junior, was an investment banker and corporation executive, who had commanded an infantry division in World War II, had been Under-Secretary for the Army under Truman and United States Special Representative in Europe under Eisenhower. It will be recollected that his report recommending US aid to underdeveloped countries in population control was rejected by President Eisenhower. Henceforth, in his capacity as Chairman of the Population Crisis Committee, he devoted his considerable energy and influence to fund raising for the IPPF and, later, for the UN Fund for Population Activities. John D. Rockefeller III, head of the family and respected philanthropist, set up the Population Council, organized the Declaration of Heads of States on Population which was presented to the Secretary-General in 1966, and was Chairman of the US–UNA population panel. As important, in a quite different circle which formed American public opinion, was the leadership given by Rev. Richard Fagley in the Protestant

Churches. So strong was the support in business, church and academic circles for UN involvement that by the time that the US–UNA panel report was published it could be openly welcomed by President Nixon.

Quite as important as the contributions made by such leaders of public opinion was of course the investment in research and the work of American scientists in developing new contraceptives which, despite their defects, were considerably more suitable for use in the developing countries than those which had previously been available.

Scandinavian influence was important because the Scandinavian countries, who had supplied two Secretaries-General to the United Nations, were trusted by the developing countries as small states without colonial records. With India and Ceylon they had the longest records as protagonists of involvement. Dr Karl Evang, Director of Health Services of Norway, who for many years carried the brunt of the battle in WHO, had first become interested in the question when, whilst in jail as a conscientious objector, he had translated a book on birth control from English into Norwegian. On its publication he was so flooded with correspondence and queries on the subject that his involvement never ceased. The Swedish Government, which was the first to give assistance in family planning to a developing country, had a broad basis of support in its initiative, including economists, politicians and social workers. The Swedish programme in Ceylon was initiated by Alva Myrdal, then ambassador to India and Ceylon, and previously a senior official in UN and UNESCO. Another Swede, Mrs Ulla Lindstrom, was one of the most formidable advocates of UN involvement in family planning both at the General Assembly and, later, in the Population Commission.

The British contribution was small in relation to the reputation which Britain enjoyed in the UN and Specialized Agencies, particularly in the period following the Second World War. Apart from Huxley, who had little influence with the British government, there seems to have been no public figure even as consistently interested in the question as had been Eleanor Rathbone in the thirties. Lord Caradon, who became British Ambassador to the United Nations in 1964, with the additional authority of having the status of Minister in the Labour Government, was the first and perhaps only senior British representative to have taken a determined positive line, and that at a later stage. Caradon's enthusiasm seems to have been mainly due to his experience of population problems when Governor of Jamaica.

Whilst the American reinforcement of the Scandinavian

initiative was of the greatest importance, it might not have been successful against strident Russian opposition to 'neo-Malthusianism' if it had not been for the steadfast and long-established Asian, and especially Indian, support.

The earliest formal proposal for the involvement of a UN agency in family planning was the resolution proposed in the World Health Assembly in 1950 by S. W. R. D. Bandaranaike, Ceylon's Health Minister and subsequently Prime Minister. Unable to obtain assistance from the UN organizations, India, Pakistan and Ceylon sought it instead from American foundations and from Sweden. Meanwhile they continued to keep the issue alive in the annual conferences of the international organizations and by pressure exercised through Asian regional bodies. There was virtually unanimity among the Asian countries in the international organizations on the question.

The Indian example was important for many reasons. India was not only the most populous member of the UN, but also, under Nehru, enjoyed great prestige as a leader of the Third World. For all the reverence shown to Gandhi, his views on sex were privately regarded as quirky and impracticable even by some of his close associates. From two fascinating accounts which exist of his meeting with Margaret Sanger,[1] it seems that she may have persuaded him to give his blessing to the rhythm method; this possibly influenced the Indian government to try it out shortly after independence, when one of his former disciples was Health Minister. But even in the early fifties, it was the rationalists and humanists, typified by Jawarharlal Nehru, a science graduate of Cambridge, who prevailed. India was the first country in the world whose government declared an official anti-natalist population policy. Whatever the shortcomings of the Indian family planning programme, the fact that India was English-speaking, at least at the official level, and open to foreign field workers made it the international laboratory on population. Once the Indian government had adopted a population policy and asked for international aid, it became increasingly difficult for the problem to be ignored in the UN agencies.

Throughout the debates in international organizations on all aspects of population, it seems that the main concern of Communist delegates was to promote the 'correct' interpretation of population trends. At the 35th session of ECOSOC in 1963, Mr Solodovnikov, the Soviet delegate, complained that 'efforts were being made to use the UN to spread propaganda . . . and to disseminate theories which were at variance with reality' and that 'it was the duty of the UN bodies . . . to speak out against

[1] One by his secretary, Mahadev Desai, and the other by Margaret Sanger herself in Homer Jack: *Gandhi Reader*, London, 1958, pp. 302-6.

CONCLUSIONS   203

Malthusian explanations of population changes'.[1] In 1966 the
Soviet delegate at the General Assembly observed: 'it was
gratifying that expert opinion had at long last begun to appreci-
ate the role which economic and social changes could play in
solving population problems'.[2]

Communist demographers, for their part, had begun to show a
much greater flexibility on the population question after the Asian
Population Conference in 1963. Several Soviet demographers
began to argue in favour of anti-natalist policies in less developed
countries, provided these were part of, and not a substitute for,
far-reaching economic and social reforms,[3] although Peter
Podyachick, for many years Soviet member of the Population
Commission, did not appear to share this view.[4]

The American conversion and the adoption by Asian countries
of population control policies did much to bring about UN
involvement in action programmes. But this in itself might have
remained only a symbolic victory if those programmes had
continued to rely on the techniques of the fifties. The technological contribution of the Americans in the development first of
the loop or coil, and then of the oral pill was quite as important.
But, as in other fields, the enthusiasm to export new techniques
was sometimes self-defeating. There is a story recounted to one
of the writers of a visit by a family planner to Africa, where he
called on his fifteenth Chief of State in as many days. 'Were you
briefed about my country or myself?' the President interrupted
mildly as the message of birth control as a panacea began. 'No,
Your Excellency, I had no time'. 'A pity,' concluded the President, 'or you might have learnt that my country is under-
populated, and that I am a Catholic.'

Such incidents seem to have caused American ambassadors in
several countries to urge the State Department to attempt to
regulate the efforts of American official and unofficial bodies, and
this in turn led the US government to seek to divert its assistance
through multilateral channels. The US in fact, having given top
priority to population control in its foreign aid policy, needed the
United Nations as much as the United Nations needed the US.

[1] OR of ECOSOC, 35th session, 1963, p. 30.
[2] OR of the General Assembly, 21st session, 1966. Summary Records of the
Second Committee, p. 443. See also H. K. Jacobson: *The USSR and the UN's
Economic and Social Activities*, Notre Dame, 1963, pp. 145-6.
[3] See for example, B. Z. Urlanis: 'Marxism and Birth Control', Paper given
at the Conference of the IUSSP, Sydney, 1967; and Y.N. Guzeraty, 'Population and World Politics', *International Affairs* (Moscow), October 1967.
Both articles are reprinted in *Studies in Family Planning*, no. 49, January 1970.
[4] P. Podyachick: 'Impact of Demographic Policy on the Growth of the
Population', in E. Szabady (ed.), *World Views of Population Problems*, Budapest,
1968, pp. 231-51.

The extent to which the resolutions of the United Nations agencies, often so bitterly disputed, affected national population policies is somewhat early to assess. In Asia the policies of several governments were ahead of the global policies of UN, though regional meetings of international agencies sometimes served to enable experiences to be exchanged at that level. In Latin America CELADE, the UN demographic training centre in Santiago, seems to have played a not unimportant part in educating key government officials as to the implication of population trends, a necessary prerequisite to the adoption of population policies. The WHO Regional Office for the Americas, which as the Pan-American Sanitary Bureau was older than WHO itself, has always enjoyed a considerable measure of independence, which it seems to have used in the late sixties to interpret the changing mandates of WHO liberally in assisting family planning programmes.

In Africa, on the other hand, Dr Quenum, WHO Regional Director, made no secret, as an African, of his dislike for foreign intervention in favour of population control policies. He referred in 1967 to propagandists who saw contraception as the means of limiting the vitality of certain peoples and of holding back the 'menacing hordes of the Third World'; he also maintained that the majority of African countries were underpopulated.[1] In Africa the UN influence seems to have percolated less through health ministries than through the close network of development economists, some of whom were able to assert the need—or at least desirability—of controlling the rate of population increase by having this written into their governments' development plans. Much of sub-Saharan Africa, even in 1968 when visited by a UN mission, was at a stage when it needed help in establishing the demographic facts before it considered population policies.

The countries of North Africa and the Middle East moved very rapidly towards population policies in the mid sixties. In some cases they helped to change UN policies: in others UN assisted the changes at the national level. In certain of them, such as Turkey and Lebanon, the changes of position were remarkably sudden and dramatic.

Paradoxically it may even seem to future historians fortunate that the attempt to involve the UN Agencies in family planning in 1948–52 failed. If the same resolutions which were passed in the late sixties had been voted in the early fifties, representatives of UN Agencies visiting underdeveloped countries as 'travelling salesmen' to promote family planning and population control

[1] A. Quenum: 'Africa and the Problem of Contraception', *West African Medical Journal*, October 1967, pp. 149–54.

might have been counterproductive in countries which were not yet ready for public discussion of the issues. Perhaps the Indian experience was necessary before international programmes could have developed.

Lord Caradon in an address to the IPPF Conference in Santiago in 1967 criticized the United Nations and Specialized Agencies because until 1965 almost no 'practical action' had been taken by them in assistance of programmes designed to reduce the birthrate. It could be argued that until the technological breakthrough which produced cheap and effective contraceptives, opportunities for 'practical action' were in any case limited. Yet even if Lord Caradon's criticism is admitted, the indirect influence of the agencies of the UN system should not be underrated. Firstly, they produced global figures which could be universally accepted showing that the world's population was in the process of doubling itself over a period of thirty years. Secondly, their legislatures provided a forum in which the debate on the right to family planning facilities and the need for population control could be staged. Thirdly, as the tide turned in favour of these measures, resolutions of the United Nations gave them international legitimacy which made it easier for national leaders to change course.

Our conclusions can only be inconclusive. If it is difficult to assess the relative importance of various factors in changes of national social policies, it is much more so at the international level. Even to obtain a serious basis for such an assessment would require access to archives of foreign ministries which will not be available for many years in relation to the period under review.

Yet perhaps the justification for the quest, however uncertain its results, is that it may help to suggest that there is an international history of attitudes to social change which can be traced, however imperfectly, through the records of international organizations.

However the roles of the actors are seen, whether of governmental representatives, international officials or the non-governmental organizations behind the scenes, and however inadequately motives can be comprehended in contemporary history for which archives are not open, the attempt seems worth making to understand what Conor Cruise O'Brien has called the 'sacred drama' on the United Nations stage.

It is in the political context that O'Brien has suggested that 'the proceedings on the East River deserve and require exacting and sustained attention if the safeguards of survival are not to be lowered.'[1] It may also be true, however, that the proceedings

[1] Conor Cruise O'Brien: *United Nations: Sacred Drama*, New York, 1968, p. 297.

of the United Nations and its Specialized Agencies concerning the major economic and social issues with which the world is confronted deserve considerably wider attention in relation to the future of mankind than they at present receive from the relatively few diplomatic and academic specialists and international officials who find them intelligible.

Appendix I

Note on Sources

Although use has been made of other works, for which references are given at the end of each chapter, the main written source of information for this study has been the documents of the United Nations system. We have made extensive use in particular of the records of the Second Committee of the General Assembly, the Economic and Social Council and the Population Commission and of the official records of WHO, UNESCO, ILO, FAO and UNICEF. For Part I extensive use was made of the records of the League of Nations.

We have made some use of the archives of international agencies. Here rules of access vary considerably between the application of a thirty-year rule on the one hand and the exercise of the discretion of the Director-General on the other. In the latter case this may allow research workers access to quite recent materials.

Most of the more important documentary material, including the proceedings of the UN General Assembly and the conferences of the specialized agencies are issued as publications. Others exist only in mimeographed form. Although the practices of different agencies vary, most of the documents are generally accessible through the United Nations and the specialized agencies or in depository libraries.

United Nations

The great majority of UN documents are issued initially in provisional form. The documents of the major organs of the UN, in particular the records of the General Assembly and its Committees and of the Economic and Social Council, are subsequently reissued in final form after correction and editing. Together with supporting documents they are published as *Official Records* (OR) at the end of each session. In this study references to the *Official Records* of the General Assembly and ECOSOC indicate the session, year and page or paragraph number. The records of the twenty-fourth and twenty-fifth sessions of the General Assembly had not appeared in final form when the study was completed. Consequently, references are to the provisional mimeographed documents.

The documents of the committees of ECOSOC, its functional commissions, the regional economic commissions and the ad hoc committees of the General Assembly are issued only as mimeographed documents. The reports which these bodies submit at the end of each session appear in final form as supplements to the *Official Records* of their respective parent bodies.

References to mimeographed documents are indicated by the appropriate UN documents series symbols. These symbols identify the issuing organ and the nature of the document. Each organ has its own symbol as follows:

General Assembly

A/–	Plenary documents
A/C.2/–	Documents of the Second Committee (economic questions)
A/C.3/–	Documents of the Third Committee (social questions)

Economic and Social Council

E/–	Documents of the Council
E/AC.6/–	Documents of the Economic Committee
E/AC.7/–	Documents of the Social Committee.
E/CN.9/–	Documents of the Population Commission

The nature of the document is shown by a series of additive symbols, the most important of which are as follows:

RES.	Resolution
–/SR	Summary records of a meeting
–/PV	Procés-verbal. Verbatim records of the plenary meetings of the General Assembly
–/L	Working document, usually a draft resolution, submitted for consideration and having only limited distribution.

Thus, for example, the symbol A/PV.1829 denotes the provisional verbatim minutes of the 1829th plenary meeting of the GeneralAssembly; E/AC.6/SR.355 refers to the Summary Record of the 355th meeting of the Economic Committee of ECOSOC: and E/CN.9/154 indicates the 154th document of the Population Commission.

Documents issued by the Secretariat bear the prefix ST/–. The symbol ST/SOA/– refers to documents of the Department of Social Affairs, which includes the UN Population Division.

Until its fifteenth session in November 1969 the Population Commission issued summary records in mimeographed form (E/CN.9/SR–). These were discontinued as part of a general policy in the United Nations of reducing the volume of documentation.

In addition the United Nations also publishes a wide range of technical reports, printed books, pamphlets, etc. In many cases these publications bear standard UN documents series symbols. However, they may also be identified by their sales number. The sales number indicates the year of publication and the broad field, for example, economic development or demography, in which the publication falls. Where appropriate the sales number is indicated in the reference.

United Nations Children's Fund (UNICEF)

Although generally considered as an autonomous body, UNICEF is in fact a subsidiary organ of the United Nations. The documents of UNICEF form part of the United Nations documents system and are issued with the prefix E/ICEF/–. The reports of the Executive Board appear as supplements to the *Official Records* of ECOSOC.

World Health Organization (WHO)

The *Official Records of the World Health Organization* contain a complete record of the documents, proceedings and decisions of the World Health Assembly (including the minutes and reports of its Committees), the decisions and resolutions of the Executive Board, and the proposed annual Programme and Budget. Resolutions adopted by the World Health Assembly are identified by the number of the session followed by the number of the resolution, e.g. Resolution WHA 18.49. The *Official Records* are numbered chronologically and are indexed.

The minutes and working papers of the Executive Board exist in mimeographed form only. They are identified by the symbol EB followed by the number of the session. Thus, for example, EB 35/ Min.13/Rev.1 refers to the corrected minutes of the thirteenth meeting of the thirty-fifth session of the Executive Board.

UNESCO

The records of the UNESCO General Conference are published at the end of each session in three volumes comprising the Proceedings (corrected verbatim records of the plenary meetings), Resolutions and Index. The working documents of the General Conference appear in mimeographed form only indicated by the number of the session followed by the letter C. Many of the key discussions on UNESCO's role in the field of population took place in the Programme Commission of the Conference. Programme Commission documents bear the symbol PRG. The symbol VR indicates verbatim record.

The documents of the Executive Board of UNESCO appear in mimeographed form only, but are available for general distribution. Documents are identified by the session number followed by the letters EX. Summary records (SR) are issued in final form at the end of each session. A record of decisions of the Executive Board is also issued at the end of each session.

ILO

The main documents of the ILO Governing Body appear in final form in the *Minutes of the Governing Body*, which are published after each session. They contain a summary record of the discussion and decisions. Reports and other documents submitted for information and discussion are included as appendices. The *Record of Proceedings* of the International Labour Conference contains the corrected summary records of the plenary sessions of the Conference and the reports of the Conference committees. The latter includes the Selection Committee in which the main discussion on draft resolutions takes place. The *Record of Proceedings* also contains the full text of the resolutions, conventions and recommendations adopted by the Conference.

The *Minutes of the Governing Body* and the *Record of Proceedings* of the Conference are indexed.

Documents of the Regional and Technical Conferences of the ILO follow a similar pattern to the *Record of Proceedings* of the International Labour Conference. Other useful sources of information are the *Studies and Reports*, a series of publications on different social and economic questions relating to labour and the *Official Bulletin* of the International Labour Office, a quarterly publication containing a summary of the work of the Organization.

FAO

A published report containing a summary of the discussions is issued at the end of each session of the FAO Council and the FAO Conference.

The documents and verbatim records (PV) of the Council appear in mimeographed form only and are identified by the symbol CL followed by the number of the session. The documents of the Conference also appear in mimeographed form only. Conference documents are denoted by the symbol C followed by the year in which the session took place. Verbatim records of plenary sessions and commissions of the Conference are indicated by the symbol PV, followed, where appropriate, by the number of Commission in roman numerals, and the number of the meeting.

An important source of information on population trends in relation to food supplies is the *State of Food and Agriculture*, an annual assessment by the FAO secretariat of trends in the production and supply of foodstuffs and agricultural products, changes in agricultural technology, etc.

League of Nations

League documents, like those of the United Nations, are identified by a series of symbols. The symbols indicate to whom the document was distributed, its date and number. Documents distributed to members of the Council carry the letter C, those for members of the Assembly the letter A and those distributed to all members the letter

M. The documents of committees and conferences are indicated by
their initials, usually in French. Thus CH (Comité d' Hygiene)
refers to Health Committee documents and C.E.I. (Conférence
Economique Internationale) to documents of the International
Economic Conference of 1927.

The records of the Council and Assembly were published in the
Official Journal. The proceedings of the Council appeared in the
Official Journal itself, issued monthly; the resolutions and proceedings
of the Assembly, including its committees, as special supplements
showing number and date. The records of both bodies are indexed.

Until the 19th session in 1932 the minutes of the Health Committee
were issued as official documents showing number, date and place of
the session and the appropriate document number. From 1932
onwards minutes were not issued. The reports of the Health Committee
to the Council on the work of each session form part of the documents
of the Council.

Many League documents were issued as sales publications either
in the *Official Journal* or separately.

Appendix II

Resolutions

1838 (XVII) *Population growth and economic development* of 18 December 1962

The General Assembly,

Considering that rapid economic and social progress in the developing countries is dependent not least upon the ability of these countries to provide their peoples with education, a fair standard of living and the possibility for productive work,

Considering further that economic development and population growth are closely interrelated,

Recognizing that the health and welfare of the family are of paramount importance, not only for obvious humanitarian reasons, but also with regard to economic development and social progress, and that the health and welfare of the family require special attention in areas with a relatively high rate of population growth,

Recognizing further that it is the responsibility of each Government to decide on its own policies and devise its own programmes of action for dealing with the problems of population and economic and social progress,

Reminding States Members of the United Nations and members of the specialized agencies that, according to recent census results, the effective population increase during the last decade has been particularly great in many of the low-income less developed countries,

Reminding Member States that in formulating their economic and social policies it is useful to take into account the latest relevant facts on the interrelationship of population growth and economic and social development, and that the forthcoming World Population Conference and the Asian Population Conference might throw new light on the importance of this problem, especially for the developing countries,

Recalling its resolution 1217 (XII) of 14 December 1957, in which the General Assembly, *inter alia*, invited Member States, particularly the developing countries, to follow as closely as possible the interrelationship of economic changes and population changes, and requested the Secretary-General to ensure the co-ordination of the activities of the United Nations in the demographic and economic fields,

Recalling Economic and Social Council resolution 820 B (XXXI) of 28 April 1961 which contains provisions for intensifying efforts to ensure international co-operation in the evaluation, analysis and utilization of population census results and related data, particularly in the less developed countries, and in which the Council requested the Secretary-General to explore the possibilities of increasing technical assistance funds for assistance to Governments requesting it in preparing permanent programmes of demographic research,

Recognizing that further studies and research are necessary to fill the gaps in the present knowlege of the causes and consequences of demographic trends, particularly in the less developed countries,

Recognizing also that removals of large national groups to other countries may give rise to ethnic, political, emotional and economic difficulties,

1. *Notes with appreciation* the report of the Secretary-General on measures proposed for the United Nations Development Decade in which he refers, *inter alia*, to the interrelationship of population growth and economic and social development;

2. *Expresses its appreciation* of the work on population problems which has up to now been carried out under the guidance of the Population Commission;

3. *Requests* the Secretary-General to conduct an inquiry among the Governments of States Members of the United Nations and members of the specialized agencies concerning the particular problems confronting them as a result of the reciprocal action of economic development and population changes;

4. *Recommends* that the Economic and Social Council, in co-operation with the specialized agencies, the regional economic commissions and the Population Commission, and taking into account the results of the inquiry referred to in paragraph 3 above, should intensify its studies and research on the interrelationship of population growth and economic and social development, with particular reference to the needs of the developing countries for investment in health and educational facilities within the framework of their general development programmes;

5. *Further recommends* that the Economic and Social Council should report on its findings to the General Assembly not later than at its nineteenth session;

6. *Endorses* the view of the Population Commission that the United Nations should encourage and assist Governments, especially those of the less developed countries, in obtaining basic data and in carrying out essential studies of the demographic aspects, as well as other aspects, of their economic and social development problems;

7. *Recommends* that the second World Population Conference should pay special attention to the interrelationship of population growth and economic and social development, particularly in the less developed countries, and that efforts should be made to obtain the fullest possible participation in the Conference by experts from such countries.   *1197th plenary meeting,*
18 December 1962.

2211 (XXI) *Population growth and economic development* **of 17 December 1966**

The General Assembly,

Recalling its resolution 1838 (XVII) of 18 December 1962 on population growth and economic development and Economic and Social Council resolution 933 C (XXXV) of 5 April 1963 on the intensification of demographic studies, research and training, 1048 (XXXVII) of 15 August 1964 on population growth and economic and social development and 1084 (XXXIX) of 30 July 1965 on work programmes and priorities in the field of population,

Recalling World Health Assembly resolutions WHA 18.49 of 21 May 1965 and WHA 19.43 of 20 May 1966 on the health aspects of world population,

Taking note of resolution 3.252 adopted on 29 November 1966 by the General Conference of the United Nations Educational, Scientific and Cultural Organization at its fourteenth session, and of paragraphs 842–844 of the programme for 1967–1968 of that organization on the subject of education and information related to population growth,

Recalling the inquiry conducted by the Secretary-General among Governments on problems resulting from the interaction of economic growth and population change, and his report thereon, which reflected a wide variety of population problems,

Commending the Economic and Social Council and the Secretary-General for convening the World Population Conference, held at Belgrade from 30 August to 10 September 1965, in which a large number of specialists in demography and related fields from developing countries were able to participate,

Taking note of the summary of the highlights of the World Population Conference,

Noting the steps taken, by the organizations of the United Nations system which are concerned, to co-ordinate their work in the field of population,

Concerned at the growing food shortage in the developing countries, which is due in many cases to a decline in the production of foodstuffs relative to population growth,

Recognizing the need for further study of the implications of the growth, structure and geographical distribution of population for economic and social development, including national health, nutrition, education and social welfare programmes carried out at all levels of government activity,

Believing that demographic problems require the consideration of economic, social, cultural, psychological and health factors in their proper perspective,

Recognizing the sovereignty of nations in formulating and promoting their own population policies, with due regard to the principle that the size of the family should be according to the free choice of each individual family,

1. *Invites* the Economic and Social Council, the Population Commission, the regional economic commissions, the United Nations Economic and Social Office in Beirut and the specialized agencies concerned to study the proceedings of the 1965 World Population Conference when pursuing their activities in the field of population;

2. *Notes with satisfaction* the decision of the World Health Organization to include in its programme of activities the study of the health aspects of human reproduction and the provision of advisory services, upon request, within its responsibilities under World Health Assembly resolution WHA 19.43, and the decision of the United Nations Educational, Scientific and Cultural Organization to stimulate and provide assistance towards scientific studies concerning the relations between the development of education and evolution of population;

3. *Requests* the Secretary-General:

(*a*) To pursue, within the limits of available resources, the implementation of the work programme covering training, research information and advisory services in the field of population in the light of the recommendations of the Population Commission contained in the report on its thirteenth session, as endorsed by the Economic and Social Council in its resolution 1084 (XXXIX), and of the considerations set forth in the preamble of the present resolution;

(*b*) To continue his consultations with the specialized agencies concerned, in order to ensure that the activities of the United Nations system of organizations in the field of population are effectively coordinated;

(*c*) To present to the Population Commission at its fourteenth session, as envisaged in Economic and Social Council resolution 1084 (XXXIX), proposals with regard to the priorities of work over periods of two and five years, within the framework of the long-range programme of work in the field of population;

4. *Calls upon* the Economic and Social Council, the Population Commission, the regional economic commissions, the United Nations Economic and Social Office in Beirut and the specialized agencies concerned to assist, when requested, in further developing and strengthening national and regional facilities for training, research, information and advisory services in the field of population, bearing in mind the different character of population problems in each country and region and the needs arising therefrom.

1497th plenary meeting,
17 December 1966.

(b) ECONOMIC AND SOCIAL COUNCIL

1048 (XXXVII) *Population growth and economic and social development* **of 15 August 1964**

The Economic and Social Council,

Recalling General Assembly resolution 1838 (XVII) of 18 December 1962 on population growth and economic development and Council resolutions 933 B (XXXV) of 5 April 1963 on the World Population Conference to be held in Belgrade, Yugoslavia, in 1965 and 933 C (XXXV) of 5 April 1963 concerning the intensification of demographic studies, research and training,

Having considered with appreciation the inquiry conducted by the Secretary-General as requested by the General Assembly among Governments of States Members of the United Nations or members of the specialized agencies concerning the particular problems confronting them as a result of the reciprocal action of economic development and population changes,

Having noted in particular the serious concern expressed in reply to the inquiry by many Governments of developing countries about the slow rate of economic growth of their countries in relation to the high rate of their population growth,

Having further noted the high priority given by the Advisory Committee on the Application of Science and Technology, *inter alia,* to 'the objective of a more complete understanding of population problems',

Commending the Economic Commission for Asia and the Far East for organizing the Asian Population Conference held in 1963,

1. *Invites* the General Assembly, the regional economic commissions and the Population Commission to examine the replies of the Governments to the inquiry and to make recommendations with a view to intensifying the work of the United Nations in assisting the Governments of the interested developing countries to deal with the population problems confronting them;

2. *Requests* the Secretary-General to circulate the findings of the inquiry to the World Population Conference and to the specialized agencies concerned, in particular the International Labour Organization, the Food and Agricultural Organization, the United Nations Educational, Scientific and Cultural Organization and the World Health Organization, with the suggestion that they take the findings into account, as appropriate, in formulating their programmes;

3. *Requests* the Secretary-General to undertake in the future, at appropriate intervals, similar inquiries on problems resulting from the relationship between economic development and population changes;

4. *Draws the attention* of the General Assembly to resolution 54 (XX) unanimously adopted by the Economic Commission for Asia and the Far East on 17 March 1964 which invites 'the United

Nations and the specialized agencies to expand the scope of the technical assistance they are prepared to give, upon the request of Governments, in the development of statistics, research experimentation and action programmes related to population';

5. *Recommends* that the Economic Commission for Latin America and the Economic Commission for Africa organize regional conferences, study the population trends as well as the economic trends connected with them and their implications for economic and social development in the regions concerned, and to communicate their findings to the Council and to the Population Commission for appropriate action;

6. *Urges the* Secretary-General and the specialized agencies concerned to explore ways and means of strengthening and expanding their work in the field of population, including the possibilities of obtaining voluntary contributions.

1351st plenary meeting,
15 August 1964.

1084 (XXXIX) *Work Programmes and priorities in population fields* of 30 July 1965

The Economic and Social Council,

Recalling General Assembly resolution 1838 (XVII) of 18 December 1962 on population growth and economic development and Council resolutions 933 C (XXXV) of 5 April 1963 on intensification of demographic studies, research and training and 1048 (XXXVII) of 15 August 1964 on population growth and economic and social development,

Bearing in mind the problems in the economic and social development of developing countries associated with the growth and structure of population and migration from the countryside to the cities,

Recalling the concern with these problems expressed in the responses of many Governments of developing countries to the inquiry among Governments on problems resulting from the interaction of economic development and population changes carried out in accordance with the above-mentioned resolution of the General Assembly,

Taking note of the views expressed by the Population Commission in the report of its thirteenth session on population growth and economic and social development and on possibilities of assisting Governments of developing countries in dealing with population problems, and in particular the Population Commission's recommendations on the long-range programme of work of the United Nations and the specialized agencies in the population fields,

Being aware that many countries lack technical personnel with specialized training in population questions and facilities for training national technicians,

Considering that there is a need to intensify and extend the scope of the work of the United Nations and the specialized agencies relating to population questions,

1. *Endorses* the recommendations of the Population Commission in the report of its thirteenth session on the long-range programme of work in the fields of population, including its recommendations with regard to the increase and improvements of demographic statistics, the strengthening of regional demographic training and research centres, and other activities to increase the supply of technically trained personnel in the developing countries, expansion and intensification of research and technical work, widening of the scope and increase of the amount of technical assistance in population fields available to Governments of developing countries upon their request, and conferences and related activities in the population fields;

2. *Draws the attention* of the Statistical Commission, the Social Commission and the Commission on the Status of Women to the recommendations and suggestions of the Population Commission relating to activities in their fields of interest;

3. *Invites* the regional economic commissions and the interested specialized agencies to give consideration to possibilities of modifying and expanding their programmes of activities in the population fields along the lines indicated by the recommendations of the Population Commission;

4. *Calls to the attention* of the General Assembly the need to provide the necessary resources, within the framework of the decisions taken to balance the budget of the United Nations, for the United Nations to carry out the intensified and expanded programme of activities in the fields of population recommended by the Population Commission;

5. *Requests* the Secretary-General:

(*a*) To consider giving a position for the work in population in the United Nations Secretariat that would correspond to its importance;

(*b*) To provide, in accordance with Council resolution 222 (IX) of 14 and 15 August 1949 and General Assembly resolution 418 (V) of 1 December 1950, advisory services and training on action programmes in the field of population at the request of Governments desiring assistance in this field;

(*c*) To consult the interested specialized agencies on the division of responsibilities and co-ordination of activities in the long-range programme of work in the population fields recommended by the Population Commission;

(*d*) To present to the Population Commission at its fourteenth session proposals with regard to the priorities of work over future periods of two years and of five years, within the framework of the long-range programme of work in the population fields.

1394th plenary meeting,
30 July 1965.

1347 (XLV) *Population and its relation to economic and social development* of 30 July 1968

The Economic and Social Council,

Noting the changes that have taken place in the world population situation in the last twenty years, caused by the considerable decline in mortality which has spurred world population growth,

Recognizing the importance of giving approprite attention to the inter-relations of economic, social and demographic factors in formulating development programmes,

Considering that the policy organs of relevant organizations in the United Nations system have stressed in their work programmes the importance of the problem,

Recognizing the need for the United Nations and the specialized agencies to assist the developing countries, upon request, in dealing with problems arising out of the current and prospective population trends, and in formulating and promoting national policies of their own choice in the field of population,

Considering that the International Conference on Human Rights held at Teheran adopted resolution XVIII of 12 May 1968 on human rights aspects of family planning, which states in part 'that couples have a basic human right to decide freely and responsibly on the number and spacing of their children and a right to adequate education and information in this respect',

Taking into account the views of the Committee for Programme and Co-ordination, which recognizes the importance of demographic research and projects, and that such research should be restricted to studies which could serve as practical tools for policy-making or for supporting field activities and in particular that the United Nations population programme should concentrate more on information programmes at the regional and country levels,

Noting with appreciation the report of the Administrative Committee on Co-ordination on co-ordination in the field of population,

Further noting the setting up of a United Nations Trust Fund for population activities as a measure to supplement the resources to be obtained from the regular budget and the United Nations Development Programme, and *welcoming* opportunities for strengthening these activities, made possible by additional voluntary resources,

1. *Endorses* the recommendations of the Population Commission, in the report of its fourteenth session, on the five-year and two-year programmes and priorities within the framework of the long-range programme of work in the fields of 'population in accordance with General Assembly resolution 2211 (XXI) of 17 December 1966;

2. *Endorses* the conclusions of the Committee for Programme and Co-ordination with respect to the United Nations population programme;

3. *Recommends* that the United Nations Development Programme give due consideration to applications submitted for financing projects designed to assist developing countries in dealing with population problems, primarily in the fields of economic and social development, including both national and regional projects;

4. *Requests* the Secretary-General, within the approved programme of work to:

(a) Pursue a programme of work covering training, research, information and advisory services in the fields of fertility, mortality, and morbidity, internal migration and urbanization and demographic aspects of economic and social development, in accordance with Council resolution 1084 (XXXIX) of 30 July 1965 and General Assembly resolution 2211 (XXI);

(b) Give special attention to further developing those aspects of the work in population fields which are of direct benefit to the developing countries, especially advice and technical assistance requested by Governments in population fields, within the context of economic, social and health policies, and where appropriate, religious and cultural considerations;

(c) Submit to the General Assembly biennially a concise report on the world population situation, including an assessment of the current and prospective population trends;

(d) Bring promptly up to date the study *Determinants and Consequences of Population Trends;*

5. *Requests* the Committee on Development Planning to give appropriate attention to the interrelation between population dynamics and economic and social growth with respect to the second United Nations Development Decade, taking into account the diversity of regional and national characteristics;

6. *Invites* the regional economic commissions and the United Nations Economic and Social Office in Beirut to prepare and consider regional reports on population aspects of economic and social development;

7. *Welcomes* the decision of the Administrative Committee on Co-ordination to establish a Sub-Committee on Population and *calls for* intensified action in cooperation with the Committee for Programme and Co-ordination to improve co-ordination and avoid duplication.

1556th plenary meeting,
30 July 1968.

(c) WORLD HEALTH ASSEMBLY

18.49 *Programme activities in the health aspects of population which might be developed by WHO of* **21 May 1965**

The Eighteenth World Health Assembly,
Having considered the report of the Director-General on Programme

Activities in the Health Aspects of World Population which might be developed by WHO

Bearing in mind Article 2 (*l*) of the Constitution which reads: 'to promote maternal and child health and welfare and to foster the ability to live harmoniously in a changing total environment';

Noting resolution 1048 (XXXVII) adopted by the Economic and Social Council at its thirty-seventh session, August 1964;

Believing that demographic problems require the consideration of economic, social, cultural, psychological and health factors in their proper perspective;

Noting that the United Nations Population Commission at its thirteenth session, April 1965, attached high priority to the research and other activities in the field of fertility;

Considering that the changes in the size and structure of the population have repercussions on health conditions;

Recognizing that problems of human reproduction involve the family unit as well as society as a whole, and that the size of the family should be the free choice of each individual family;

Bearing in mind that it is a matter for national administrations to decide whether and to what extent they should support the provision of information and services to their people on the health aspects of human reproduction;

Accepting that it is not the responsibility of WHO to endorse or promote any particular population policy; and

Noting that the scientific knowledge with regard to the biology of human reproduction and the medical aspects of fertility control is insufficient,

1. *Approves* the report of the Director-General on Programme Activities in the Health Aspects of World Population which might be developed by WHO;

2. *Requests* the Director-General to develop further the programme proposed:

(*a*) in the fields of reference services, studies on medical aspects of sterility and fertility control methods and health aspects of population dynamics; and

(*b*) in the field of advisory services as outlined in Part III, paragraph 3, of his report, on the understanding that such services are related, within the responsibilities of WHO, to technical advice on the health aspects of human reproduction and should not involve operational activities; and

3. *Requests* the Director-General to report to the Nineteenth World Health Assembly on the programme of WHO in the field of human reproduction.

Thirteenth plenary meeting,
21 May 1965.

19.43 Programme activities in the health aspects of population which might be developed by WHO of 20 May 1966

The Nineteenth World Health Assembly,

Having considered the report presented by the Director-General[2] in accordance with resolution WHA 18.49;

Bearing in mind Article 2 (1) of the Constitution;

Noting the part played by economic, social and cultural conditions in solving population problems and emphasizing the importance of health aspects of this problem;

Noting the resolution 1084 (XXXIX) of the Economic and Social Council, the discussions at the Second World Population Conference and the subsequent discussion during the twentieth session of the United Nations General Assembly;

Noting that several governments are embarking on nation-wide schemes on family planning;

Noting that the activities of WHO and its Scientific Groups have already played their part in collecting and making available information on many aspects of human reproduction;

Recognizing that the scientific knowledge with regard to human reproduction is still insufficient; and

Realizing the importance of including information on the health aspects of population problems in the education of medical students, nurses, midwives and other members of the health team,

1. *Notes* with satisfaction the report presented by the Director-General;

2. *Reaffirms the policy statements contained in the consideranda of resolution WHA 18.49;*

3. *Approves* the programme outlined in Part III of the Director-General's report[1] in pursuance of the operative part of resolution WHA 18.49;

4. *Confirms that the role of WHO is to give members technical advice upon request, in the development of activities in family planning, as part of an organized health service, without impairing its normal preventive and and curative functions, and*

5. *Requests* the Director-General to report to the Twentieth World Health Assembly on the work of WHO in the field of human reproduction.

Fourteenth plenary meeting,
20 May 1965.

20.41 Health aspects of population dynamics of 25 May 1966

The Twentieth World Health Assembly,

Having considered the report of the Director-General;

Welcoming particularly the references therein to provision of training;

Recognizing the urgent nature of the health problems associated with changes in population dynamics now facing certain Member States, especially in the recruitment of suitably trained and experienced staff;

Recalling resolutions WHA 18.49 and WHA 19.43;

Reiterating the considerations expressed in these resolutions;

Considering that abortions and the high maternal and child mortality rates constitute a serious public health problem in many countries, and

Believing that the development of basic health services is of fundamental importance in any health programme aimed at health problems associated with population,

1. *Congratulate* the Director-General for the work accomplished during 1966;

2. *Approves* the report of the Director-General;

3. *Expresses* the hope that it will be possible for WHO to continue its activities in this field along the principles laid down in resolutions WHA 18.49 and WHA 19.43; and

4. *Requests* the Director-General:

(*a*) to continue to develop the activities of the World Health Organization in the field of health aspects of human reproduction;

(*b*) to assist on request in national research projects and in securing the training of university teachers and of professional staff; and

(*c*) to report to the Twenty-first World Health Assembly on the work of WHO in the field of human reproduction.

Twelfth plenary meeting
25 May 1967

21.43 Health aspects of population dynamics of 23 May 1968

The Twenty-first World Health Assembly,

Having considered the report of the Director-General on health aspects of population dynamics;

Noting with satisfaction the development of activities in reference services, research, and training, and the provision of advisory services to Member States, on request, on the health aspects of human reproduction, of family planning, and of population dynamics within the context of resolutions WHA 18.49, WHA 19.43, and WHA 20.41;

Emphasizing the concept that this programme requires the consideration of economic, social, cultural, psychological and health factors in their proper perspective;

Reaffirming the considerations expressed in these resolutions;

Recognizing that family planning is viewed by many Members States as an important component of basic health services, particularly of maternal and child health and in the promotion of family health and plays a role in social and economic development;

Reiterating the opinion that every family should have the opportunity of obtaining information and advice on problems connected with

UNPQ—Q

family planning including fertility and sterility;

Agreeing that our understanding of numerous problems related to the health aspects of human reproduction, family planning and population is still limited,

1. *Congratulate* the Director-General on the work accomplished during the year 1967;

2. *Approves* the report of the Director-General; and

3. *Requests* the Director-General

(*a*) to continue to develop the programme in this field in accordance with the principles laid down in resolutions WHA 18.49, WHA 19.43 and WHA 20.41 including also the encouragement of research on psychological factors related to the health aspects of reproduction;

(*b*) to continue to assist Member States upon their request in the development of their programmes with special reference to:

(i) the integration of family planning within basic health services without prejudice to the preventive and curative activities which normally are the responsibility of those services;

(ii) appropriate training programmes for health professionals at all levels;

(*c*) to analyse further the health manpower requirements for such services and the supervision and training needs of such manpower in actual field situations under specific local conditions; and

(*d*) to report on the progress of the programme to the Twenty-second World Health Assembly.

Seventeenth plenary meeting
23 May 1968

Index